WE CANNOT FORGET

Genocide, Political Violence, Human Rights Series

Edited by Alexander Laban Hinton, Stephen Eric Bronner, Aldo Civico, and Nela Navarro

WE CANNOT FORGET

Interviews with Survivors
of the 1994 Genocide in Rwanda

EDITED BY SAMUEL TOTTEN
AND RAFIKI UBALDO

RUTGERS UNIVERSITY PRESS

NEW BRUNSWICK, NEW JERSEY, AND LONDON

Library of Congress Cataloging-in-Publication Data

We cannot forget : interviews with survivors of the 1994 genocide in Rwanda / edited by
Samuel Totten and Rafiki Ubaldo.

      p.   cm. — (Genocide, political violence, human rights series)

Includes bibliographical references.

ISBN 978–0–8135–4969–9 (hardcover : alk. paper) — ISBN 978–0–8135–4970–5
(pbk. : alk. paper)

    1. Genocide—Rwanda—History—20th century.   2. Tutsi (African people)—Crimes
against—Rwanda—History—20th century.   3. Rwanda—History—Civil War, 1994—
Atrocities.   4. Rwanda—History—Civil War, 1994—Personal narratives.   5. Rwanda—
Ethnic relations—History—20th century.   I. Totten, Samuel.   II. Ubaldo, Rafiki.

   DT450.435.W4 2011

   967.57104'310922—dc22

2010028687

A British Cataloging-in-Publication record for this book is available from the British
Library.

Visit our Web site: http://rutgerspress.rutgers.edu

Manufactured in the United States of America
Typesetting: BookType

We, Samuel Totten and Rafiki Ubaldo, dedicate this book
to the survivors of the genocide in Rwanda. We are humbled
by their resilience, tenacity, and goodwill as they go about
reestablishing their lives in the shadow of the nightmare
to which they were subjected. We are also humbled by the warmth
they showed us as we probed into their lives, and are grateful
for their willingness to share their stories so that current and
future generations can learn what it is to face genocide up close.

CONTENTS

WE CANNOT FORGET

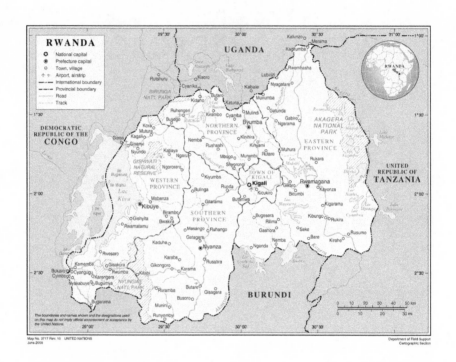

RWANDA

- ⊛ National capital
- ⊛ Prefecture capital
- ○ Town, village
- ✦ ✦ Airport, airstrip
- — International boundary
- — Provincial boundary
- — Road
- — Track

DEMOCRATIC
REPUBLIC OF THE
CONGO

UGANDA

UNITED
REPUBLIC OF
TANZANIA

BURUNDI

NORTHERN
PROVINCE

AKAGERA
NATIONAL
PARK

EASTERN
PROVINCE

WESTERN
PROVINCE

SOUTHERN
PROVINCE

GISHWATI
NATURAL
RESERVE

NYUNGWE
NATL PARK

BIRUNGA
NATL PARK

⊛ Kigali

TOWN OF
KIGALI

Lac
Kivu

29°30   30°00   30°30   31°00   1°00
1°30
2°00
2°30

Ruhuru   Kisoro   Cyanika   Kabale   Nyagatare   Kafunzo   Merama
Kagitumba
Rwempasha
Lubirizi
Butaro   Muvumba
Kidaho   Katuna
Kirambo   Cyamba   Mulindi   Getunda   Gabiro   Ngarama
Ruhengeri   Byumba   Muhura
Busogo   Kinihira   Kinyami   Rutare   Rukara
Kora   Nemba   Rushashi   Mbogo   Murambi
Mutura   Kagaho   Ngaru   Shyorongi
Gisenyi   Goma   Kabaya   Ngororero   Kiyumba   Gikoro   Rwamagana   Kayonza
Nyundo   Bulinga   Runda   Kicukiro   Bicumbi   Kigarama
Mabanza   Gitarama   Butamwa   Kibungo   Rukira   Rusumo
Kibuye   Birambo   Bugesera   Kibungo   Sake   Kirehe
Bwakira   Masango   Ruhango   Gashora   Bare
Gishyita   Gatagara   Nemba
Rwamatamu   Kaduha   Nyanza   Ngenda
Rwesero   Karaba   Rusatira
Kamembe   Gisakura   Gikongoro   Karama
Bukavu   Cyangugu   Rwumba   Kitabi
Cyimbogo   Karangera   Butare   Gisagara
Nyakabuye   Bugumya   Ruramba   Busoro
Bugarama   Munini
Runyombyi

The boundaries and names shown and the designations used
on this map do not imply official endorsement or acceptance by
the United Nations.

0   10   20   30   40   50 km
0   10   20   30 mi

29°00   29°30   30°00   30°30

Map No. 3717 Rev. 10   UNITED NATIONS
June 2008

Department of Field Support
Cartographic Section

INTRODUCTION

In one hundred days, between April 6 and July 4, 2004, extremist Hutu and their followers murdered between five hundred thousand and one million Tutsi in Rwanda. The genocide was largely carried out with rudimentary farm tools (such as machetes; *massues,* a traditional weapon fitted with nails sticking out from the head of the club; and hoes) versus modern, high-tech weapons, thus its appellation, "the machete genocide."

While many leaders and officials around the world, including those at the United Nations and in the United States, claimed that the genocide happened so quickly that it could not have been prevented, such claims are now perceived as disingenuous at best, and unconscionable lies at worst. In fact, throughout the early 1990s, Human Rights Watch (HRW) documented the ever-increasing tension and violence in Rwanda, and in doing so, issued one report after another that could, and should, have served as genocide early-warning signals to the international community. Unfortunately, and sadly, most of HRW reports and warnings went unheeded.

In this book we present the first-person accounts of eleven survivors. They reside in different parts of Rwanda and endured different experiences. What they have in common is continuing sadness and difficulties in daily living, but also amazing resilience.

EVENTS LEADING UP TO THE GENOCIDE

Genocide is a complex phenomenon, and no genocide erupts out of a vacuum. While no genocide is inevitable, all have antecedents. In the case of Rwanda, one has to reach back at least 125 years to even begin to understand what contributed to the ever-changing conflict between the Tutsi and the Hutu.

Some historians portray the relationship of the Hutu and Tutsi in precolonial times as one of harmony and equality. That, however, was not the case.
Initially, and generally, the Tutsi migration into Hutu regions was peaceful,
but over time the situation disintegrated as the Tutsi conquered the Hutu in
a series of battles. Subsequently, the Tutsi assumed rule of large swaths of the
region and, ultimately, controlled significant factors of life therein, including
the all-important ones of land, cattle, and labor.

At one and the same time, the Tutsi and Hutu began speaking the same
language, Kinyarwanda, practicing the same religion, living and working
side by side, and even intermarrying. Generally, the division between the
people of Rwanda broke down according to their occupations: the Tutsi
were largely cattle-herders, administrators, and soldiers; the Hutu were
farmers; and the Twa (otherwise known as Pygmies, and the smallest
population group in Rwanda) were foragers. Interestingly, depending upon
one's status in society (ownership of land and cattle, marriage into a family
of prominence, etc.), individuals could, and did, switch classifications
(from Hutu to Tutsi and vice versa). Furthermore, a host of entities within
Rwandan society contributed to keeping the peace between the various
groups, with the clan system possibly being the most significant when it
came to resolving conflict among them. Some scholars have argued that
up through the mid-nineteenth century, clans were much more prominent
and significant in identifying who was what in Rwandan society than were
Tutsi-Hutu-Twa classifications. Furthermore, Catharine Newbury (1988)
argued that although the terms "Hutu" and "Tutsi" were used in precolonial
times, their meaning and significance were vastly different from their more
modern use. In fact, Newbury (1988) noted that "ethnic identity" actually
differed in different periods of time and from one region to another, and
that there was no universal definition of ethnic identity.

Just prior to the arrival of the European colonialists in Rwanda, King
Rwabugiri, a Tutsi (who reigned from 1860 to 1895), tightened his control of
the country and carried out major reforms. The changes he instituted resulted
in an increased emphasis on "ethnic" differences in Rwanda. Regarding the
latter, Newbury (1988) noted that:

> With the arrival of central authorities, lines of distinction were
> altered and sharpened, as the categories of Hutu and Tutsi assumed
> new hierarchical overtones associated with proximity to the central
> court—proximity to power. Later, when the political arena widened and
> the intensity of political activity increased, these classifications became
> increasingly stratified and rigidified. More than simply conveying the

connotation of cultural difference from Tutsi, Hutu identity came to be associated with and eventually defined by inferior status. (n.p.)

Over the next one hundred-plus years, the impact of the latter had a devastating impact on generations of Rwandans.

King Rwabugiri created and oversaw a well-organized kingdom: a Tutsi king overseeing a threefold chieftaincy system (one dealing with military issues, one with land, and one with cattle). In earlier years, Europeans had believed that Africans were inferior to themselves; however, after witnessing what the Tutsi had created, the colonialists were extremely impressed.

In 1885, when European powers met in Berlin and negotiated the partition of Africa, Rwanda was turned over to Germany. Colonialists, first the Germans and then the Belgians, perceived the Tutsi, versus the Hutu or the Twa, as more like themselves: lighter skinned, more organized and adept at administrative tasks, and natural rulers. As a result, the Germans and Belgians largely retained the hierarchy they found in Rwanda, with the Tutsi in the seat of power.

This all related to the theory that the Tutsi were of Hamitic origin, which led Europeans to view them as "advanced beings," that is, more similar to themselves and to Semitic peoples than most other Africans (and certainly more similar than the Hutu and Twa). For the colonial administrations, the Hamitic theory underscored their bias and belief that the Tutsi were born to rule over the Hutu populace. While maintaining the infrastructure of the traditional administration, the German administration ruled through Rwanda's king.

The arrival of the first Catholic missionaries in Rwanda in 1900 set in motion a long and contentious relationship between Christianity and the traditional belief systems of the Rwandese. Ultimately, this relationship had a profound and negative impact on the relationship of the Hutu and Tutsi.

After the defeat of Germany in World War I, Rwanda became a protectorate of the League of Nations to be governed by Belgium. Following the lead of the Germans, the Belgian colonial administration and the Catholic Church continued to support the privileges accorded the Tutsi. In 1931, however, the Belgian colonial administration, in collaboration with the Catholic Church, deposed King Musinga and replaced him with his son Rudahigwa. The Catholic Church, which engineered the removal of the king, viewed him as an obstacle to the Christianization of Rwanda.

Gradually, the Belgians "systematically removed Hutu from positions of power and excluded them from higher education, which was the [main means] of preparation for careers in the administration. Thus they imposed a Tutsi monopoly of public life not just for the 1920s and 1930s, but for the next generation as well." Understandably, Hutus came to resent their second-class treatment, which led them to "experiencing the solidarity of the oppressed" (Des Forges 1999, 35, 38).

Following a census in 1933 and 1934, the Belgians introduced mandatory identification cards that denoted individuals as Hutu, Tutsi, or Twa. Thus began the formal divisions between the three main groups residing in Rwanda. During the 1994 genocide the ID cards became death warrants for the Tutsi.

Over the next twenty-five or so years, between the mid-1930s and late 1950s, various fissures erupted between the Tutsi elite and the colonialists, the Tutsi and the white clerics, and the Hutu and Tutsi. As colonialism gradually ground to an end in Africa and as the United Nations pressured Belgium to create a more just society in Rwanda, the Belgians provided various opportunities for the Hutu to step out of the shadow of the Tutsi. These ranged from naming Hutu to various administrative positions in Rwandan civil society to admitting more Hutu students into secondary schools. Hutus were also elected to various government advisory councils. The creation of such opportunities, though, resulted in disenchantment among both the Tutsi and Hutu. The Tutsi despaired over losing power, and the Hutu decried the limited opportunities granted them. As a result of such frustrations, both the conservative Tutsi and radical Hutu plotted how they could gain control of Rwanda. The conservative Tutsi hoped to push aside the Belgians before majority rule became the norm in Rwanda (which, they knew, would result in the Hutu gaining the upper hand since there were vastly more Hutu than Tutsi in Rwanda), and the radical Hutu were intent on gaining power before the Belgians withdrew from Rwanda. While moderates (who organized political parties whose aims were to bring together Hutu and Tutsi) existed in the country, they were pushed aside by both the Parmehutu, the party that appealed primarily to Hutu, and the Union Nationale Rwandaise, the party that appealed primarily to the Tutsi.

In *The French Betrayal of Rwanda*, Daniela Kroslak (2008, 23) argues that "After the Second World War the reinforced predominance of the Tutsi was reinterpreted by a new clerical generation of Flemish priests who, in the light of their own history, sympathized with the subordinated Hutu and branded the Tutsi feudal exploiters, which by then they were. This, too, kindled debate in the late 1950s before Belgium's departure in 1959 and Rwanda's independence in 1962." Notably, the Catholic Church, of which over 60 percent of all Rwandans were adherents, switched its allegiance from the Tutsi elite to the Hutu elite—and did so prior to the Belgians' switching allegiance. In doing so, the Catholic Church helped to bring about the Hutu revolution.

In 1957, nine Hutu intellectuals published a political pamphlet entitled The Bahutu Manifesto, which denounced the "Tutsi monopoly" and affirmed that the Hutu constituted the rightful "race" of Rwanda. Part and parcel of the manifesto was that the Tutsi constituted a foreign and Hamitic race. The Bahutu Manifesto received the support of both Catholic missionaries and the colonial administration, the latter of which was growing uncomfortable with the demands for independence by the ruling Tutsi elites. Tutsi elites countered that the Tutsi were, in fact, the legitimate founders of the Rwandan state. Following in the steps of the Bahutu Manifesto, Hutu intellectuals created Parmehutu, the Party for the Emancipation of Bahutu.

While receiving medical treatment from a Belgian physician in 1959, King Rudahigwa died under mysterious circumstances, which increased the level of fear among Tutsi elites, who already believed that the colonial administration aimed to curtail their demands for independence. Violence erupted around this event, as well as others, leading to an ongoing spiral of attacks and counterattacks. Ultimately, some two thousand Tutsi were murdered and thousands of Tutsi families fled from the country in fear. A UN special commission conducted a study in Rwanda and reported that "racism bordered on 'Nazism against the Tutsi minorities' and that the government together with the Belgian authorities were to blame" (Melvern 2004, 7).

Dismissive of the accusations, the Belgians removed half the Tutsis serving as local authorities and replaced them with Hutus. This opened the door for even more overt racism against the Tutsi. Melvern (2004, 7) writes that "for the next three decades Rwandan political life would fall under the influence of a monstrous racist ideology that preached intolerance and hatred."

That same year, the so-called Hutu Social Revolution took place amid tensions between the Hutu and the Tutsi. By this time, the Belgian administration and the Catholic Church had switched alliances, and in doing so cut their ties with the Tutsi ruling classes and began supporting Hutu politicians who were more concerned with the abolition of the monarchy than ongoing colonialism.

Around this same time, an attack on a Hutu leader in Gitarama by a group of young Tutsi sparked off widespread violence against the Tutsi in the country. Thousands of Tutsi were killed while thousands of others were forced into exile.

Ultimately, municipal elections in 1960 resulted in the Hutu elite's gaining total leadership of Rwanda. Subsequently, in 1961, the monarchy was abolished and Rwanda became a republic. In 1962, Rwanda received independence from Belgium and a Hutu elite took over the leadership of Rwanda. Gregoire Kayibanda, the leader of Parmehutu, became the first president of independent Rwanda.

Beginning in 1961, Tutsi refugees carried out attacks on Rwanda, "an effort they would repeat ten times over the next six years" (Des Forges 1999, 39). Taking advantage of the attacks, Hutu leaders in Rwanda issued a clarion call to all Hutu to stand behind the government, took even greater control of the government reins, and continued to remove Tutsi from any positions of authority. Hutu officials also carried out attacks against Tutsi still residing in Rwanda. During this period, a minister in President Gregoire Kayibanda's cabinet was assigned to supervise the planned killing of Tutsi. It is estimated that between ten and fourteen thousand Tutsi were killed during this period (Melvern 2004, 9, 10). Tellingly, in 1964, British philosopher Bertrand Russell called the killings of Tutsi the most horrible extermination of a people since the Holocaust.

Des Forges (1999, 40) notes that "by 1967, when both the incursions and the attacks within Rwandan ended, Tutsi were at risk of attack for the simple fact of being Tutsi." It is estimated that between the early 1960s and 1967 approximately twenty thousand Tutsi were murdered and that more than three hundred thousand were forced out of Rwanda. In 1963, exiled Tutsi, who had been carrying out periodic attacks against the Hutu government in Rwanda, intensified attacks from neighboring Burundi. The attacks prompted the Hutu-run government to kill Tutsi still residing in Rwanda. By the end of the 1960s, half of the Rwandan Tutsi had fled the violence in Rwanda and were leading lives in exile.

In a coup d'état in 1973, Major General Juvénal Habyarimana ousted President Gregoire Kayibanda. Habyarimana, a Hutu from the north of Rwanda, accused Kayibanda and the southern Hutu elite of practicing regionalism and dividing the country. Purportedly, Kayibanda had favored the Hutu from his region of Rwanda, while ignoring and disenfranchising Hutu from the rest of the country. A different accusation was leveled against the Tutsi: that their presence in both government administration and the nation's schools largely exceeded imposed quota policies aimed at correcting historical injustices against the Hutu majority. Slightly before and during the 1973 coup, Tutsi were purged from both public schools and the National University of Rwanda. This resulted in another flood of Tutsis fleeing into exile.

In 1975, Habyarimana created the MRND (Mouvement républicain national pour la démocratie et le développement). Three years later, in 1978, MRND was declared the only political party allowed in Rwanda. From that point forward, every Rwandan was made a de facto member of the party, and no opposition to the MRND or Habyarimana was allowed.

Four years later, in 1979, Rwandans in exile created the Rwanda National Union (RANU), whose express goal was to end the stateless status of Rwandan refugees. Nine years later, in 1988, they created the Rwandan Patriotic Front (RPF).

Over the years, the number of Rwandan refugees in neighboring states (Burundi, Uganda, and Tanzania) ballooned to well over a half million people. With the exception of Tanzania, where refugees were welcomed, the vast majority of Rwandan refugees in the other countries were treated poorly and lived marginalized lives.

On October 1, 1990, angry at its continued exile and frustrated with the Habyarimana government's refusal to allow Tutsis to return home to Rwanda, the RPF attacked Rwanda from Uganda, thus igniting a civil war. According to Filip Reyntjens (1996, 246), "The RPF incursion allowed for the manipulation of ethnicity [by the Habyarimana government in Rwanda] and thus put the Tutsi population in [Rwanda] in great jeopardy." In fact, the Habyarimana administration reacted, in part, by carrying out a fake attack of its own on Kigali, the capital of Rwanda, and then carrying out wholesale arrests of approximately thirteen thousand Tutsi, asserting that such individuals were supporters of the RPF and constituted a fifth column of sorts. Then, throughout the 1990s, "test massacres" of Tutsi took place in regions such as Bugesera and Kibirira.

Alarmed at the violence in Rwanda, the United Nations pushed the combatants to engage in peace negotiations. The latter were held in Arusha, Tanzania. In July 1992, the RPF and the Rwandan government agreed to a cease-fire, and in August 1992 both sides agreed to the first round of agreements that would become commonly referred to as the Arusha Accords.

Cosponsored by the United States, the Organization of African Unity, and France, the talks addressed a number of key issues: power sharing between Hutu and Tutsi via the establishment of a transitional government, the dismantling of the military dictatorship of President Juvénal Habyarimana, the establishment of the rule of law in Rwanda, the repatriation and resettlement of refugees, and the integration of the RPF and FAR (Forces armées rwandaises) into one Rwandan military force. Violence in Rwanda, though, continued unabated, and in January 1994 the U.S. Central

Intelligence Agency warned that if it continued up to half a million Rwandans could die.

In July 1993, Melchoir Ndadaye, a Hutu, was elected president of Burundi, but not three months later, he was assassinated by four Tutsi hard-line soldiers. Not only did the assassination result in a prolonged civil war between the Tutsi and Hutu in Burundi, in which an estimated two hundred thousand people were killed, but it had profound ramifications in Rwanda. As Des Forges (1999) asserted:

> The movement known as Hutu Power (pronounced *Pawa* in Kinyar-wanda), the coalition that would make the genocide possible, was built upon the corpse of [Burundi president Melchior] Ndadaye. The doubts about RPF's intentions, sown by [its] February 1993 attack [on Rwanda] and fed by the extent of RPF gains at Arusha, ripened following the assassination of Ndadaye in Burundi. As one political leader commented during the genocide, "Who didn't have his eyes opened by what happened in Burundi? [They] elected President Ndadaye [a moderate Hutu], who really wanted Hutu and Tutsi to live together, but you know what they did [to him] . . . ? (p.137)

On the evening of April 6, 1994, the Rwandan presidential airplane carrying the presidents of Rwanda and Burundi, who were returning from meetings in Dar es Salaam about the Arusha Peace Agreement (also referred to as Arusha Accords), was shot down by a missile over the Kigali airport. All on board were killed. Immediately, roadblocks were put in place across the city of Kigali and the systematic slaughter of Tutsi began. Between April and July 1994 some five hundred thousand to one million Tutsi were killed, along with pro-democracy Hutu. On July 4, 1994, the RPF took control of Kigali and put an end to the genocide.

INTERVIEWING SURVIVORS OF THE 1994 GENOCIDE

The genesis of this book was an initial research project that we (Totten and Ubaldo, the interviewers and co-editors) conducted in Rwanda during the summer of 2006. At that time, we were conducting a qualitative study of survivors' perceptions of the *gacaca* process (an indigenous form of local justice in Rwanda that was adapted in the late 1990s and implemented in the early 2000s to try alleged perpetrators of the 1994 Rwandan genocide). During the course of our research, we found ourselves asking more and more questions about each individual's personal history in relation to their life prior to the period of genocide, particularly in relation to their interactions with Hutu neighbors and officials in their village. Such information added immensely to the context of the interviewees' perspective of gacaca, and provided powerful insights into what transpired prior to and during the genocidal period.

Various individuals said they greatly appreciated that we were interested in their complete stories, and that we did not simply ask, in a quick and perfunctory fashion, about what they had experienced during the genocide. They inferred that other researchers and journalists spent far less time speaking to them and really getting to know who they were or what they thought, felt, and had experienced prior to, during, and following the 1994 genocide. Such comments prodded us to consider the possibility and value of conducting in-depth interviews with a wide range of survivors.

While many fine analyses had been published about the Rwandan genocide, relatively few books of interviews were available (e.g., *Into the Quick of Life: The Rwandan Genocide: The Survivors Speak* by Jean Hatzfeld; *A Time for Machetes: The Rwandan Genocide: The Killers Speak* by Jean Hatzfeld; *Intimate Enemy: Images and Voices of the Rwandan Genocide* by Scott Straus and Robert Lyons). The latter books, we knew, either included excerpts of interviews (Straus and Lyons) or contained relatively short interviews (the two books by Hatzfeld). As powerful as the information and stories in the latter books are, they do not provide in-depth and detailed stories about the survivors' experiences before, during, and in the aftermath of the genocide. Nor do the aforementioned accounts even begin to approach the detail found in many of the accounts and oral histories of such genocidal tragedies as, for example, the Armenian genocide, the Holocaust, or the Cambodian genocide.

Eventually, and prior to the conclusion of the study of the gacaca process, we decided that it would be worthwhile to conduct detailed interviews with an eclectic group of survivors who had resided in different parts of the country, and had vastly different experiences.

Ultimately, we conducted the interviews over a period of a year and a half (January 2008 through August 2009). Each interview in this book took between seven and fifteen hours to conduct. In every single case, interviews were conducted over a period of two or more days.

THE INTERVIEWEES

All the interviewees included in this book are survivors of the 1994 Rwandan genocide. Since the survivors' backgrounds (e.g., the parents of some survivors were both Tutsi, while others had one parent who was Tutsi and one who was Hutu), experiences (e.g., some had been attacked by extremist Hutu prior to 1994, most had not; some victims fought back, most did not; some managed to escape to Burundi or the Congo, many did not), and insights were vastly different, we chose to focus solely on the stories of survivors, and not perpetrators. Even those who sought sanctuary in the very same area often had vastly different experiences, and this is understandable when one realizes that in many cases tens of thousands of people congregated at churches and sector offices.

We interviewed twenty-four individuals (male and female, ranging in age from twenty-two to their early sixties) from all walks of life (e.g., uneducated and educated; the unemployed, farmers, educators, business persons, journalists, and activists; impoverished and "middle class"; married, widowed, never been married) who had lived in different parts of Rwanda during the genocide. We chose eleven of the most detailed and informative interviews for inclusion in the book.

As is often the case with interview projects, some of the interviewees were only able to complete the initial session as other commitments at home, work, or gacaca forced them to bow out. This was extremely unfortunate as some of the individuals (one who is now a member of the Rwandan parliament, one who was a journalist and had sought sanctuary at the Hôtel des Mille Collines during the genocide, and another who served as the head of the gacaca in his area) had very interesting backgrounds and stories to tell. Unfortunately, two of these individuals were among our oldest interviewees (one was in her late forties and the other was in his late fifties), and since they were unable to sit for complete interviews, our final sample is skewed toward those who were quite young during the genocide.

The criteria used to select interviews for inclusion in this book were as follows: a rough balance between females and males; those who came from homes composed of different ethnicities (e.g., a Tutsi mother and father or either a Tutsi father and Hutu mother or a Hutu father and a Tutsi mother); individuals who were various ages during the genocide (e.g., children, teenagers, young adults in their twenties, and older adults in their forties and fifties); people who resided in different parts of Rwanda during the genocide (including the east, west, south, and north, as well as in cities, towns, and villages); those who had vastly different experiences during the genocide (e.g., those who sought sanctuary around or in churches; those who witnessed Tutsis engaging in combat with Hutu extremists or did so themselves; those who could provide a detailed account of the killings in Ntarama or Murambi); and those who could provide unique views into the post-genocide period (e.g., the dynamic of former perpetrators or perpetrators' families living side-by-side in the aftermath of the genocide, and the psychological, economic, and other hardships that survivors continue to face some fifteen years after the genocide).

Finally, it is notable that nine out of the eleven interviewees chose not to reveal their true names, and they did so for a variety of reasons. Several feared that those who killed their families or the families of killers might come across the interviews, and in their fury strike out at the interviewee(s). Others were nervous that their criticism of the government's treatment of survivors in terms of housing and psychological assistance might result in some sort of retaliation. A couple of interviewees felt that revealing their true identity could damage their future career because of their revelations about how the 1994 genocide has deeply affected their life. One of the interviewees said: "Imagine you were an employer and you heard my story of strong trauma after the genocide, would you take the risk to employ me?" Others felt it was unwise to have their name revealed since they detail situations involving relatives, friends, or neighbors who hid with them during the genocide and felt this could endanger their rescuers' lives. Finally, a number of female interviewees revealed such intimate details about themselves that they chose to use a pseudonym.

Conducting the Interviews

Most of the interviews were conducted in Kinyarwanda. When an interviewee was fluent in English, then English was used.

During the course of the interviews, the interpreters (Rafiki Ubaldo, Angelique Murenzi, and Ernest Mutwarasibo) did not translate stumblings such as "ums" and "ahs," but were faithful to the word usage and sentence structure of the interviewees. Thus, where certain words or phrases in an interview are not absolutely clear, explanations and synonyms have been added, in brackets, for the purpose of clarification.

Concomitantly, any mumblings by interviewees that were not critical to the interviewee's story were deleted for the sake of readability. The same is true of any questions the interviewees may have asked in response to questions posited by the interviewer. When interviewees added something of interest that was germane to a question, such information was included in the interview, along with an editor's note.

The questionnaire consisted of thirty-two questions that probed a host of issues related to the interviewees' experiences in the pre-genocide, genocide, and post-genocide periods.

Conducting the interviews was grueling for both the survivors and us. Any survivor of genocide who relates his or her story faces a difficult, if not excruciating, task. In almost every case, as a survivor tells his or her story, the story automatically and inexorably results in the recall of horrific memories and vivid scenes of horror (including those during which they may have witnessed the brutal treatment, if not murder, of loved ones). In some cases, the survivors experience an unnerving and very real sense that they are living the horrors all over again. It was primarily due to the latter reasons that we always informed the interviewees that they were not obligated in any way to be interviewed, and promised them that any time they wished to end the interview for the day, or altogether (regardless of whether the interview was completed or not), that it was their absolute right to do so. There were, in fact, many cases when interviewees asked if we could end the interview for the day and pick it up the next. Sometimes this happened repeatedly with the same interviewee. As a result, some interviews were conducted over three and four sessions (sometimes with weeks separating the sessions). There were also several interviewees who asked if the interview could be halted altogether, either because they simply found it too grueling to reveal their stories in such great detail or because they felt they had revealed enough of their story and saw no point in continuing to talk on and on about their experiences, thoughts, and perspectives.

Numerous times interviewees broke down and cried, and either excused themselves for fifteen or twenty minutes in order to regain their composure or asked us if we would simply sit and keep them company. In one case, an elderly female survivor asked us if we would hug and hold her (which we did).

Since the interviews always took two or more days to conduct, it allowed us to check back with each interviewee to see how they were doing emotionally. In almost every case, the interviewees voiced an interest in continuing their interviews, which was a sign to us that the interviewees were holding up emotionally and found at least some value in relating their stories. Those who could not commit to meeting again to continue their interviews did so due to major obligations or conflicts in their schedules. When we returned for the second (and, in some cases, third and fourth) portion of the interview, it was as if we were returning to see a friend. In fact, upon our return, conversation during the first fifteen to thirty minutes often revolved around issues unrelated to the genocide and pertained to more personal and social issues or concerns.

The interpreters also faced extremely difficult circumstances. Not only were they doing double work (translating the questions from English into

Kinyarwanda and then translating the interviewee's response from Kinyar-wanda into English), but since they were survivors, the stories being told affected them to a far greater extent than they would have had they not experienced the genocide at first hand. Many of the stories related by the interviewees invoked vivid and horrific memories for the interpreters— memories of threats, attacks against one's home or village, and beatings or killings of their loved ones and friends. At various times, the interpreters sat in silence for minutes at a time in order to collect themselves, emoted (either by swearing and commenting in English or tearing up), or simply asking to quit for the day.

Key Issues and Themes

The interviews included in this book provide in-depth stories and, in some cases, revelatory information about the pre-genocide, genocide, and the post-genocide periods. Delineated herein are the major issues and themes that are addressed in a fair amount of detail in various interviews. Since it is a given that all the interviewees spoke about the violence they faced and witnessed, this is not discussed under a separate category.

Discrimination against Tutsi

Initially, every interviewee was asked to recall when they first realized that some in Rwandan society perceived Hutu and Tutsi as being different. Generally, the interviewees begin by talking about being ordered, at school, to stand up and identify him or herself as a Tutsi or Hutu. Many speak about how they were not sure what ethnicity they were, and either had to be told by their teacher or had to go home and ask their parents or grandparents. Many also speak about what they perceived as the slanted history they were taught, with the Tutsi demonized and blamed for many, if not most, ills of Rwandan society.

Likewise, numerous interviewees comment on how each year, beginning in 1990 until the commencement of the genocide in April 1994, became ever more tense and volatile: Tutsi were suspected and accused by Hutu of being Rwandan Patriotic Front (RPF) supporters; the creation of Hutu Power groups (extremists in favor of Hutu exclusivity) contributed to ever-increasing divisiveness within Rwandan society; and *Kangura* (an extremist newspaper) and Radio-télévision libre des mille collines (RTLM) (hate radio) spewed their venomous anti-Tutsi rhetoric.

One interviewee after another describe how he or she, as a Tutsi, felt like a second-class citizen in Rwanda. A majority of the interviewees note that in the two to three years preceding the genocide they had absolutely no recourse if Hutu insulted or assaulted them. Many claim that Hutu harassed or harmed Tutsi with total impunity.

Relationships between Tutsi and Hutu prior to 1990

Most of the interviewees state that prior to 1990, Tutsi and Hutu in their villages and towns largely lived in peace, even though the government and various officials at different levels treated Tutsi as second-class citizens. After the invasion by the RPF in 1990, though, relationships between Tutsi and Hutu neighbors became strained, largely due to ongoing propaganda by Hutu extremists and the resulting fear by many Hutu that the intent of the RPF was to expel Hutu from Rwanda, subjugate or exterminate them.

Ever-increasing Violence prior to 1994

Every interviewee comments on how the violence against Tutsi increased in 1990, right after the Rwandan Patriotic Front attacked Rwanda. Interviewees comment on how individuals (be it themselves, their fathers, or brothers) were arrested, beaten, and tortured; children were harassed and beaten when they went to fetch water; and teachers slapped and denigrated Tutsi children for various minor infractions, which they overlooked when committed by Hutu children, or just out of pure spite and cruelty. In some cases, harassment by teachers was so cruel that Tutsi children refused to return to school.

Some interviewees comment on how certain relatives chose to leave Rwanda and move to another nation, generally Burundi or Uganda, in order to escape the ever-increasing violence. Others note that brothers or other young men in their villages left home to join the RPF.

Many mention the virulent messages issued in *Kangura* and RTLM, and how the hateful messages encouraged and prodded Hutu to distrust Tutsi and treat them as enemies. Likewise, many mention the fact that Tutsi were described in disparaging and dehumanizing terms such as *inyenzi* (cockroach) and *inzokas* (snakes) by *Kangura*, RTLM, and fellow Hutu villagers—terms that suggested Tutsi were dangerous and needed to be dealt with harshly.

Governmental Efforts to Meet Survivors' Needs

The vast majority of interviewees note that they believe the current Rwandan government has been fairly proactive in its attempt to meet the dire needs of genocide survivors. Furthermore, numerous individuals note and comment on the creation and implementation of special programs that address all of the following needs (and more) of the survivors: school fees, the construction of new houses, medical care and medication for females who were raped and infected with HIV/AIDS during the genocide.

At one and the same time, many interviewees point out that a good number of the programs have been underfunded or not managed very well. As a result, many survivors report how they, or their loved ones and fellow survivors, remain in dire need of assistance—in terms of psychological counseling, funds for college, blocks of land on which to build a home, materials with which to build a house—which has not been forthcoming.

The continued lack of housing for genocide survivors is a major problem. During the genocide, most homes and buildings were either destroyed or dismantled piece by piece and carried off by Hutu fleeing from the incoming Rwandan Patriotic Front (the military arm of the Tutsi rebels). Although the current Rwandan government has promised to provide survivors with their own homes, it is now more than sixteen years on and many survivors continue to wait for the promise to be honored. A female survivor who lost her husband and five of her seven children and has moved from place to place since she does not have her own home said: "FARG [Fonds national pour l'assistance aux rescapés du génocide] has built 100 houses [around her area] but those houses have no toilets and no kitchens. The contractor who built the houses was corrupt and stole the money and didn't complete the houses. And besides that, about 200 more houses are needed here. FARG forgets that life doesn't stop with physically surviving in '94."

Loneliness of Survivors

When the interviewees speak of the murder of their fathers, mothers, brothers, sisters, grandmothers, grandfathers, cousins, and children, and the fact that they miss their relatives' presence in their lives, the sense of their loneliness is palpable. Many of the youngest interviewees, particularly the orphans, speak about how they are totally alone in the world, with no one to love them, care for them when they are in need, or to provide guidance. Those who lost husbands or wives and children talk about the sorrow of being widowed and without their children, and how utterly empty they feel. Several comment that once their family members were murdered, often in front of them, they felt as if they, themselves, had died. Numerous interviewees said that since they are already dead inside (emotionally, socially, spiritually), they would prefer being dead physically.

A twenty-six-year-old male survivor, who lost his mother and two brothers in the genocide (and whose father died shortly after), said: "Before the 1990s I was happy, I led a normal life, enjoyed affection from my parents. I had a very nice life. I was blessed as I had my parents, my brothers, and my extended family. Now, today, I feel sad. It's hard for me to cry when someone dies. When a friend's parent dies and they have one left, I think, not because I am mean or selfish, but I think, they are lucky."

Ongoing Psychological Suffering

The vast majority of the interviewees comment at length about the psychological suffering they continue to experience some sixteen years after the end of the genocide. They say the memories of the horrors to which they and their loved ones and friends were subjected (including witnessing the machete attacks on their loved ones, being chased and hunted down by Hutu, being raped by Hutu, nearly drowning in rivers filled with dead bodies) never leave them. They talk about their perdurable sadness, their ongoing anguish over the loss of loved ones, and acute trauma.

When the interviewees refer to "trauma," they are not referring to depression, no matter how serious or profound such depression might be, but something else altogether. They are, in fact, referring solely to those incidents and events when either they, a loved one, friend, or fellow community member suffers a psychological attack (or state of panic) that results in their crying for days on end, screaming or yelling as a result of some incident or sound that brings back vivid memories of what they witnessed or experienced during the genocide, or when they must be hospitalized in order to receive medication to ameliorate their post-traumatic stress.

For example, a female survivor/interviewee in her mid-thirties, who lost her entire family (mother, father, brothers, and sisters), reports the following:

> My aunt is traumatized as a result of the genocide. She had seven children, and now she only has two. They were all killed, as was their father, her husband. She constantly cries and shouts a lot. The worst case we've seen was during a memorial service [when] she began shouting and crying and it sounded as if she thought the war was on again. That day she got help from a trauma counselor, but the rest of the time [throughout the year] she receives no help. Only when there are active signs of trauma [showing up in public, making incoherent sounds] can she get help. Other times, she can't get help because there are no signs. Crying is not enough of a sign. Besides she does not have enough money to go get help every time she cries.

Significantly, then, when the interviewees speak about the great difficulties survivors (both themselves and others) face, they are not taking into account how most survivors may, in fact, suffer, to some degree, from clinical depression. Indeed, they are not taking into account that profound depression causes one to live life bereft of joy, hope, or any sort of happiness, and constitutes a serious malady that impacts how one perceives the world and life itself. And unless they are specifically questioned how about they feel about daily life or their existence, interviewees are generally not inclined to broach such issues or speak about them. Equally significant, most do not seem to understand, let alone appreciate, that clinical depression can and should be treated by professionals through both counseling and medication.

When questioned about how they feel on a daily basis—happy, fair (a mixture of happy and sad), sad, depressed—the vast majority of the interviewees reply with the equivalent of "so-so" to "sad." Only a few interviewees speak about living in a cocoon of desolation, though the words and countenances of many of the others suggest that they, too, might experience such misery.

A few of the more educated interviewees comment that psychological assistance for survivors suffering from post-traumatic stress is minimal in Rwanda. While the government and various nongovernmental organizations have specialists to conduct trainer of trainer programs in cities, towns, and villages, to enable local people to serve as counselors, the number of counselors compared to those in need of assistance is infinitesimal. The overall problem is exacerbated by the fact, as mentioned above, that many survivors do not seem to realize that the daily depression, anxiety, and overwhelming sadness they experience is potentially treatable, and thus do not seek help. Over and above that, many survivors are so impoverished that they cannot afford the relatively small amount of money to travel by bus to seek the help of a counselor. Thus, tens of thousands likely live forlorn lives that are awash in an overwhelming sadness that leaves them feeling largely bereft each and every day of their lives.

Heavy Weight on the Shoulders
of the Widows, Children, and Orphans

Almost to a person, the interviewees comment on the heavy weight of responsibility they carry on their shoulders. Widows, orphans, and children who have been forced to accept the mantle of main provider all comment about the need to fend for themselves and their families, and the need to do so with little to no assistance of any kind from anyone else. The young also talk about weighing the advantages of trying to attend school (secondary school and/or university) versus making sure that they and their loved ones (or those they are taking care of, such as younger orphans or extended-family members) have adequate housing and enough to eat each and every day.

Among the host of problems and challenges the interviewees speak about dealing with are grinding poverty, a lack of education, and joblessness. A twenty-six-year old interviewee, who is an orphan, with a university education, reports that after searching for a job for well over a year he has all but given up hope that he will eventually find a decent job: "For a whole year I would buy newspapers twice a week looking for jobs, spending money on application letters. I've applied for so many jobs—more than a hundred—I've quit counting. I'd apply for five jobs a week. Whenever I came across a position related in any way to my [discipline] I'd apply. . . . I even went to banks to see about getting a loan so I could begin my own business, but they wouldn't give me a loan because I didn't have a steady job." One can only imagine how isolated, frustrated, and hopeless such an individual feels—one who is totally alone in the world and had the fortitude to earn a university degree in the aftermath of genocide only to remain financially destitute with little to no hope that his life will get any better any time soon, if at all.

Appreciation for Gacaca

There is no doubt that the vast majority of the interviewees, certainly in the 90 percent range, seemingly feel positive about various aspects of gacaca. It is also a fact, though, that many of the interviewees seemingly, and simply, reiterated the government's position about gacaca's value in regard to emptying jails (by allowing those génocidaires—those who carried out killings during the genocide, many of whom are still serving prison sentences—who plead guilty, fully divulge their crimes, and ask for forgiveness in a genuine manner to have his or her prison sentence cut in half), and ending divisiveness (purportedly by treating all citizens of the country fairly, that is, bringing the perpetrators to justice, and ending impunity, but at the same time allowing those who confess and ask forgiveness to be accorded forgiveness by halving their prison sentences).

Even those who do not believe that gacaca is as valuable as the government purports it to be in regard to truly holding perpetrators responsible for their actions and ending impunity comment that gacaca is helpful in helping to locate the "bones" [remains] of loved ones and getting at, even if only partially, the truth in regard to what happened to one's loved ones during the genocide (meaning, how they were killed, where, and when), and who was responsible for harming or killing their family members.

As for the question as to whether gacaca actually contributes to the reconciliation of the victims and former perpetrators, that was another matter altogether, and many of the interviewees held vastly different views.

While most interviewees believe gacaca contributes to ending impunity and assists families in locating their loved ones' remains, their views that gacaca will bring about reconciliation between the victims and their killers is extremely mixed. Some think it might, others are dubious, and some are outright disdainful and dismissive of such a notion.

A twenty-six-year old man who lost his entire family whispered: "Reconciliation? There are many things I [would] look at before I'd consider reconciliation taking place. I may try to reconcile with one person but [looking extremely sad and depressed and trying to say something but not finding the words] . . . I think reconciliation is only possible for a person who wasn't hunted, who didn't lose all his family, and didn't experience all these horrors, because that picture is hard to erase from your brain."

Although reconciliation is still a work in progress and can't be said to be a fact of life in Rwanda, people (former perpetrators, the family of perpetrators, and survivors) do live side-by-side, often work side-by-side, travel on the same small vans that serve as the main forms of transportation in the country, obtain water at the same sources, purchase goods at the same tiny stores, and do so, for the most part, in a civil manner day in and day out, month after month and year after year. Perhaps that is all that can be expected sixteen years after such a massive and catastrophic genocide. Indeed, possibly that, in and of itself, is a miracle of sorts.

Ongoing Fear for Their Lives

While most of the interviewees speak appreciatively of the current security situation in Rwanda (i.e., the efforts of the current government to maintain a relatively peaceful society), many say that they do not feel welcome in the villages they lived in prior to or during the genocide. Many who continue to reside in the same village in which they grew up comment that the families of génocidaires are unfriendly, if not outright mean and spiteful, toward them. Various survivors remark that the families of génocidaires either totally ignore them, despite the fact that they live in close proximity to one another and frequently see one another; cast angry looks at them; spew harsh comments when passing the interviewee's/survivor's home; or leave threatening messages under their doors. Some of survivors/interviewees voice a desire to move to another part of Rwanda, while others say they wish they could leave Rwanda altogether. In both cases, a lack of financial wherewithal precludes their moving.

Numerous individuals who no longer reside in their original village say that they actually fear returning home; and indeed, they fear that their life would be at risk should they return. Some even say that they are not willing to remain in their village at night, out of fear that someone might murder them under cover of darkness.

Some interviewees currently studying at the National University of Rwanda state that they feel uneasy attending the same school as former Hutu, and that during their initial matriculation at school, feared they might be killed (particularly while asleep). Some comment that they have no idea whether some of their fellow students actually took part in the killings in 1994 and that makes them nervous about attending classes with or sleeping in the same dorms with such individuals. Some also say it is unnerving to attend classes and live in dorms with the children of those who are currently imprisoned for having committed atrocities during the genocide.

According to the interviewees, among the many reasons for the ongoing tension between survivors and others (be they verbal or written insults or threats, menacing looks, or more hostile actions such as destroying their gardens or stealing the garden produce) are as follows: ongoing hatred, toward Tutsis; resentment that the survivors were not killed during the genocide; fear that the survivors might reveal something at gacaca about the crimes the génocidaires committed; ongoing genocide ideology; and possible guilt over what they had done during the genocidal period (be it attacking Tutsis, taking part in the killing process, or failing to assist the Tutsi). The latter, of course, is conjecture on the part of the interviewees.

Tied to the aforementioned fear of many interviewees is their sense that the "genocide ideology" (the extremist Hutu mindset that demonizes all Tutsi) lingers among many former Hutu. Speaking of such, a woman who lost her husband and five children said: "I see genocide tendencies in the comments made by local people about the national government. Every time there is a policy to implement, Hutus in the neighborhood will makes comparisons with the former government [the Hutu-dominated government during and prior to 1994, which supported the Hutu extremists], mostly saying that things were perfect with the former government, the Habyarimana regime. That is what scares me most."

The International Community's Response
to the Genocide and Its Aftermath

Interestingly, most of the interviewees did not voice bitter thoughts or feelings toward the international community for watching the genocide unfold and doing little to nothing to halt the atrocities. That is not to say that they don't greatly regret the lack of effective international action. Still, their main concern is centered around what the international community can, and should, do today to "atone" for its callous and unconscionable disregard for the lives of hundreds of thousands of Tutsi and thousands of moderate Hutu.

Many interviewees speak about the need for political leaders as well as "average" citizens from abroad to visit Rwanda in order to appreciate the devastation wrought by the genocide as well as to gain an understanding of the plight of the survivors in the post-genocide period. The interviewees also suggest the need for members of the international community (nations and individuals) to help provide funding and materials for the erection of solid homes for the survivors; funding, training, and personnel to address the psychological needs of survivors; and funding (scholarships) to help survivors matriculate at a Rwandan university, if not a U.S. or European university.

Lack of Attention to Key Issues and Concerns in the Interviews

There are numerous issues that very few (and, in certain cases, none) of the interviewees address in the interviews. Among the most significant are: insights into Hutu resentment at the decades-long discrimination against them by the Tutsi in the colonial and early postcolonial years; the real fear experienced by Hutu as a result of the 1990 RPF attack on Rwanda and the possibility of their being slaughtered by the RPF; and the equally real fear of the RPF taking over the country and forcing Hutu into servitude and second-class citizenship again. While some interviewees allude to some of the above concerns, none address them directly or in any detail.

It is possible that the interviewees have not considered such issues or, if they have, do not consider them all that important in light of the tragedy that befell themselves and their fellow Tutsi. Or, it is possible that the interviewees have thought about such concerns but dismiss them as inconsequential (when, in fact, they are anything but).

CONCLUSION

No one can really gain a true sense of the horror of genocide without coming face-to-face with it. That is, no one can sense the abject fear, the chaos created by jeering and callous killers, the unfathomable sorrow of seeing loved ones brutalized and murdered, the stench of rotting bodies, the horror of being hunted down, or being brutally beaten and slashed and left for dead.

It is equally true that no one can really gain a true sense of the devastation, loss, suffering, and ongoing hardship experienced by survivors in the post-genocide period without coming face-to-face with such. For many of the interviewees/survivors whose stories are presented in this book, extreme sadness and a lack of hope are their daily companions. The horrors suffered and witnessed by them never seem to fade; indeed, these are something that the interviewees seem destined to live with day in and day out for the rest of their lives. As a survivor of the genocidal massacre at Murambi said:

> As for my wife and five children, I do not know exactly how they died. The women and children were inside the classrooms [half-built classrooms located on the compound in Murambi, where ten thousand or more people were encouraged to seek shelter and then slain in a massive orgy of violence that lasted half a night and almost all the next day]. What I do know is that they must have been killed in a very horrible way because the *Interahamwe* [the youth wing of the Hutu extremists, who were extremely violent and led the way in carrying out the genocidal killing] went in the classroom and slashed them with machetes, cutting off limbs and killing them with massues. What is unbearable is the memory of hearing my children [he said "my children" but must have meant all of the children huddled therein] and their begging for forgiveness even though they had nothing to ask forgiveness for.

While no single book is capable of providing a comprehensive picture of a genocide, the interviews included in this book present a vivid snapshot of important aspects of the Rwandan genocide by those who suffered through it and survived. The interviews present intricate details and harrowing images of what individual Tutsi experienced and witnessed during the events leading up to the 1994 Rwandan genocide, at the center of the maw of the genocide, and in its aftermath. They also provide remarkable insights into various relationships that Tutsi and Hutu had prior to the genocide, the foreshadowing of genocide vis-à-vis the violence carried out by the FAR and the Interahamwe in the wake of the RPF's attack on Rwanda in 1990, the ever-increasing hatred and threats issued by *Kangura* and RTLM, the fear aroused by the downing of Habyarimana's plane. Likewise they provide powerful insights into the killing processes carried out in various areas of Rwanda, the reactions (good and bad) of Hutu in response to the attacks on their Tutsi family members and friends, the ways in which different individuals managed to survive the savagery, the return to Rwanda to face the utter destruction wrought by the perpetrators, and the host of difficulties that never seem to dissipate in the post-genocide period.

As one reads story after story of horror, one begins to appreciate the words of one interviewee: "We aren't survivors, we're victims."

ROSE MARIE MUKAMWIZA

DATES OF INTERVIEWS: January 31, February 1, 2008

LOCATIONS OF INTERVIEWS: Huye/Rukira/Gahenerezo

INTERVIEWER: Samuel Totten

INTERPRETER: Rafiki Ubaldo

LANGUAGE IN WHICH INTERVIEW WAS CONDUCTED: Kinyarwanda

BIRTH DATE OF INTERVIEWEE: 1953 (interviewee does not know month and day)

AGE DURING THE GENOCIDE: Forty-one years old

PLACE OF BIRTH: Huye

PLACE OF RESIDENCE DURING THE GENOCIDE: Huye

ETHNICITY PRIOR TO THE GENOCIDE: Tutsi

NUMBER OF IMMEDIATE FAMILY MEMBERS KILLED IN THE GENOCIDE: Husband, five children, mother, father, six brothers, three sisters, and all of their children

CURRENTLY RESIDES WITH: Her two children

The night of the crash of President Habyarimana's plane [April 6, 1994], we heard about it on the radio. He had been causing conflict between Tutsi and Hutu so when I heard he was killed I thought maybe now there can be peace between Tutsis and Hutus.

Before the shooting down of the president's plane, I had gone to Kigali to visit my aunt. She lived in Nyamirambo. While I was there I was dressed traditionally. I dressed my hair so it was piled high and dressed in a *kitenge* [a multicolored flowing gown with a flowing shawl. It is a traditional dress that all women in Rwanda wear for wedding ceremonies and other celebrations; however, when a rural woman goes to the city she often wears such a dress as it constitutes her best set of clothing], and my aunt [in Kigali] told me not to dress that way anymore because it drew attention to oneself and that this was dangerous. Also, she said, since people would assume I was from elsewhere, they would ask about my identity. She told me this because some Hutus in the neighborhood had already begun going around identifying houses of Tutsis. Although they [the Hutu] were not yet attacking people in their homes, Tutsis were being beaten up in restaurants and bars.

Later, a man, a neighbor, visited my aunt's home and noticed that I was not from the area and asked where I was from. I said I was from Butare, and he said, "There are a lot of Tutsis in Butare." My aunt became afraid because he was her neighbor and she feared he would assume that she was Tutsi. That evening, RTLM [Radio-télévision libre des mille collines, the extremist Hutu radio station, which broadcast hateful messages about Tutsi, and urged Hutu to kill Tutsi during the period of the genocide] denounced a Tutsi in Kigali. I don't remember the name, but they accused him of going to visit the RPF [the Rwandan Patriotic Front, the rebel force primarily comprised of Tutsi] in the eastern part of the country [in Murindi] they controlled, and transporting Tutsi to where the RPF was located so they could join in the fight against the [Rwandan] government.

On the 9th of April, [back in Huye] I went to work in the fields, and there I saw local authorities mobilizing for a meeting of all people in the sector. We gathered at the office of the sector, and once at the office they told us to separate into groups, Hutu and Tutsi. They announced that there was insecurity [a potential for war] in the country, and it was caused by Tutsi. The decision was made to search all of the houses of Tutsi in order to locate any weapons brought in by Tutsis from the outside. Once that was completed we were allowed to go back home.

Sometime afterwards, around the 21st of April, at three in the morning, local officials and Interahamwe [the extremist Hutu youth group that was instrumental in carrying out the genocide] told everyone—Tutsis and Hutus—to leave their homes. They [the Interahamwe] were scattered all over the hills, blowing whistles to wake us up, and as we looked out to see what was happening we were told to get out of our homes right away. The excuse they gave us was that the homes were not safe to stay in because there were robbers coming to rob us and take all of our belongings. We were told to go to Tonga [a forested valley relatively close to her village] where we would be safe, but that if we stayed [at home] we could be hurt. At Tonga, from early in the morning to almost noon, the authorities checked everyone's identity card to see who was Tutsi and who was Hutu. Then, it was announced that Hutus had to go back home and Tutsis had to remain. Now that we were separated, we knew what followed: death.

We, all the Tutsis, began running. My family and some others ran to Matyazo [about ten kilometers from Tonga]. Others went elsewhere.

When we got there, we went to a health care center and we were told by the military that if we gathered there we would be safe because they were guarding it. Once inside, we were given food, and they also gave us water and we spent the night there.

We had believed that the killing was between political parties, and since we were simple people and not members of political parties we believed the soldiers would protect us. So, we spent some days there. We went there on Wednesday, we spent Thursday there, and then they—soldiers, Inter-ahamwe, and other members of the local population—started to kill us on Friday.

All those soldiers and others stormed the place. They had machetes, *agafuni* [hoes], guns, grenades, stones, spears, and *massues* [a clublike weapon with nails protruding from the head].

They were standing outside the fence and they said, "Those of you who do not wish to be hacked to death with a hoe or massue, throw a goat or chicken over the fence, and you will be shot." [Interviewer's note: In other words, if they produced a goat or chicken they would be killed quickly, but if they failed to do so then they would be hacked to death and suffer more.]

So everyone began running around grabbing goats and chickens to throw over the fence. It was a chance to get shot.

The doors and gates remained locked and as soon as there were no more goats and chickens to throw over the fence, the single shots stopped, and they forced open the doors and gates and began killing people with machetes.

Frightened and shocked, we, many of us, lay down, and then they began to kill us. I was hit in the head with a massue. It cracked my head open. [She reached up and pulled back a bandana she was wearing to point out the deep slash where she had been hit.] I was also slashed with a machete on my left leg.

Some men stood up and began to fight, and I saw my husband struggling with a man with a machete. The man . . . I saw the man cut off my husband's arm from the shoulder. He [her husband] was close to our children, and when he fell down, a soldier threw a grenade toward him. Our children, who saw their father being hurt, had taken a blanket and covered themselves with it. When the grenade exploded, it killed my husband and five of my children. One of my other children got hit with fragments of the grenade, but lived. One was not hurt. When the grenade was thrown, along with others that were thrown into the crowd, everyone, screaming and running, scattered everywhere, trying to find a way out of there.

I, too, ran, and as I was running toward the fence I fell into a garbage dump [sump]. It was about two meters [six feet] deep, but I [positioned myself] so

I could sit and see out of it. I spent the night there, not knowing where my children were or if they were even alive.

On Saturday, the military came with prisoners who wore pink caps with a red cross, and large [bulldozer] tractors to collect dead bodies and bury them. I don't know how many were killed, but there were people there from Nyaruguru, Matyazo Nyarutovu, Ngoma Mpare, and Huye. So there were many, many people. Maybe up to fifteen thousand. There [had] hardly [been] any room to sleep, and the space your body took up was all the space you had. Again, I don't know how many people were killed, but I can tell you that after the genocide only ten people told the story of Matyazo.

While the tractors, two of them, pushed the dead into piles, soldiers were going around to check to see if people were dead. The prisoners collected bodies the tractors couldn't reach and were throwing the bodies into the back of big trucks, [into] which the tractors were also dumping people.

Somehow, a soldier saw me and ordered me to get out of the garbage pit. I told him I couldn't because I was unable to move. He told me he was going to shoot me, but I begged him to spare me and said I would try to get out. Finally, I managed to crawl out by using my elbows. I was lucky that my tendon was not cut [points to her Achilles' tendon].

I asked the soldier, "Where do I go?"

He replied, "Go to hell or go to heaven. Don't you know where Tutsis go?"

So, I walked out toward the main door that had been forced open, and on my way out I saw the blanket we had brought with us and under there were decomposing bodies.... As I kept walking, I came to many children, and two of them were my children. So I ... think that some of those decomposed bodies were my other children.

I could tell them [those who were alive] by their clothes. One, who was two and a half, was covered with blood and the other one, who was four years old, was filthy and depressed and had been beaten with a club.

At first, my children refused to hug me because my head and clothes were covered in blood. [Interviewer's note: At this point in the interview, and as an aside, the interviewee shared the following with us: "I saw a white girl who was killed there. Her mother was Rwandan, but her father was a European. I saw her when she was alive inside the compound and later when she was dead."]

My four-year-old, Claire, addressed me, "Old woman ... old woman ..." Both looked very frightened of me.

I said, "Claire, I'm not an old woman, I'm Mama."

It took several minutes for my children to recognize me, and then more time for them to allow me to approach them. After they did, I took the youngest on my back and looked around, wondering what we should do.

I remembered that living nearby was the family of the teacher of my oldest son, and so we went over to them. This family was Hutu, but kind. The teacher, who was pregnant, brought holy water and started to clean the wounds of my youngest child, believing that God would heal her. And she covered her wounds with a clean cloth.

We, my two surviving children and I, then continued on to the university hospital in Butare to get my wounds taken care of. On the way, we came across Interahamwe who had guns and who were walking toward us.

They asked, "Where are you going?"

My head and face were still covered in blood, and I was still in my dress that was also covered with blood and my leg was bleeding badly and I was limping.

I told them, "I'm a Tutsi woman, but my husband is a Hutu soldier." I also said, "My children were killed because they mistakenly followed Tutsis [to where the Tutsi had been ordered to go so they could be killed]."

They asked me about myself and I said, "I'm a Tutsi and I was shot." Still, they allowed me to continue.

At the hospital was my brother-in-law, Emmanuel, who was a driver for the hospital [and who had managed to hide there]. I asked a secretary at the window for him, and he came and helped us to get food and soap and clean clothes so we wouldn't look like people who escaped [a massacre], otherwise they could finish us off.

He asked his co-worker to take us to another area where other displaced people were staying within the hospital compound, and that's where we spent the night. The following morning I went to see my brother-in-law, thinking he might help us to get another portion of food, but I learned that he had been killed that same night by soldiers.

I went back to the camp [compound], and there was a woman who had been slashed on both arms and she had bandages but it was smelling very bad because no one had changed the bandages. She had a baby six months old and couldn't care for it, and thus I told her I would do so. The woman with the baby had seventy thousand Rwandan francs and she helped us purchase food from kids selling it on the street. It was very difficult to find food, but she had money to buy it with and thus we were able to purchase some.

We spent two weeks at the hospital, but we were living in terrible conditions. The surroundings, the whole area, became like a large toilet and it became poisonous [unsanitary] for the hospital.

During those two weeks, the Interahamwe and soldiers entered the compound to locate men to kill. They came in the night with torches [flashlights] to find them. They also entered to find girls and when they found one they'd grab their breasts to see if they were still firm, not like older women, and if they [their breasts] were firm then they would take them to rape them.

After two weeks the hospital was so filthy, and because of that the *préfet*, Sylvain, the *bourgmestre*, Joseph Kanyabashi, and the doctors at the hospital made us move to the prefecture. They brought a small red truck and they transported us to the prefecture headquarters. The truck came three times to transport everyone. The next day all of the bourgmestres of Butare came to the prefecture to bring every displaced person back to their commune of origin. Our bourgmestre, Ruremesha Jonathan, and two policemen, Bizimana Joseph and Xavier, aka Ndisonzeye, brought us back to Huye. It was now mid-May.

At Huye commune we spent the night outside, and the next morning, they [the bourgmestre and the councilors of the sector] held a meeting on how to kill us. In daylight, in front of us, they held such a meeting. The discussion was right in front of us. Some were arguing they should kill us right there, but some said, "If we kill them here in the commune then it will smell very bad in the commune." There was nothing we could do because the police were there with the Interahamwe. So, one councilor said, "The best idea is to send every displaced person to his sector where the Tutsis could be killed and dumped in latrines."

Even the owner, a Hutu soldier, of this house [where she currently resides with her two surviving children] was in that meeting. They lined up all the councilors and every one had to queue up behind his councilor.

Every councilor asked his people, "Which family will house you because your house is destroyed?"

Everyone gave the name of a neighbor where they could possibly stay. My councilor asked where I would go, and I said I was not sure but I would try a friend.

He said I could stay in the commune, but I suspected they would kill me in the night so I went down to Tonga with my children. When we reached the forest we went down a hill and tried to find a place to hide. That night it began to rain, pour down, and I was afraid my children would die because of the cold and rain. It rained until three in the morning or so. Torrents of water rushed down the hill and we remained wet all night long.

In the morning, we walked up the hill and as it was getting sunny and warmer we took off our clothes and went naked and started to dry off. My children started to get warm and eventually they fell asleep. The youngest, Jane, woke up and cried a lot because she was hungry. A man, Gaspard Seba-hire, heard her and approached us. He asked us how long we had been there and if we had food to eat. I told him we arrived the previous night and that we didn't have any food. After a long time, about fifty minutes, he returned with a crowd of Interahamwe. Before they reached us, one of the Interahamwe climbed a tree so he could detect exactly where we were, and I called out to him, "You do not have to climb a tree, we are here."

There were about nine men, and one of them was a man who owed money to my husband—my husband had had a small shop [a small roughshod metal kiosk where he sold sugar, salt, rice, milk powder, flour, cosmetics]—and this man saw it was me, and he said, "Please don't kill her. We can send her to Nyanza where she comes from originally." They argued and then they all left, but two men came back and said they wouldn't leave without raping me. [Interviewer's note: The interviewee began weeping and Rafiki got up and hugged her tightly for several minutes.]

They raped me and left me there. I was devastated, hungry and cold, and . . . [again, she breaks down weeping]. Gaspard came back and told me to leave and go to Nyanza where I had come from. [Crying and voice cracking] So, I left and we went to Nyanza. My husband had property and a house there once.

Once we got there I learned that two of my children, two of the boys, had escaped the killing in Matyazo. When they had separated Hutu and Tutsi at Matyazo, a women with Hutu identification was let go and my two boys followed her: Jean Paul Uwimana was eleven years old and Augustin Kubwimana was eight years old. When they saw me they came running and hugged me and asked me, "Momma, you are alive?"

I asked them how they managed to remain alive, and they told me they had lived with a cow herder who took care of them. I told my boys that we should remain where we were and not run away, and if they should kill us at least we will be together. But the boys were frightened by what I said, and ran away.

I then took my two little girls, and I headed toward the nearest roadblock and told those at the roadblock—the Interahamwe—"I am tired of running, so you can kill me." There were ten of them, and I knew them all as they lived on the same hill as I had at one time, and they told me, "Before we kill, you have to tell us the secrets you have of the RPF," and I told them, "I don't know anything."

Then they asked me, "Didn't the RPF tell you how they would come back to Rwanda?" Since my husband had a small shop and had some money, they figured he should have such knowledge.

I said, "No, I don't know."

Then they said, "Put your children in the trench so we can kill you alone."

Then a man called Gakuba Evariste, around forty-five years old, grabbed me and pulled me to the ground and raped me.

Claire, my older girl, saw me beg not to be raped, and then watched as I was raped. She was so traumatized by it that even after the genocide, she would ask what those men had been doing to me. She had watched as I was raped the first time, too. In the middle of that, four men—Nsengiyumva, Gatabazi, Musonera, Nsabimana, aka Cyumbati, and Ribanje—came up, talking about how they had killed my two boys.

Gakuba had heard them coming, and he had run away.

And then the four men all raped me in front of my children. [Rose Marie began weeping again, and Ubaldo and Totten could no longer ask any questions and sat in silence fuming at what she had been subjected to by the men. Continuing to weep, she began holding her head and said she couldn't go on, and then said, "Please don't go. Can we talk about who you are?" We talked for about ten minutes and then she said she needed to rest, and we left.]

———

That man I spoke to you about yesterday, Gakuba, in the middle of 2007, he wrote me a letter from the prison. He was in the prison here at Karubanda, and he wrote asking for forgiveness. He was asking for forgiveness because he knew he hurt me and that my children got killed because of his actions. He was begging God to forgive him. Nothing he said in the letter, of course, changed the course of events. When someone asks for forgiveness he should be forgiven. In my particular case, forgiving or not forgiving would not bring back my husband and children. I have not answered the letter, but sometime later I got a notice from gacaca [the structure developed for communities to try the individuals accused of allegedly committing crimes in their area during the genocide] that I needed to testify in his case. He mentioned to gacaca that he had asked me to forgive him, and the court asked me if I had forgiven him, and I said, "Yes, I have," and he was released. From then on he never came to my house or tried to communicate with me in any way. He now lives in Tonga.

The procedure of gacaca is difficult. Yes, the person in prison asks for forgiveness, but what is the context of that forgiveness? It's just a ceremony because they [the prisoners] are all told to ask for forgiveness. Additionally, there is not even a symbolic compensation for lives that were lost. Of course, there is no price for the lost ones, but I think that if my husband was still alive or my [extended] family was still alive, my children would be able to attend school and we'd have a home of our own and . . . But they are no longer here and I am alone, without any help. What I call compensation would be the principle, for example, to pay for the schooling of survivors without selecting them based on their scores. FARG (the Victims of Genocide Fund, which is primarily financed by the Rwandan government and is responsible for providing homes, health care, and schooling for the impoverished survivors of the 1994 Rwandan genocide) is meaningless for me today because it is paying for schooling based on rankings—who achieved or did not achieve this or that grade; it does not pay for people due to having survived.

Gacaca does do some good. The trials of the accused sometimes provide information about where and how people were killed, and where their bodies were dumped.

As far as the process of reconciliation, it comes down to individuals. It is up to the guilty one to think about the crime and ask for forgiveness of the victim. One can tell if a plea for forgiveness is genuine or not. Some people truly apologize and you can tell from their different expressions—some cry, others kneel in front of you, and they ask for forgiveness by confessing that they committed the crime and express how sorry or sad they are.

It's complicated. For example, in the very beginning when Gakuba wanted to apologize he sent me a message that he wanted to talk with me, and when I went to the prison's fields in the valley [near her home] he wanted to give me a bucket of carrots. I refused. He asked me what he could do for me, and I asked him what he thought he could do for me. He said, "Once I get out of prison I will visit you as much as I can so our two families can resume our friendship as before." Well, he got out of prison, but I've never seen him here [her home]. So, he was released—but he lied. People of Integrity [the panel of judges] at gacaca asked the people of their population [sector] if they were satisfied with his confession and they said they were and he was released.

In front of gacaca he really acted sad for what he had done, and I believed him. *Now*, I think he only wanted to get out of prison.

You need to realize, I feel a need to see, face-to-face, the person who did these things to me; not, of course, for social reasons but to ask him face-to-face, "You know what you did to me, how would you feel if this had been done to your wife?"

I'm a living shame, but I know the cause of my shame is *theirs, the rapists*, and I would like to see him *to make him really think about what he did*. It was not enough to hear him give his testimony. Like I said, it was more of a ceremony. I want to see him now, in normal circumstances, as he's out of prison and we would not be in gacaca, and have him face me so I can ask him that question . . . , "Imagine men doing to your wife what you and the others did to me."

So, I would like to meet him regularly, and ask him that question and remind him of what he had done. And to ask him, "Do you know how much my heart is broken?" That would be my punishment for him.

Some ask if I would have rather had Gakuba tried in a classical court [formal court; also referred to in Rwanda as national court] where he could have been condemned to death. [Through June 2007, Rwanda had the death penalty, and various génocidaires who were tried prior to June 2007 could be and were sentenced to death for the crimes they committed during the 1994 genocide. However, in June 2007, Rwanda abolished the death penalty, and thus any génocidaire tried after that could not be sentenced to death, and any of those in prison who had already been sentenced to death could not be put to death.] Look at it this way, if I were dead I would not have this pain I live with, and if he were killed he would not feel the guilt or pain for what he did.

After the genocide, the RPF took us to Save [on the way to Kigali, about ten kilometers away], and Jeanne [one of her daughters] kept asking me, "What were those men doing with your *pipi* [pee pee]?" She constantly asked that question and I told her, "That's another problem with the war, like how they killed people. That was their way of killing me."

Today, she [Jeanne] is grown up, and she knows what happened to me and she knows I walk around with shame in front of her. But it is not my fault.

I've been traumatized three times, and it happened to Jeanne two times, and we know for Claire it happens every April. [Interviewer's note: By "traumatized," the interviewee is referring to those periods when she or her daughters cannot stop weeping, begin yelling or screaming as a result of the memories of the horrors of the genocide, and/or have to be hospitalized for a day or two in order to be tranquilized. Most Rwandans do not consider that they suffer ongoing trauma due to their perdurable sadness; for them, such sadness is simply the life they lead.] One day Jeanne saw a man shot by a local defense force [local guards who provide security for towns and villages today], and the memories of '94 came back. She cried and screamed, ran away from school, and came here [their temporary home] crying and speaking jumbled words that made no sense, along with "They're killing us! They're killing us!"

The second time we went to a memorial event in Huye [to a cemetery where survivors are buried] where she saw human bones as they were burying victims who had been recently uncovered, and she ran away crying out, "People are dying! People are dying!" I, along with many others, ran after her and when we caught up with her, our neighbors took her to the hospital in Butare for trauma counseling. She spent two days there.

Claire, who is eighteen, as I said, experiences trauma when the commemoration period begins. She cries, endlessly. This is during the official period of commemoration, beginning in April, when we hear sorrowful songs on the radio. That causes the trauma to erupt. She doesn't cry all day long, but often throughout the day and night. If she hears something that provokes her, if she hears something sad, she will break out weeping. Still, she goes to the commemorations because if she didn't she'd feel her [dead] father and our other relatives would not be proud of her.

Two years ago, when she was sixteen, Claire, during the April commemoration, went into her bedroom, closed the door and refused to speak with anyone or even eat. When we tried to bring in food to her, she wrote a note and placed it above her bedroom door: "Leave me as I am! And leave me in peace!" She then went back in her room and continued to refuse to talk to anyone or to eat.

Every April she wakes up in the morning, bathes, and goes back to her room for the rest of the day and evening. For the whole week. We know to leave her alone. What else can we do?

Sometimes they bring her from school because she's been crying and goes mad [begins screaming], is uncontrollable and talks incoherently. This can happen any time of the year.

As I said, I've been traumatized three times. In my heart there is a huge number of coffins, as many as the number who were killed. I have constant stomach pains and headaches.

One night I went to bed, and I had a nightmare and the nightmare was that the genocide was taking place, and the whole story of my life during the genocide came back and I was searching for something to save me but there was no one. It was around three in the morning, and I abruptly woke up. I opened the [front] door [of the house,] and I started to cry and scream for help and I ran out onto the dirt path. Some neighbors came to assist me because they thought I was being attacked, and they calmed me and brought me back home. I was in such a trauma I didn't even recognize them, and I tried to resist them. I don't recall how they got me back home. Back at home they began to pray because they thought I had been attacked by demons. But it didn't help me because I could see among those people who came here were Hutu, and I thought they were there to kill me and I started to beg: "Please don't kill me! . . . Please don't kill me!" They replied, "We are here to pray for you, not kill you."

The second time, I went to Sovu [a hill nearby] for gacaca, and a prisoner gave testimony about how he killed a child. He described how he hacked the child with the machete, and many people, including me, began to run in all directions because we were so traumatized and it brought back horrible memories. Many of us went to hide in the health care center. They quickly gathered us in the hall, and tried to convince us there were no killers there. I stayed there for about six hours before I was calm enough to leave.

The third time, some relatives came to tell me that my aunt—the only aunt I had—had died. My heart was beating hard and I had a very hard time breathing, and I went to the hospital because I was suffering very badly. They gave me some pills—kind of orange—and I slept all day for two days.

After the genocide, I got a job with CARE Australia. I spent three years with CARE—from 1995 to 1998. It was in Ngoma. There was an orphanage there, and I was taking care of small children [whose parents had been murdered during the genocide]. I'm a mother, so it was not difficult for me to take care of the children.

Those who were very small didn't know what had happened, but those who were older did and were very sad. The youngest thought we were their mothers.

One thing that brought me back to life was CARE Australia, because they gave us a salary and health care. The health care was more important than the money. I had wounds and they treated me very well—and my children, too. Our wounds were still open, and we had not had medical attention. My wounds had become infected and those of my children as well. It was the policy of CARE Australia to give jobs to widows as a result of the genocide and others who had special needs.

I remember when the war was over [the period of genocide, in early July 1994], a friend gave me five thousand Rwandan francs, but I refused the money because I didn't know what to do with the money. *I was lost.*

There were two things that motivated me to return to life—my two children. They had to be looked after in the best way I could. The fact that I was still alive and that I didn't want to give any satisfaction to those who wanted me dead or to think I couldn't take care of my personal life also motivated me.

But, listen, I have a problem in my heart. I am a jealous person. I shall explain. Have you seen in Rwanda how people go on holidays? Have you seen how men and women go to weddings? And go out together on weekends? Have you seen how men buy nice clothes for their wives? When I see all that, I want to take my children and leave the country, but I can't. I, we, have nothing. I have no husband, my children have no father.

In 2007, Nyiramugwera Bernadette, who is the wife of one of the men who raped me, got angry at me and began to make plans to kill me. She plotted with three men. Rwabuzisoni Cyprien, one of the men, came to tell me what was going on. He was freshly released from prison, and my thinking is that at a certain point he knew he could go back to prison and so he told me that Bernadette sold a cow and gave the three men money to kill me.

I told him, "Look, this could be regarded as a false accusation unless you write down their names and what they're planning to do, and then sign the paper." He did that, and I took it to the police, and the police arrested all of them. Cyprien confirmed that he wrote the statement and signed it. He was going to have to make his accusation in court, but he committed suicide. Then, the local leaders created a curfew around my house [a zone, basically, which no one could enter past a certain time in the evening] because they feared for my life, and the curfew is still on [in effect] through today.

Bernadette later got jailed again because gacaca discovered that she had hired Interahamwe to kill a child in 1994. The parents of the child had left cows and tools in Bernadette and her husband's possession so Bernadette had to make sure the child was not around to claim the cows and tools. [The little boy's parents had already been killed in the genocide.] Bernadette told the boy to go to the banana plantation and hide there. Some minutes after the boy left, Bernadette called out to the Interahamwe that she just saw a "cockroach" [an *inyenzi*], and they came and killed the boy. This story was told by the killers themselves in the gacaca. She received nineteen years in prison. She's fifty-three now so I don't think she will make it out.

Now, no one right now is threatening me. People are friendly to me for the simple reason that I want it so. I'm friendly to everyone. It is difficult to respond negatively [to one who is friendly]. *But I am alone! So, how am I to think about safety? It is not safe in my heart!*

Look at my small restaurant [a small, filthy hovel without electricity or water], for example. People know I'm Tutsi, and many of my customers are Hutu. If they didn't consider me friendly they could think I might poison them.

Also, I have a reputation for saying the truth in gacaca. I do not fabricate stories and many Hutus respect me for that. Obviously, if I had been taking sides in gacaca that man would not have warned me about the plot to kill me. Also, you need to realize that the people in this area elected me to be president of gacaca so they obviously trust me. It's not possible to corrupt me because no amount of money can wash away my shame [as a result of having been raped during the genocide].

The government is not doing enough for us [the survivors of the genocide]. Look at this house, for example. It's not my property. I could be pushed out at any time. If they [the owners of the house] ask me to move out, I will not have any other place to go. FARG has been talking about building houses for us, and it's now fourteen years since '94.

I think I have to tell the other side of the story, too. Some survivors got houses, but sold them and ended up back in poverty. But I understand them, too—imagine if they [the government] gave you land miles and miles away from the land you own and cultivate. So, if you build a house on the land they give you, you do not have anything to eat.

In this area [Huye, where she resides], FARG has built a hundred houses, but those houses have no toilets, no kitchens. The contractor who built the houses was corrupt and stole the money and didn't complete the houses. And besides that, about two hundred more houses are needed here.

FARG forgets that life doesn't stop with physically surviving in '94. For example, our friends who were young then are still getting married and their families are growing up, and their extreme poverty should not prevent them [the children of the survivors] from having a family. And orphans would like to have their own homes.

Imagine, also, orphans of genocide who were taken in by other families. They are now grown up and need their own homes.

I'd change the Rwandan bureaucracy if I could—it needs to be improved. For example, the country is encouraging people to create jobs themselves, and we're trying to find jobs to do. But when you start a small business, the bureaucrats come and inspect you [the facilities of the business], and they give you many tasks to do before allowing to you continue your business. They've ordered me to close my small restaurant for sanitary reasons—not having clean water, a modern kitchen, a nice roof so there is more light, a modern toilet. So, how can they expect me to survive if I close my business? I don't have the means to purchase or build a modern kitchen or toilet. We were given two weeks to fix the restaurant! If they come back and find you have not done anything, they will force you to close.

One last thing I must say, I see genocide tendencies in the comments made by local people about the national government. Every time there is a policy to implement, Hutus in the neighborhood will make comparisons with the former government [the Hutu-dominated government during and prior to 1994]—mostly saying that things were perfect with the former government, the Habyarimana regime. That is what scares me most.

[As the interviewer and interpreter were about to leave, at the end of the interview, the interviewee said:] I consider you [Totten and Ubaldo] friends, and one day you can come back and we can take a picture of us and I can leave it for my children.

UMULISA

DATES OF INTERVIEWS: May 7, 13, and June 2, 2008

LOCATION OF INTERVIEWS: Kigali

INTERVIEWER: Samuel Totten

INTERPRETER: Not needed

LANGUAGE IN WHICH INTERVIEW WAS CONDUCTED: English

BIRTH DATE OF INTERVIEWEE: January 7, 1975

AGE DURING THE GENOCIDE: Twenty years old

PLACE OF BIRTH: Muvendo

PLACE OF RESIDENCE DURING THE GENOCIDE: Butare, Karubando

ETHNICITY PRIOR TO THE GENOCIDE: Tutsi

NUMBER OF IMMEDIATE FAMILY MEMBERS KILLED IN THE GENOCIDE: No immediate family; more than one hundred extended family members

CURRENTLY RESIDES WITH: Husband and baby son

As I grew up, I discovered that many of my family members were living outside the country. For example, my auntie and uncle moved to Burundi in 1977 because the [Rwandan] government was killing Tutsi. They went to Bujumbura. My grandmother told me that she [the auntie] had a very difficult life there, but when she decided she wished to return to Rwanda she was not allowed to do so by the authorities at the time [the government of Rwandan president Juvénal Habyarimana]. Even when my grandparents went to visit her, they could not cross at the border [the official border crossing between Rwanda and Burundi], but had to cross [secretly and stealthily] through the bush. No one who had gone into exile could return at the time. They could not do so until after the [1994] genocide.

My grandmother told me how the [Hutu-dominated] government tried to kill her brother, how they burned her house, how she had to hide her children, and how my grandfather was put in prison. My grandmother *always* told the story over and over about how they wanted to murder her brother. They tried to kill him in the 1960s. They wanted to kill him just because he was a Tutsi. At that time, the government, the Hutus, had no reason to kill Tutsi, but when they wished to cause trouble between people they would burn Tutsi houses down or kill Tutsis.

They [the killers] beat him [her great uncle], and threw him in the River Nyabarongo, between Kibuye and Gitarama, hoping he would drown. They thought he died, but he didn't and he swam across the river. He hid and waited until after the troubles were over and then returned home. Later, though, during the genocide he was killed.

So, you see, I heard these stories when I was young and I understood that Tutsi could be beaten and killed at any time, and their houses could be burned, for no reason at all, just because they were Tutsi. I began hearing these stories when I was ten or eleven.

Each year when I was in primary school, the teacher would have the Tutsis stand up and the Hutus stand up. So, from a very early age I knew I was Tutsi. This was every year, at the beginning of the year. Always, there were only three or four Tutsis. This process began in primary one or primary two. And if you said you didn't know, they [the teachers] would say, "Go ask your parents." The first time I didn't know.

The teachers, as I recall, didn't say anything as we stood, but I do remember what was said about the kings of Rwanda, who were Tutsi, when we were studying the history of Rwanda. What was said about the Tutsi was not positive, the kings were said to have been bad and cruel, to have killed people [Hutu].

Also, my father, who was a very smart man, was, when he was young, in a competition that the French held in regard to who spoke French best—this was when he was in secondary school. The prize was that he got to fly in an airplane around Rwanda. He did very well in secondary school, but because he was Tutsi he was not allowed to go to university. At that time, one just wrote an application to get into university—there were no national examinations and school scores [grades] were not considered. He completed the application, but was not admitted to school [the National University of Rwanda (NUR) in Butare], solely because he was Tutsi. Many others in his [secondary] school who were not as intelligent as he was, but were Hutu, were admitted.

So, I, since I knew this story, I knew even if I was first in my class I might not make it to secondary school or the National University of Rwanda. He [her father] told this story [about not getting into NUR] over and over again.

He wanted to go to university so badly, and he wanted, encouraged, us [his children] to go to university, to even get a Ph.D.

Since he was not allowed to go to university, he went on to become a pastor. I'm not even sure he wanted to be a pastor, but he did want to continue his education. So, he went to the School of Theology of Butare, something like that, but it was not recognized as a university. He attended for four years. He spoke Kinyarwanda, French, and English. He served as a parish pastor, but he also started two small businesses—he owned a small bus [to transport people] and a shop selling rice, beans, and other commodities. That allowed him to provide for his family. But he was also very committed to his work as a pastor. Then, later, in the 1980s, he moved the family to Kigali, where he worked for the Bible Society, as a pastor and as a translator, translating the Bible from other languages into Kinyarwanda. He worked with a group of people [fellow translators], and he particularly enjoyed that work because he could apply his intellectual skills.

I knew that even if I passed the national examination [that it was quite possible and quite likely that] I could not be admitted to the university because I was Tutsi—if they [government officials] overlooked that I was Tutsi or didn't know that I was Tutsi, then I could. But I knew they knew that I was Tutsi and would not overlook me by mistake, so I felt that the only way I could go was by a miracle of God.

The only jobs open to Tutsi [under the Habyarimana government] were nursing and education [teaching]. No matter how smart, no matter how talented, no matter how hard you worked, you had no choice. And not only that, but those jobs were poorly paid.

Every application you made for university in Rwanda at that time [prior to 1994], you had to put whether you were Hutu or Tutsi. At that time there were no private universities [other than those that were religious based], so the government controlled the universities and who got into them.

In primary eight, I sat for the national examination [for admittance to a secondary school]. I ended up being accepted at a church school, École des sciences infirmières, a girls' boarding school in Kibuye. I was not satisfied because I was doing nursing and not something that would be better for me—such as mathematics.

Even at that school it was very difficult for a Tutsi to gain entrance because only 14 percent of Tutsis were allowed to attend [secondary school] at that time. The percentage was based on the percentage [of people] comprising each ethnic group—Tutsi, Hutu, Twa. It was said that there were 85 percent Hutu in the country, 14 percent Tutsi, and 1 percent Twa.

I was in the first year of secondary school [1991], which was during the time the RPF [Rwandan Patriotic Front, the rebel group primarily comprised of Tutsi] was fighting the Rwandan army in this country, and thus the tension between groups [Hutu and Tutsi] was bad. I was always worried, [and] not sure if I would ever again see my parents [due to Tutsi being killed around Rwanda, and the fact that her parents resided in Kigali and she lived a relatively great distance from them].

When you go into nursing, you go to the hospital to practice what you learned in theory, and one day we went to the hospital for a practical [practicum] with a group of about ten students. I think I was the only Tutsi in the group. As we were walking together, talking, our teacher, a Hutu, said to me, "You do not look like you are going to work" [walking like a person motivated to work] and sent me back to the school. He also wrote a disciplinary referral on me, gave me a zero out of a hundred for the day, and even wrote in my school transcript that I was not a good student. This was a man who I had seen beating Tutsis, girls, without any reason. He used a curtain rod, the thick ones, made of wood, to hit the girls, *hard*, for no reason at all.

I felt very sad and I was crying, but I was more afraid than anything. I feared what he could do. So, I was very scared because I thought he could do more than just send me back to the school. I feared he could beat me, fail me, kick me out of school, and ruin my record. [In fact,] he even gave me a zero in his department [specialty area], public health. The other teachers were not as open [openly hostile to Tutsi students] as that.

What was very difficult for me [to stand] was history because we were learning about how Tutsi were not good to Hutu during the period of the kingdom [rule of kings]. There were about three of us [Tutsi] out of thirty-five students. I remember I could not even look at the teacher in the eyes because everything he was saying bad about the Tutsi I felt he was saying about me—that I was no good, that I was bad. I didn't even want to be there. I couldn't even answer him when called upon. I was also asked [forced] to learn [Rwandan] history such as this story he told us: when a Tutsi queen wanted to stand up, a spear [with the points facing downward] would be placed on Hutu children's chests and she would get up by applying pressure to the spears and the spears would cut [kill] the children. For me, I thought the story was not true, but I couldn't argue. No Tutsi could. And also, the RPF [Rwandan Patriotic Front] was attacking at this time [and thus, made it even more difficult for Tutsi students].

At this time, they [the government and Hutu teachers] made up these stories to show the Tutsi were no good [in order to place them in a poor light, and to create additional tension between the Hutu and Tutsi]. It all was part of the national curriculum, and it was the same at the primary and secondary levels, only with more information at the secondary level.

As I said, I was very good in maths [mathematics], but I had the same teacher for history and math that year, and so my math scores went down, too.

After the RPF attacked the country, students in our school became active in political parties and began to join the Interahamwe. The students were supported by those teachers in the school who were extremists. Even some of my friends joined the Interahamwe. In fact, one of my very best friends joined the Interahamwe. Her father was a soldier, an officer, and she said that the Tutsi would be killed at any time. She may have known the plan of the government, the army.

Even the [Hutu] girls prepared to fight. Even the words of those [the girls] who joined the Interahamwe were very scary. For example, she [her friend] used to say, "We will kill you!" She was serious! But then, in the next minute, she would make a joke, and I could do nothing.

She would even touch my nose [rub it]. Everyone made a distinction between Tutsi and Hutu based on how they looked [including the shape and size of one's nose], so she would rub my nose without making comment. I, of course, could not do anything. Yes, I could have pushed her or complained and possibly nothing may have happened; but, since you were young you heard how they [Hutu] could kill you, and that you lived at the grace of the Hutu—so you just hoped to be allowed to live and didn't want to do anything to upset them.

People outside the school did the training of the Interahamwe. It was not done on the school grounds. Also, since the school was a boarding school, the girls only got training outside during vacation.

[One day,] the headmaster saw me and a friend talking—we were just talking about general things, nothing about the war or the Rwandan Patriotic Front, and he told us, "You are not allowed to be together alone." We didn't say anything and we separated ourselves. We could guess why he said it—that he suspected us of supposedly exchanging information about the RPF or something like that or suspecting us of being like spies. We could not know for sure. We couldn't ask, and we didn't ask because we knew we could be killed at any time and we didn't want to bring ourselves trouble.

Even those who were not interested in politics began to divide themselves into separate groups—Hutu and Tutsi. There was a particular program on Radio Rwanda [the national radio station during the Habyarimana years, which generally toed the party line; not to be confused with Radio-télévision libre des mille collines, the extremist radio station] and it was the program for the MDR [Mouvement démocratique républicain or Democratic Republican Movement], and they could, and did, say anything they wanted. For example, they would say, "The Hutu have to be together" and "Hutu have to ban together to defend themselves," and, even, "Kill Tutsi." When political issues were discussed on the radio—Radio Rwanda—they, the Hutu students, would talk about them, openly.

The semester before the genocide the Interahamwe began to attack and kill people. I had friends and relatives living near the school who had to move because they were being threatened, and they warned me to be very careful.

At school, in the dormitory, there were very strong gates and they locked them at night with big locks, and so I worried all the time because I knew that if they [the extremist Hutu] wanted to kill us, they could. And in that dormitory there were only two Tutsi, two of us, out of a total of twenty-four students [all of whom were Hutu].

The situation was bad all over the country. Even Kigali [the capital of Rwanda, where her parents resided] was bad; in fact, it was worse. I used to think [plan], "If they kill my parents then I must go to my grandmother's"— because she lived near the school.

I had one friend who I could talk with, a fellow Tutsi, and we used to hide and talk. We had to [talk]! Other students [Hutu] began referring to themselves as Interahamwe, and we didn't know what to do. We knew that in other schools, such as the one my cousin attended, students began to beat Tutsi, even before the genocide. That was a school in Gisenyi, in the north, where they even killed one [student, a Tutsi].

Just before our Christmas and New Year break, tension at school increased. There continued to be threats to kill us, but outside school, people were being threatened even more often by the Interahamwe. They [the Hutu] were very aggressive, yelling, screaming, hitting the others [the Tutsi]. Even young Hutus threatened Tutsi adults.

My grandfather told me about a man who was a very close friend of his and when they passed in the street, the man, who was in a car, passed by my grandfather without acknowledging him. This man, who even cared for me when I was young, [had] joined the Interahamwe. He was the man who trained them. During the genocide he killed many people.

Prior to the genocide, [this man] even visited me at school. He was the director of another school, and he came by just to check up to see how I was. But in the months [immediately preceding the genocide], he quit visiting or inquiring about me.

Tutsi, even adults, feared going out at night, after dark, because it was very dangerous. Men, particularly, quit going out at night, to the bars, fearing they would be beaten or killed. This was in December 1993, and January, February, and March 1994, just before genocide.

I remember, during the holiday, we [she and her friend, a fellow student] traveled from school to Butare, and it was very difficult because there were roadblocks and they [the police] would check identity papers. When they saw you were Tutsi they would glare at you in a frightening manner. My friend showed her identity card, which [identified a person as Tutsi or Hutu or Twa], and one man, I remember, stared at her very meanly. For some minutes he refused to allow her to get back in the minibus. I showed them my student I.D., which didn't list whether you were Hutu and Tutsi. I looked young so I was lucky they didn't ask me. The roadblocks had originally been set up by the French and [Rwandan] gendarme in 1990 after the RPF first attacked. Later, I don't know why, the French quit guarding the roadblocks so only the gendarme did. Then, during the genocide, the Interahamwe [manned] the roadblocks.

At that time, in Butare, many Tutsi children [young people, including teenagers] experienced great difficulties in their villages and at school, and many young Tutsi began joining the RPF. I had friends, boys, who joined the RPF. Me, I was young, and a girl, and I didn't think it was wise to join the RPF or to go out into the bush with all men. Some girls did.

At home, our parents didn't want to scare us so they didn't talk about the situation in front of us. But we had four aunties in Kigali who decided to move from their homes because of the threats and dangers, and one thought of moving to Butare because Butare was considered safer because there were about 45 percent Tutsi there and the préfet of Butare was a Tutsi.

Hutu began killing people in Kigali—not in large groups, but a person here and a person there. So, even though my parents didn't want to scare us by talking about the situation, we knew, due to our aunties' situations, that the situation was very dangerous.

Even though school was very difficult [due to the various dangers posed by the Hutu], I had no other option but to continue; remember, I said I was attending a government school and government schools were the best schools—so I returned. But it was difficult because I didn't know if I would [ever] see my parents again [since they lived a relatively far distance from here, and people were being killed all around the country].

For me, the new semester was even more difficult than the semester before. You didn't know if you were going to be able to finish school. Also, there definitely was more tension between [Hutu and Tutsi] students and more tension between Tutsi students and Hutu teachers. And then there were all the bad things on the radio [Radio-télévision libre des mille collines], and in the newspaper [*Kangura*, a screed published by a Hutu extremist whose sole purpose was to denigrate the Tutsi].

At school, all the Tutsi, we grew closer—like family members—because we had no one else. We were all afraid—of what might happen—even with the RPF; I mean, we didn't know who they were, whether they would do anything good, whether they would win the war—and if they did, who knew what would happen then. We [also] became like family with the Tutsi on the outside [of the school compound], when we visited the hospitals and elsewhere.

We didn't really know much about the RPF. On the radio, we often heard that the RPF was a weak army, [and so we did not know] whether they would be able to come and save us. We knew many were Tutsi because we had friends who joined, but many of us did not follow politics so we did not really know [much about the overall situation].

Almost the entire semester [January, February, and March] was the same—the same tension between students, the same tensions between certain teachers and students, the radio messages [of hate broadcast by RTLM]. But in March, the tension was so high I began to think: If I can only leave school. Just move out of school and go live on the outside. I wanted to go home, but I knew my parents would say, "Stay there, be patient." It was also toward the end of the semester, so I [forced myself] to be [patient]. On the outside, the Interahamwe came from Kigali and it became more violent, and everywhere you went outside of school you would hear about the violence, the threats, the fear, and how dangerous it was.

One day I went to a friend's house and we listened to the RPF radio [station, which was called Radio Muhabura], and it was comforting because they were saying they would make the country better. [They were saying that those] people [Tutsi] outside the country [in exile] could come home. Mainly, these thoughts were expressed in songs. Also, during the genocide, on the radio, the RPF talked about how they would save people.

I remember reading *Kangura*, and I was scared at what I read, and I thought, "Now things are very serious!" I don't remember where I first saw it—in Butare or Kigali—but I think I saw it in a big bus station. I read it many times, and I made a point of looking at it when I could, especially since I knew it was saying terrible things about us [Tutsi]. I remember reading the Hutu Ten Commandments in *Kangura*, and I was especially shocked how they defined who you were if you had a Tutsi father and a Hutu mother—that is, if you had a Tutsi father and a Hutu mother you were a Tutsi, but if you had a Hutu father then you were Hutu. To me, if you had one parent who was Tutsi and one Hutu, you were just mixed. But they [the Hutu extremists] did not see it that way. And even when your father was a Hutu and your mother a Tutsi, you were not considered a full Hutu. In other words, they [the children] were not completely accepted. I remember feeling very isolated because it created a distinction between us [Hutu and Tutsi], and it scared me. For me, it was clear the [Hutu] Ten Commandments were talking about Tutsi, [espousing] hatred for [all] Tutsi.

I remember looking at the cartoons in *Kangura*, and how they dehumanized (I didn't know that term, or use it, at the time) the inyenzi [cockroaches] and the *inkotanyi* [a reference to the RPF troops] and Tutsi, and it made me feel much the same way as it did when we studied history in school—the way they [*Kangura*, history textbooks, Hutu extremists, Hutu teachers] talked about you.

I also remember how they [the Hutu extremists] called people in Rwanda inyenzi [cockroaches] and *inzoka* [snake]. They often said that a snake can give birth to a snake, so any snake [Tutsi] was bad, dangerous, no matter how young.

I felt sad being called such a kind of animal you had no connection to; maybe if they called you lion, it makes sense [e.g., the sense of bravery being implied]—but if you are called a snake, it's an animal that is very dangerous and people don't like to live with it. But you didn't know what to do, and there is nothing you [could] say.

Being called an inyenzi also bothered me because it's [being] pointed out you are dangerous and you need to die. And everyone hates them in Rwanda because they get in our cupboards, and you try to do everything to get rid of them.

Just before April 6th [the day President Habyarimana's plane was shot down over Kigali], tensions increased even more. The president was attending a meeting about the peace agreement [the Arusha Accords], and everybody was watching to see the outcome of the meeting. It was a meeting to discuss, I think, the agreement with the RPF, and the Interahamwe were not in favor of power sharing with the RPF. There was discussion on the radio, in the newspaper, and people were saying, What will happen when the RPF comes?" "What will happen if Habyarimana signs the peace agreement?" "What will happen if he doesn't sign it?" and "If they agree to share power will the Interahamwe kill everyone? At school, the students, the Hutus, would openly discuss such questions and say what they wanted. They also openly discussed what their parents said. But, again, Tutsi just kept quiet. We would discuss it, if we could, when we found ourselves alone, in secret.

On April 6th, I was on holiday, Easter holiday, back in Butare. I was at home, alone. My father had to go to Kibuye for a church meeting, and my mother, who was in Kigali, decided to come home that day when she heard my father had to be away. When we woke up in the morning [April 7th] we heard on the radio that the president's plane had been shot down. Because my dad was not there, my sister, twenty-two, went to sleep with my mommy, and they turned on the radio and heard that the president's plane had been shot down and that no one was allowed to go out of the house.

We had a radio at home, but the plane crash was not announced on the radio until the morning. And even those people in Kigali, who knew about the crash, if they were Tutsi, wouldn't dare make calls to people about it—we had fixed lines, no cell phones—because they would be scared, afraid that their conversations may be listened in on and that they may be accused of being involved [in the downing of Habyarimana's plane].

Even prior to the genocide, and then during the genocide, my aunties and uncles would use different names, because we believed that there was a central location where all conversations of everyone were recorded, and that they could go back and listen to any conversation and they would have your number. I don't know if that was true, but that's what people thought. So, instead of, for example, saying "Hutu," they [her relatives] would use the name of a Hutu who they both knew was a Hutu—so they might say "Freddie" meaning "the Hutus did this or are doing . . ."

We have seven children in our family and all of us were there [in Butare], plus my mother, my cousin, the houseboy, and a guard. So, there were eleven. After two weeks our dad came and another cousin who was living in Butare Town. She came because it was very dangerous [in Butare Town] where she was living.

Remember, my father was in Kibuye, at my school—it was a church school—and roadblocks were everywhere; and everyone knew my dad, because he was from that area, and they knew he was Tutsi and they could've killed him when they saw him. Perhaps, if you tried to pass a roadblock and said you had lost your identity card, they might let you pass. But he couldn't, because everyone knew him. So my father remained in the church; fortunately, the decision had not yet been made to kill the pastors. The pastors there were from all over Rwanda, and were both Tutsi and Hutu. Most were Hutu. Actually, there were five Tutsi out of fifty pastors. Some even brought their families, out of fear for their safety, to the church compound. One was my father's uncle, and out of fear he brought his entire family there, and they, all of them, his entire family, were killed, except for him.

The main pastor, the president of the church, Twagirayesu, was an advisor to Habyarimana. His family members killed many Tutsi in the area, and he was there when all the killing was going on. His family members were among the main killers of Tutsi in the area, and he had the power to prevent the killing.

I would say he was Interahamwe, and one of the main advisors to them. I don't know for sure, but I think that is true.

My father was there [at the church] for two weeks, during the beginning of the genocide. Some Tutsis, who lived near the school/church, including my grandfather and uncle, my mommy's brother, brought their families to the school seeking safety. About two weeks after the genocide began, they [the Interahamwe] came to the church to kill the pastors and their families.

While still in Kibuye, our father called and told us that many people were being killed, and that, in fact, our grandfather, my mommy's father, had been killed. So we had no idea how he would get to Butare, or even if he would. We knew so many people there, and we knew many of them who were killed. Also, they [the Interahamwe] got on the radio and thanked the people [Hutu] of Kibuye for getting so involved in killing the people in the area.

One day he [her father] heard someone yell, "They are coming to kill Tutsi!" and he jumped out of the window of the guesthouse he was staying in and he hid in a kind of bush. He stayed in the bush during the night and slept there. He was with other Tutsi pastors. Many, but not all the [Tutsi] pastors and their families jumped out of the [windows of the] rooms. Those who didn't were caught and killed. My uncle jumped out the window and got away, but his family didn't and all were killed.

In the morning, all those who survived, they went to the church president and asked him what they should do. They knew they could not hide themselves for long. He gave them a car to take them to Gitarama, where there was another church school, and he wrote a letter to the government telling them that he was sending the Tutsi pastors to this school, Remera Rupoma. Remember, this man was educated, he knew what was going on and what he was doing. Before they reached the main road in Gitarama, before they got to the school, my father decided it was not a good idea to go to the school and leave us alone in Butare. He got out of the car, but all of the other pastors went to the school, and later all of them got murdered at that school.

That [getting out of the taxi] was very dangerous to do; there were no [other] taxis, and so many roadblocks. The lucky thing is that the RPF was fighting in Kigali, so many people were leaving Kigali, especially Hutu, and going south. So there were so many people on the road that not even those at roadblocks could check everyone's identification, and so that's how he managed to get to Butare.

My father came by foot, and when he was tired he would get a bike [hire a person with a bicycle to transport him a distance] and then he would walk again. When he got to Butare his eyes were very red and he was very tired.

Our father did not explain how, exactly, he made it back or how long it took him, but it must have been very dangerous. I believe he returned mainly by road, but since he had experienced many wars, he may have attempted to avoid the roadblocks by going up in to the hills when he approached one.

Our father, since he had just returned to Butare on foot, he had a much better understanding of what was happening than we did since we had remained in the house those two weeks.

From the beginning, our mother told us that God told her not to be scared. I don't know if it was that or she knew if we jumped out of the window out of fear, we could get killed. While it was also true we could get killed staying in our house, she tried hard to keep us safe.

When she heard her father was killed she felt she could not grieve in front of us because it would scare us and . . . Perhaps she forced herself into denial, but she tried not to show her grief for the sake of us, her children.

What was most shocking was that anyone would think of killing him [her grandfather] because he was a pastor for many years and helped so many people. In Kibuye, people didn't even call him pastor but papa—and his wife, mama [as a sign of respect]. Even though they wanted him dead, they had to call people from the outside to kill him because no one there would kill him. They also killed my grandmother and my cousins, who were living with my grandparents.

My mum said God told her to stay in the house with the family, and that she, we, would be safe. It was like Noah and the ark when God told him to stay on the ark and he would be safe, and that's what he did. From the very beginning of the genocide my mum told us this. When my father returned to Butare and wanted us to leave for Burundi they disagreed, a lot, on that. My father tried to explain to her how serious the killing was outside, but, again, as a Christian, he was not totally against, if I can say [put it this way], the prophecy of my mother. But, at the same time, he knew that it would be very difficult to get to Burundi, especially with such a large family.

Shortly after he arrived home, within two days, the killing started in Butare. One day before [the killing began], my father went into town [Butare Town]—we lived on the outskirts [of Butare Town], near the prison in Karu-banda—to purchase rice. He purchased enough rice for three months—a big bag, about fifty kilograms or even larger, and a large bag of beans. The next day the killing started seriously. From that point, it was impossible to go out, to go to purchase food, because it was so dangerous. So, within two days of [her father] getting home, we had no choice but to stay for it would've been impossible for us to make it to Burundi.

All day we had to remain in the house. At night we could enter the compound [of their home,] but not out in the open.

We had a Tutsi guard and a cook, a young Hutu male, in his early twenties. He [the guard] was a Christian, a good Christian, and he stayed with us the entire time, until the genocide finished. He was the only one who could go out of the house. At one point we could not get water—we had had running water but at some point it was cut off—and he was the only one who could go fetch it. Water, during the genocide, for our family, became a problem because our cook had to fetch water for drinking, cooking, bathing, and the toilet. We did not have the luxury of a toilet that flushed automatically [without pouring water into the toilet]. We didn't bathe every day, but that was still a lot of work to fetch—so much water—and he, the cook often got tired [lugging the water]. And when he got really tired, he said he would only fetch water for cooking, and if we wanted more water for bathing or the toilet then he would charge a hundred francs a trip. But we had no money and could not go to the bank. So . . . what was most difficult for me was to be forced to watch my father give up authority in the face of the boy's demands. The boy would often use language that was inappropriate and refuse to do certain work; and my father, knowing that if the boy got irritated he could bring the Interahamwe to our home to kill us, would do, say, nothing. The boy would humiliate my father, and there was nothing my father could do.

I think this boy, at some point, was confused. At home, our home, he knew he had to obey [normally], but then when he went out and saw the other Hutus were stealing anything they wanted, running [manning] roadblocks, bossing people around, getting rich, he was a bit confused. He would even come back and tell us what the Hutu were doing, how they did anything they wanted to anyone.

I say he was conflicted because at times he would say, "I'm not going to fetch water unless you pay me," but later, I guess, he would think [about the matter, and the situation of the family], and he would go fetch the water.

He had to go to fetch water at Gahenerezo, down the hill in the valley, and it's a bit far. He'd carry one or two jerry cans, twenty liters each, and he'd have to go two or three times. I think God used him because nobody else did that type of job for Tutsi during genocide.

During the day and night, we, our family, would pray—we were Christians—two of us would pray for an hour and then two others would pray for the next hour. It was the only way we could get peace and maintain trust in God—and we prayed for water because it was a very big problem.

One night, in May, I had a dream in which I saw a table knife and it was dripping water, just drops, not running [or flowing,] and we filled everything [cups, bottles, the bathtub] in our house, every container we had. Two days later, the director of the prison, Karubanda, called my father on the phone to tell him that once a week, every Friday, Electrogaz [the utility company] would be sending water to the prison so there was a chance he could provide us some water in our house. Electrogaz was going to open the pumps up for the prison because the prisoners could not go down to the valley and fetch enough water for the prison.

He knew we were Tutsi, but he didn't choose to kill us. He even, sometimes, gave us some food. I remember one day he gave us a sack of beans. Because he was a very important Interahamwe nobody questioned him about our house [about why their house was always quiet and untouched] as nobody would think that Tutsi would be allowed to remain living in the area so close to him.

Also, just before [the] genocide, the prison was guarded by a gendarme and there was one gendarme who liked my little brother, who was six years old. He [her brother] had a deep voice, and the gendarme would call our house a lot just to talk to my brother because he just liked to listen to his voice. During the genocide he [the gendarme] did not want to join the killing. During genocide he would call us, and tell us the plans of [the] Interahamwe.

The day before the killing was to start in Butare, the [new] president [Dr. Theodore Sindikubwabo, an aging pediatrician and politician from Butare, who was recommended by the MRND] made a speech that was recorded and played on the radio, and during the speech he said there was peace and everyone should go out in the morning and go back to work. But the plan was that the Interahamwe would be at roadblocks that were set up to catch all of the Tutsi who were out [of their homes]. So many people were killed that day. If the soldier had not called and told my father that we needed to stay in the house, I am very sure my father would have gone out to shop because we had very few supplies at our house.

In Butare, there were many people [Hutu] who did not want to be part of the killing—some because they didn't understand [why the killing was being perpetrated] but some because they didn't want to kill—and they [the killers] even had to bring in lots of Interahamwe from Ginkogoro on the big green buses, Ontracom, over five buses, and even a plane with Interahamwe from the north, to convince people, local people, to join the killing. As the buses came into Butare they began shooting in the air. We heard that. That was around 22nd of April.

One day, in late May, Interahamwe came to attack our area and began to attack our neighbor's home, and the prison director heard about this and came in from town [Butare Town] and opened up the prison and got some prisoners to chase them away before they began to attack our home.

Eventually, water began coming on Friday to our house, but it wasn't enough because the prison got the water first and by the time we got it, there was very little flowing through the pipes, more of a trickle. So, we would fill everything up we could, Fanta bottles, cups, and gourds.

Some Fridays, though, the water that would come out of the tap had blood in it. When they [the génocidaires] killed people they would throw them into the river, and the river water would be collected in big water tanks. It was not red-red like blood, but when you put it in cups or bottles it was tinted red. The rest of the week, when the water had to be fetched, we would try to forget the blood in the water.

At one point, in the middle of the genocide, in May or June, the director of the prison let out of prison those whose sentences were almost up. I think he let them [Tutsi prisoners] out, go, and return to their villages and homes so they could be killed. But there was an old man, maybe in his fifties, who was to be let out but insisted on staying in prison because he had no family to return to, and so the director took the old man to his [the director's] house to work as a servant. One evening, the old man left the compound at the director's home, and those at the bar, across from the director's home, saw him and remembered they had not killed the Tutsis in the prison.

The killers went to the prison, and that night there was very loud singing. It was very strange because though different groups within the prison—church organizations, scouts, the Red Cross—always sang when they met, this night everyone was singing, very loud. They were singing the normal songs they always sang, but longer and louder, much louder.

The next morning, a man, a Twa, who was a prisoner [a trustee who was allowed outside the prison walls] and often came to our home and crawled under the front gate in order to pick up leaves from a tree that served medicinal purposes, visited us and told us, "We killed all the Tutsi last night." He thought we were Hutu and so he told us. He didn't figure out we were Tutsi even though our gate was always closed and he always had to crawl underneath it to get the leaves.

In late May there was a lot of killing. We could look out the window and see, on the opposite mountain, houses burning. And in front of our house, in May, two men were killed. Right in front of our house there was a roadblock, and when the two men came up, we heard gunshots. At that time, I think, they had killed most of the people in the area and began searching houses for any Tutsi who had not been killed yet.

In late May or the beginning of June, around noon, two men—one a soldier in uniform with a gun [a rifle], and the other one who was dressed regular [in civilian clothing], came [crawled] under the gate and forced the door [to the house] open and made all of us—all my brothers and sisters and two cousins, my dad and mum and the guard and the houseboy—leave the house and enter the yard in front of the house. They let the houseboy, who was Hutu, go, and told the rest of us, "We are taking you to kill you at the museum," which is where they took lots of people to kill them because there is a forest behind the museum.

My father apologized, "Please forgive us, we are sorry!"

Before the genocide you [Tutsi] knew you had no rights and could die [be murdered at any time]. People, before genocide, made you feel as if you deserved to die. That's just the way it was, the way people thought, how they had been conditioned to think. So, to ask for forgiveness was almost as if we were apologizing for living, for existing. My father said, "Please forgive us. . . . Please don't kill us." Then my mother started singing, a song from the book, the hymnbook, and no one helped her sing even though we all knew the song. I can't remember the song; I just remember it was from the church book. The two men just stood there and didn't stop her.

I was mostly thinking of how they were going to go about killing us. I was thinking, Does my father have enough money to pay to have us killed with guns? and, If not, we're going to be killed with machetes. [Interviewer's note: Victims often paid to be shot in order to be killed quickly versus being hacked to death with a machete.] It cost about five thousand Rwandan francs to be shot, and I wasn't sure my father had that much money.

Suddenly, my mother quit singing, and the soldier took the other man aside and talked to him and they both came back and one said—I don't remember which—"Go back to your home."

And then the other said, "Others will come and kill you."

My father thanked them, offered money—he didn't have much, maybe one thousand or two thousand Rwandan francs—and wanted to accompany them out the gate, but they said, "Be quiet." There were other killers in the street, and they didn't want them to know that they had left Tutsi behind alive.

No one in our family had a word to say. We just thanked God, and then later, waited for the next group of killers to come. We all went back in the house and locked the door in the sitting room, kept quiet and later began to talk and praise God.

June seemed a bit quiet, but we didn't know what was happening. What I thought was: Are we going to stay in this house forever? Are we going to be the only survivors? Are we going to get out and flee to Burundi?

As we stayed there, we listened to the three radio stations—RTLM, Radio Rwanda, and the RPF station, Muhabura. We listened to all three of them in order to try to figure out what was happening in the country. Radio Rwanda gave very general information, but RTLM and Muhabura gave very exact information. For example, RTLM would say, "The inyenzi are now in Nyanza. The small inyenzi are now in Nyanza. [Interviewer's note: The interviewee explained that "They would say 'small inyenzi' to suggest that the RPF was weak and would be easy to kill, and by emphasizing smallness it suggested to people, the Hutu, there was nothing to be afraid of, nothing to fear."] Go and kill them!" So, we knew the RPF was in Nyanza.

So, on the radio, you could learn that the RPF was getting close, and that gave us hope. We were hoping that the RPF would come in from Burundi and reach Butare.

So, things in Butare were a bit peaceful because the killing had already been done. During this time I began having dreams about peace, and this was quite confusing because we had no idea if peace would come or when it would come. One dream I had is that we were met by soldiers, but soldiers who didn't have ranks [chevrons] on their shoulders [sleeves], and they didn't ask for identity cards [as the Rwandan military and Interahamwe constantly did] and they were caring. And they had different uniforms from the other [the interim government's] army, and I met them in the street, which meant that I was out [of the house and free to move about].

Another night I woke up in the middle of the night and a voice said, "Peace with you," and I was confused and went back to sleep, not thinking much of it. Later the same night, I heard a voice say, "John 20–21." Again, I went back to sleep, not paying much attention to it because I had been reading the Bible a lot. I figured in the morning I'd look it up. Also, I was sharing my room with my two sisters and a cousin so I didn't want to wake them. In the morning I looked up the verse in the Bible and read, "Again, Peace be with you." Jesus said this right after he had been resurrected.

After reading this, I believed peace would come. I didn't know when or how, but I believed that there would be peace. I didn't know if we would go to Burundi or what would happen when the RPF arrived. Remember, I knew they were Tutsi, but I didn't know them. It wasn't that we didn't trust them, we did; but we didn't know how they would recognize us as Tutsi or if we would recognize them as Tutsi. Also, some people had changed their identity cards. For example, either my sister or cousin had changed their identification card by taking a razor and cutting off the X which marked whether they were Tutsi, Hutu, or Twa and then drawing the same size X through Hutu. She thought that if we were taken away she could show her card and claim we were all Tutsi. Many people did this. Some threw their cards away. For me, I didn't think we could be saved [and thus didn't bother altering her identification card], but my sister or cousin thought she could jump out of the window and escape and nobody would know who she was. But not me.

Our houseboy heard that the Interahamwe were looking for my cousin. Everyone in Butare knew her because she worked at the small lodge, at the restaurant, behind Hôtel Faucon. They began to wonder where she was since they had not seen her body. And so they began tracking where she had been, and just as Interahamwe were coming to our house to get her, the RPF, which had already arrived and had come to the prison because the prison is at the entrance to Butare, caught them.

In late June, French soldiers came to Butare and said they wanted to help all of the religious people get out of Butare, Hutu and Tutsi, but mainly they seemed to want Tutsi. So, they came and took the religious, such as the Catholic nuns, to a camp in Gikongoro. The director of the prison said because my father was a pastor, he would contact the [French] soldiers so they could take us to Gikongoro. My father refused, politely, saying, we had a big family and it would be difficult to care for everyone. My father feared—unlike before—leaving the house, believing it might be too dangerous. In Gikongoro, Tutsi and Hutu were put together and some Tutsi were killed. Even at road-blocks on the way to Gikongoro, Tutsi were pulled out of transport [trucks, buses, and cars] and killed.

Toward the end of June, people, masses of people, Hutu, began fleeing from Rwanda to Congo. RTLM was pleading with people not to leave Rwanda, telling them to be brave, not leave their villages, to stay and resist [the RPF].

The houseboy would go out and see what was going on, and he would come back and tell us that the roads were full of people fleeing to the Congo. The people around us—our neighbors, the [Seventh Day] Adventists behind us, and the family who lived in front of us—fled to the Congo. Even though the woman [head of the latter family] was Tutsi, she had many friends who were Interahamwe and she went with them. The director of the prison opened the prison, and let all the prisoners out and when he did, all of the prisoners and guards fled.

A few days before the RPF took over Butare, they arrived in Save, about ten minutes from Butare on the way to Kigali. French soldiers arrived on a plane that was army color [camouflaged], and they took over the control of the town and fought the RPF. That was discouraging, because when we heard the RPF was in Save that was encouraging, but now that we heard the French were involved we feared they might push the RPF back. The French were there to help the Hutu, to protect them, and began fighting the RPF. We could hear the fighting. But the RPF continued to come toward Butare.

On Sunday, FAR [Rwandan army] soldiers came up just behind our house and were discussing the situation, saying that the RPF was very strong and that they, the FAR soldiers, could not resist them. And now, we could hear the fighting close by, down in the valley and close to the prison.

Then it was very scary because the fighting was taking place close to our house and nobody else was there. We didn't know what to do—everyone was praying.

When I looked at my two young brothers, six and seven years, they were very scared. And my mum told us to pray, I think, to try to prevent us from being scared and from trying to run away. So I began praying for my brothers. Again, I got another vision—this was during the day—and I saw the throne of God and He was sitting in His robes looking at our house as if He was protecting our house. I believed He was protecting our house. And I saw that vision twice that day.

The fighting eventually passed the house, and it became quiet around three or four [in the afternoon]. This was July, around the 1st. Then one of our friends, who was a Hutu, called and told us that the RPF had taken the place [Butare]. That was Sunday night. You could tell that someone had taken the place because it was very quiet. But we still remained in our house, just waiting for what would come next.

Then, two days later, the RPF came to our house with a young boy who had been hiding in a house near us with his grandmother and sister—the whole time they hid they only had water and sugar to drink and eat—and a prisoner who had been let out of prison but didn't leave the area and remained in Butare and joined the Interahamwe. When they entered the yard, the young boy came up to the door and knocked first. The RPF waited in the street. It seemed that they did not want to scare us. That was very exciting—to see the soldiers, just like I saw in the dream. And even more, we were [going to be] out of food in one day. We asked if they had food and where were they going to take us. They took us to the prison, and there they gave us bananas and we also heard that we were not the only survivors.

The RPF took all the survivors—those who they thought were not in a safe place, orphans, and those who didn't have homes or were refugees from other towns and villages—to the Butare stadium and brought food for them there. When we heard about the survivors, my sister was so excited that there were other survivors that she went to see them all in the stadium. In the stadium, there were hundreds of people, maybe three hundred.

The RPF was concerned for our security and suggested we go to the stadium, but my father insisted that we be allowed to stay [at home], and so they let us. Shortly, the RPF came to live in the director of the prison's house. That was very good, very exciting.

A week later, the RPF took the people from the stadium to Save, and they took us there, too. They wanted to check out the entire town [of Butare] because Interahamwe kept coming back from Gikongoro to kill people. So they [the RPF] took us all there, checked the entire town, and then we were allowed to return. Those who were orphans, whose houses had been destroyed or were refugees, they stayed there [Save] until the RPF found houses for them.

It was very exciting being at Save. We were safe, we had food, but the best was that we had security. We stayed in the room of Catholic brothers—there was a Catholic center at Save, two schools, a church, a convent, and a big center for Catholics. There, we got to meet and talk with the RPF and to thank them.

When we returned to Butare, many people began flooding across the border, returning to Rwanda, refugees from 1959 and 1973. It took a while before life got back to normal because there was no work, schools were not in operation, and there was no food in stores. The RPF encouraged us, everyone, to go to people's gardens and eat that food and not sell it because everyone was in need. And the RPF helped, and so did many international organizations. So we all—except for my father who went back to serve as a pastor—stayed home for a month. And after a month, mum opened a shop where she sold milk and so that's when we began to have work.

Also, this was the time when mum began to help children. She officially started her organization [the interviewee insisted that the name of the organization not be mentioned out of fear of various repercussions, especially possible attacks by past extremists] in 1995, but even before that she helped children—orphans of the genocide—by providing them with food and finding families for them.

A big part of my extended family was killed. On my father's side, only he and his sister were the ones left from his family. More than fifty of them I can remember, whose names I know, were killed in his family.

One of the most difficult aspects of this [the killing of all her family members on her father's side] was that my grandfather was killed and thrown in a latrine, and after genocide my auntie returned to Kibuye and knew the place where he had been killed and put some signs [markers] and left immediately because it was not safe. Later, she returned with my brothers in 1995, and the neighbors showed them where my grandmother was buried and my auntie placed some flowers there. In 2001, the family was ready to bury my grandmother in a dignified way with a ceremony and my auntie and two brothers and cousin bought a coffin to put the bones in and went to Kibuye where they dug up the whole area searching for the bones. The reason they waited until 2001 is because the area was not safe to return to, especially to search for [the remains of] your relatives.

They dug all day, into the evening, until a neighbor came and told them that the killers had dug up the bones and thrown them in a river, Kiraga, so no one could dig them up and try to find out who the killers were. So they returned home without her bones and we had a ceremony, which all of our relatives and friends were waiting to attend, where we had her photographs and some flowers but not her bones. That was very hard on my father; he was not able to cope with that, not all the way up to the day he died. He talked about it over and over again, commenting on how very sad he was.

On my mum's side, close to fifty people, who I knew, were also killed. One of the saddest aspects of that was that my grandfather was a pastor and [had] helped many, many people but they killed him. He hid himself and his family in a church, and they entered and killed him and his family.

My uncle, my mother's brother, had both of his arms cut off before they threw him in a river. The killers first cut off one of his arms, and then told him to hold it with his other arm as they took him to the river. Then they told him to put both his arms [his stump and one good arm] over his head, and they cut off his other arm. They just wanted to torture him. Someone after the genocide told us what had happened to him.

After the genocide we were able to bury my grandfather and grandmother on my mum's side, along with five of my cousins who were killed with them. A neighbor who recognized what my grandfather and grandmother had done for her buried them all by herself—no one else was there or helped her—in the trash pit behind her house. I don't know if it had trash in it or not, but she put them there and covered them with dust. After the genocide she informed our family she had buried them, and we went up there and dug them up and reburied them in a compound—not at the church but near it. We had a formal ceremony in 1996 with a proper burial. They were all buried together—in one grave—a private grave, not a public grave. There was another man who was Tutsi, a friend of my grandfather—there were only a few Tutsi in that area—and he had told my grandfather he wanted to die with him and so he lived with my grandfather and grandmother and cousins during the genocide and was killed along with them.

Other relatives are buried in mass graves, but [at various times] the neighbors of our relatives during genocide would tell us, "They are buried here," and then, "No, they were buried there," so we don't really know where they are buried. Others, cousins, were thrown in a river, Nabonongo, and a marker has been placed near the river and we go there [every year during commemoration] and have a small ceremony even though their remains are not there. We do not know what happened to many of them.

Just after [the] genocide, for a period of time, I feared people were following me, that someone was going to attack me, that someone was going to kill me. And during memorial period [April through early July] I also have had a hard time trying to understand what happened to us [the Tutsi people]. During commemoration I only [allow myself to] see survivors and no one else, no other community members.

Africa is built around families, extended families. We lost so many family members it's like . . . I . . . we . . . don't have a family anymore. We have our immediate family, but not our grandfathers, grandmothers, aunts, and uncles so . . .

Those relatives from the extended family who have no family members left, we take care of them. For example, my mum has three cousins living with her and she must care for them, house them, clothe them, feed them. Most significantly, it has been very difficult psychologically for the children to live with mum because they lost their parents and brothers and sisters. It wasn't, isn't, a normal situation, living with their aunt, and at first they were hard to control. Two are sisters and one is a cousin to the sisters.

The worst aspect of life after genocide is missing aspects of my family. As a child, on holiday, we went to visit our extended family, our grandparents and aunts and uncles and cousins. We didn't leave the country to visit other parts of the world. Now, for fourteen years, we don't go anywhere.

Eventually, I chose to work with mum's organization, because the organization supports orphans, and I wanted to help because it was not their choice to lose their parents, and I understand that as a child you can't advocate for yourself, you can't get things done yourself, and need help. Also, I do it because I feel I am serving God because He helped me survive. And this is a way to honor that help. As a Christian you should ask yourself, "What would Jesus do in this situation?" And I believe God always wants to show love, so I do the activities I do to show that God is love. For example, even HIV/AIDS-infected children who are abandoned by their families, I want to show them love through what I do for them.

While I am the staff manager of our organization, I work specifically with HIV-infected children who are orphans of the genocide. I develop and coordinate programs for them. I train staff to provide one-on-one counseling for them. I also develop health-education programs and provide training for that as well. I also offer one-on-one counseling. I work with two thousand orphans on AIDS prevention programs, and I work with 217 orphans who have AIDS, conducting counseling and health programs.

The main challenge for us is that we work with very poor people. So, yes, they have HIV/AIDS, but they also do not have food, decent homes, clothes, education. When I see a HIV child about to die and didn't do anything to get the HIV [in other words, contracted HIV as a result of his/her mother having been raped during the genocide], it is very sad and I often take the sadness home with me.

It is also a struggle for me to see or hear about those poor families who, when they learn that a child is HIV infected and already do not have enough food, take the food from the HIV-infected child who is going to die and give it to the other children . . . [The interviewee paused, deep in thought.] When you are helping people, you feel you survived for a reason. You didn't survive for nothing.

Seeing survivors who are struggling without adequate housing, with nothing, is also terribly difficult. For example, I know twenty-four students—twelve males and twelve females—who are all living together in a very small house that is falling down. There is so little room they have to put their suitcases in the living room; the bedrooms are not big enough for their possessions. Also, they have no power [electricity] and no water, and I don't think they [the government] have plans to put it in there.

To me, gacaca, if it is conducted in a proper way, is important. In fact, whether gacaca hearings are done well or not, you can get important information about the genocide from them. For example, you may find out how your family members were killed, who killed them, all the details and that's very important for a survivor, for our grief, healing. Also, I think that is very important for reconciliation. If I didn't know who killed all my relatives I would [have a tendency] to think that all Hutu in Kibuye were . . . are killers. But when I know the names of the killers, who killed my family members, then, even if I sometimes think all Hutu in Kibuye are killers, I know that that's wrong. I may hear about Hutus who did good things, whereas if I hadn't heard that in gacaca, again, I may think all Hutu are killers.

I think that gacaca is acting as [a sort of] prevention because if someone comes and encourages some to kill, they [the latter] may think [twice], realizing that anything they do will become public and be discussed in public. And so, that may prevent them from listening to certain leaders.

It is also a healing tool, because when you stand and say what you want about killers and the killers stand and say what they want to say it might help to lead to reconciliation. This is one side [of gacaca]. I believe all of this happens or can happen, but there is another side.

On the other side, one concern of mine is that there are judges who are not educated. I think to make judgments one must have education, and even a basic understanding of the law. I do think everyone can give testimony, yes; but judge, no.

Another point of concern [deals] with those areas where they killed everyone [meaning, there is no one left to provide testimony so killers are apt to get off due to a lack of evidence provided in witness testimony]. Also, sometimes you find those People of Integrity [the formal name of gacaca judges]—even if they didn't take part in the killing, or where their participation [in the genocide] may have been [peripheral]—who have some connection with those who killed.

Also, many [survivors and witnesses] won't get up and tell the truth about what happened because they fear what might happen to them. Even those who did not participate in the killing often do not get up and testify out of fear of being hurt.

Also, those in charge of gacaca can make it very difficult for survivors. For example, in the gacaca [hearing] of my grandparents, we traveled all the way to Kibuye just to be told that the hearing was cancelled and to return the next week. The last time I went there they told us they did not get enough information to make a decision so they told us to return the next month. Now, to go there we need a four-wheel Jeep, which costs around one hundred thousand Rwandan francs [about US$200], and sometimes we need to take people for the different cases—my grandmother's and my grandfather's—so we may need to take two Jeeps.

Apart from the money, you must take the day off from work. Sometimes when it's during the rainy season you do not know if you can make it back because the road is not good. And there is no hotel to stay at.

If I look at the government's position, it makes sense to allow the génocidaires to confess to their crimes in gacaca and ask for forgiveness and to reduce their sentences by half. The government does not have the funds to keep all those prisoners in jail [at one point it was estimated that there were 150,000 imprisoned for allegedly taking part in the genocide] for their full sentences, and the families of those in prison often have difficulty finding enough [money and food]. So, to allow the prisoners to go free can help their families earn more money and thus have more food.

From the survivors' point of view, if the guilty confess and tell the truth [about what they did during the genocide] and ask for forgiveness in a genuine manner, it helps the healing of survivors. It is good to know where your people died and where, maybe, to find the bones [so one can] bury them. And if they [the killers] are really genuine, some survivors will forgive them.

On the other hand, there is not enough punishment to give someone who killed your family. Even if the prisoner is kept in prison for his full sentence, it is not enough. So, what I am trying to say is that while there is not enough punishment for a killer, half a sentence is even worse. Maybe the equal punishment would be to kill him and his family as he did your family, but even that would not be enough because it would not bring back the people who were killed.

If *people are genuine* then I think gacaca can lead to reconciliation. But a lot of times people say they are sorry because they just want to get out [of prison]. I think that less than 50 percent of those who have testified have said the truth, and that doesn't help reconciliation. For example, when we went to gacaca most of those who were on the mountain where my grandparents were killed said they didn't know things [facts about the murders], and of those who gave information, only some of it could even be used by gacaca [to establish the truth]. Now, if people really told the truth, you could possibly feel closer to those people—and feel something really like reconciliation. It is very difficult to judge how many are being genuine. And if it's not truly genuine then there's no hope! Who is genuine? It's a very small percent.

I'm very sure some people in my *quartier* [section] of Kigali still have genocide ideology. People have not admitted it to me openly, but if people don't tell the whole truth in gacaca then I think they still have genocide ideology. When you do [have] discussions with people, you see they still have genocide ideology. Even some people don't admit there was genocide or try to compare it with other killings, such as a person being killed by someone [during a typical homicide].

I would say that the government has done a lot for survivors but . . . for example, the government pays for secondary school for orphans and university tuition but it does not have enough money for everyone. Because of limited financial resources, the government fixes a score of three on the national exanimations in order [for a survivor] to qualify for a scholarship, and a three is not easy to get, not at all—and especially for survivors of genocide who are orphans and who have no one to care for them, guide them, or who suffer from trauma.

To even give the same national exam to orphans and children, survivors with parents, is not fair. How can you give the same exams to them? Not even talking about survivors, think about children who go to school in Kigali and those who go to school, for example, in the hills of Huye or where my father was brought up, the hills outside Kibuye. How can you compare the teachers when most wish to live in the city and those who end up in the rural areas may not be the best? I am speaking about being motivated; they [many of those teaching in rural areas] didn't get the jobs they wanted, they are getting paid less than those teachers who teach in the cities, they do not have the same didactic materials for teaching, and the parents of the children may not be able to help their children so the situation is frustrating for the teachers.

The government has also built houses for survivors, even if it has not built houses for all the survivors and even though many of the houses are not built well. For a long time, there was no follow-up [by the government] to make sure the houses were strong [well built], but now the government is following up to make sure the houses are strong [will not collapse in five years as many have].

The government also pays for health insurance for survivors—the poorest survivors. But again, it is only the poorest of the poor who are getting the help, but many who are poor—very poor—[but not the poorest of the poor] are not getting any help, assistance.

I know that the government takes one percent from everyone who works, to support FARG [Victims of Genocide Fund], but that is not enough—not to meet all the needs of survivors. I think they need to develop a new means of involving more people in helping survivors—even some survivors can help because not all survivors are poor. Many who have money are not motivated to give, but if there was a plan then they could help. Some people would give, some would not, but it would still be a means to motivate people to think about giving to help survivors, to support them. They, too, could contribute to healing and reconciliation. The donors could feel closer to the victims by giving something to them, and the survivors might not feel so alone. They could [come to understand] that there are people who care for them, and are trying to help them. And it is not only about giving money, but going to visit them.

As for the mental health of survivors, I feel is it is neglected. I say that because what has been done to help survivors in other areas—such as educating, housing, and justice—has been concrete, but I don't think any tangible effort has been made in mental health. Without a good state of mental health, one cannot fully benefit from the other areas of help. Untrained staff cannot provide mental health support. The people who are providing mental health assistance for survivors—the majority of them—only received a couple weeks' training. Not only are there not enough [counselors,] but also the competence is not enough to treat people suffering from severe trauma. Such individuals may do more harm than good.

Various organizations have tried to train counselors, but the training was weak, and those who went through it could cause serious problems due to a lack of competence. The government is the only one that can establish schools [or departments in universities], and mobilize the international community to help with this [providing assistance to those with severe trauma and training competent practitioners].

After 1994, we, the country, had one psychiatrist. Now we have, I think, less than ten psychiatrists for the entire country. After genocide we didn't have any mental health nurses, but now the country operates a diploma [three-year] program, but with no specialization in trauma counseling; so the assistance trauma victims receive may not be adequate.

Of those who enter university, some will go on to get a university degree and change their focus. Also, the mental health nurses who are practicing are working mainly for hospitals or big organizations in cities, and thus you cannot find them at the community [or rural] level.

I think a proper trauma counseling course should be required of all those being trained—doctors, nurses, social workers—in order to provide proper support when they come into contact with patients who are suffering trauma. That would allow people all over the country to receive help because there are many doctors, nurses, and social workers around the country, and this would result in those at the grassroots level being able to provide assistance.

ANONYMOUS

DATES OF INTERVIEWS: April 19, April 20, and June 8, 2008

LOCATION OF INTERVIEWS: Iris Hotel, Kigali

INTERVIEWER: Samuel Totten

INTERPRETER: Not needed

LANGUAGE IN WHICH INTERVIEW WAS CONDUCTED: English

BIRTH DATE OF THE INTERVIEWEE: December 25, 1973

AGE DURING THE GENOCIDE: Twenty-one years old

PLACE OF BIRTH: Nyarugturu (Southern Province)

PLACE OF RESIDENCE DURING THE GENOCIDE: Mubuga-Gikongoro

ETHNICITY PRIOR TO THE GENOCIDE: Tutsi

NUMBER OF IMMEDIATE FAMILY MEMBERS KILLED IN THE GENOCIDE: Father, mother, one sister, and more than two hundred other relatives

CURRENTLY RESIDES WITH: Wife and baby son

In 1990, when the Rwandan Patriotic Front (RPF) invaded Rwanda, the government leadership at the time [members and followers of the president, Juvénal Habyarimana's government] made a kind of generalization: they said all Tutsis living in Rwanda were supporting the RPF and they referred to them as *inyenzi*. I am talking about the leadership at the central level making [such] statements on the radio [Radio Rwanda], and the leaders at the regional and cell levels repeating what they heard on the radio. In fact, even before 1990 there were rumors going around about a possible war brewing [between Habyarimana's government and the RPF].

I had a lot of family members who fled Rwanda in 1959, and then in 1963 and again in 1973. [All three dates refer to periods when the Tutsi came under attack by Hutus and ended up fleeing the country and seeking exile in such places as Uganda and Burundi.] My uncle came back from Bujumbura [the capital of Burundi] to visit us, his family, in 1988. This was when my grandmother and grandfathers were still living; they were his parents. While visiting, he went to a bar to have a drink. There [at the bar in Ndago, a small, remote commercial center, in Commune Mubuga] he met a man, a judge, a Hutu, who asked him, "Can you tell me the day you [the Tutsi] will kill us?"

My uncle replied, "We killing you? Or you killing us?" From there, they exchanged bad words.

My older brother, the first born in our family, was working at Electrogaz [the distributor of water, electricity, and gas in Rwanda] here in Kigali, and in 1990 his boss was a Hutu from our area, and when the war started he sacked my brother. My brother had to come back home because there was tension in Kigali. My brother was working in the construction department at Electrogaz, where he was a very, very junior member of the company. I understand my brother was not alone in being sacked, that a number of Tutsi, who were all referred to as *inyenzi*, were also sacked.

As the days and months got worse [as tensions increased], my brother finally decided to flee to Bujumbura to join my uncles and aunts who had fled [there] previously. As the war progressed, the propaganda got worse and the local Hutus became more aggressive and would abuse and beat people. So, my brother, who had skills, decided, when he couldn't get his job back, to go elsewhere.

At this time I was in senior three and living at a boarding school. During that time, I received news from home that my brother was chased out from his job, and the one [his boss] who sacked him had been our neighbor.

During the early 1990s we lived in terrible fear. My father worked for the commune as a driver, and he had to interact with many people. The harassment was constant. And the situation was only getting worse.

In the village, as the tension grew, Hutus would actually tell Tutsis, "We will kill you! We shall eat your cows! We will burn your houses!" and Tutsis would personally gather, meet in local pubs over beer, and discuss these threats and rumors. When I visited home I would hear about such discussions.

At school I also was harassed, as were all Tutsis. The school I attended was College du Christ Roi [a Catholic school based in Nyamata, in the Southern Province], and it was a prestigious school and used to be frequented [attended] by children of senior government officials. So, at that time, when we were at school, following the holiday, we would hear terrible things that they heard at home from their parents—senior ministers, high-level military officials—and they would repeat such things at school: "All Hutus should protect ourselves because the Tutsi are going to kill us." The thing is, what they were thinking [or essentially saying] is that "If the RPF continued to attack, we will kill everybody—all Tutsi in the country—and that they [the RPF] will find no one alive." This was a mechanism used to try to repel the RPF, and actually the Hutu did kill Tutsi all over the country just as they said they would.

In 1991, at Nyanza, people would stay outside their homes because of threats that Hutus would come and kill all of them. Also, at this time, people were killed—hundreds, I do not know the exact number—in Bugesera [in Eastern Province]. This was a test of genocide [a testing out of the killing process and how people reacted, both within the nation and internationally]—how the Hutu could carry out mass killing. This was done in another place [as well], Kibirira [in Northern Province].

Ayisi David, whose father was Mbonabaryi, a member of parliament and the brother-in-law of Habyarimana and the brother of Agathe Uwilingiyimana [a moderate Hutu politician, who was not trusted by the Hutu extremists and who served as prime minister of Rwanda from July 18, 1993, to the day she was assassinated during the outset of the 1994 genocide], attended our school. Ayisi, who was in level three when I was in level five, would walk around school with a long knife in a sheath. All of the authorities at school, of course, knew this as they would see the knife because it hung from his belt. One time I saw him pull the knife, hold it in the air as if he were going to stab something, and tell a Tutsi [fellow student], "I will kill you!"

Since we were not in the same class I was not around him and we did not live in the same dorm, but I also made a point of avoiding him. He had lot of prestige among Hutu students because he carried that knife and was allowed to do so by the authorities of the school. Tutsi students feared him terribly.

At the school, there was a priest, Hormisdas Nsengimana, who is now detained at the ICTR [International Criminal Tribunal for Rwanda] in Arusha [Tanzania]. He was involved in the killing of thousands of people, including his fellow priests, so he's now being tried as a top-level *génocidaire*. At the time, he would come into the classroom and he would say, "You Tutsis are drunk on peace," meaning, "you are fools because you feel safe." Most of the students in the school were Hutus, so this was a way of inciting the other pupils [Hutu] against us [Tutsi].

After the genocide I made a joke with a friend: "The reason I didn't die in 1994 is because I had died before, psychologically died before. The death refused me because I had died before." All I heard for years in school was, "You are stupid! You are a cockroach!"

At the age of seventeen I had only seen one dead person—an old person in our village and I went to the burial. So, when we, the Tutsi, would hear that we were to be killed [by extremist Hutu], when someone told us they would kill

us, that was terrible to hear and would cause us great fear, and so we would
flee from those who threatened us in that way.

As the years went on, the insecurity of Tutsis increased. In 1992, when
the RPF proved it was stronger than the government, threats increased. I
remember on the 8th of February 1992, the RPF launched a very heavy attack
on the government and the RPF arrived within fifteen kilometers of Kigali
and from that time [forward], the international community said [to the
Rwandan government],"Negotiate! Negotiate because you are facing a strong
opponent." It was clear to everybody that the government was weaker than
the RPF. But the government kept up its threats on the radio that if the RPF
kept up its attacks it would find *no* Tutsis in Rwanda. So, the increase in the
insecurity of Tutsi was very high.

In 1993, something bad happened to me. I was outside school—we were
at a sports event—and one of the pupils, a Hutu, who was chosen as pupil
representative, said, jokingly, "Why can't we make two teams—one of the
armed forces of RPF called inkotanyi and one of Interahamwe?" The other
Hutu kids said, "Yes, that's great!" And so then they decided to reconstitute the
group into two teams. There were only six Tutsi but twenty-two Hutus.

Someone said, "How can we make a team—the team of cockroaches are
few?" So, they said, "Let's give them five people, but from the south." There
was some tension between the Hutus of the north [which was where President
Habyarimana was from] and the Hutus of the south, so the northerners would
not want to be with those from the south. And so that's what they did, and
then we played. Our team got a goal, and one of the players on our team said,
"Because we won over the Interahamwe, let us take the ball and go back to
the dormitory and they will remain shamed." The comment was a joke, but
the defeat and the words made the Hutus angry, and someone said, "Do you
see how the cockroaches act, how they are malicious? Do you see how they
do?" So, the kid who suggested the idea of the game went to the director of
the school and told him, "The Tutsi brought politics into sport. They beat us
in the game, said humiliating things, and took the ball and went back to the
dormitory." As a result, four of us were suspended from school for two weeks
by the director, the one who is now at the ICTR.

The director told my father that I was bringing politics to the school,
that I was a troublemaker and an inyenzi. My father just listened and said, "I
punished my son and told him I did not want him to do such things in the
future." My father, of course, knew I had done no such thing, but everyone
knew that priest and knew he was a sadist and you did not argue with him.

Once I returned to school, life went on as it used to be [tense but livable],
but then 1994 came, when we were on holiday. RTLM (Radio-télévision libre

des mille collines) was beginning to mobilize, over the air, Hutu to kill Tutsi. As we listened to the broadcasts, the issue in the family was how we could escape. We lived very close to the border with Burundi, only about thirty kilometers [away].

In the rural areas, the Hutu had organized militia into cells, and thus after the shooting down of the president's plane, the leaders [of the Hutu-run government] instructed the general public [meaning the Hutu] to set up roadblocks. At the same time, RTLM told people they should remain in their homes.

At this time began the systematic burning of Tutsi homes. After the houses were burned to the ground, there were messages over the radio informing the community that Tutsis, all of the Tutsi, should gather at the same place— churches, halls at administrative offices in communes, sector offices, schools, and other public structures or anywhere there was a large space where people could gather—so that they could be protected. But such gatherings of people supposedly to provide protection was really [a means to bring them together] to kill them.

During the burning of the homes, the militia were raping, killing and eating the cows, and stealing personal property. It was, really, pure anarchy.

My father was killed on 12 April. We, my entire family and our neighbors, left our homes on the 10 April, heading toward the district hall of the commune. There we stayed for a night, inside. There were about a thousand people there—so many people were inside others could not get in so they stayed in the area outside of the hall. Right away, guards—policemen of the government and Interahamwe—were placed around the area so they could be ready to kill us.

During the night of 10 April my father told us, "They are lying to us. They are not going to protect us, they are going to kill us." It was a Hutu who had told him this—as a warning. The Hutu said, "Please don't allow yourself to be lied to, you are not going to be protected, you will be killed." On the same night we saw indicators of what was going to happen. The guards prevented people from fetching food, wood, and water. So people had no food, no water, no movement, nothing!

Now, controlling this crowd—all of these people with all these children, all milling about—the police and Interahamwe told everyone, "If you attempt to leave, you will be killed." There were hundreds of guards—and they had weapons, AK-47s, big [powerful] weapons.

During this time, we received some news, that in a neighboring church, militia, the military, the police, and the gendarmerie attacked the church with grenades, throwing them into the group of people, and as the people fled, scattered in all directions, the militia, with traditional weapons such as machetes, cut [sliced and chopped] people to death. Some men in our camp said: "We are going to die the same death" [be killed in the same way as all the others], and so the men began to plan how we could all get out of that camp. They said that because we were a big crowd we should all rush in one direction; and [since] the police would shoot at the crowd, they would have to shoot until they had no bullets left and as many bullets as they had that's how many people would be killed and then the rest of us could escape. And so that's what we did. The military was still in the process of surrounding the camp so there were only guards, who were spread out [trying to contain the crowd of people]. As we fled, the militia shot at us, and hundreds of people were killed. Most of those who were killed were old ladies and old men and children and people who were sick or disabled, because they could not run fast. As we all fled, the militia chased us and killed us with machetes and massues, and other traditional weapons.

Those of us there fled toward Burundi. Eventually, we arrived at a place called Cyahinda, a Catholic mission, and there, already gathered, were thousands and thousands of people. There were lots of guards—policemen and gendarmerie—and they forced us to enter there and join the crowd. Most, though, refused to join the crowd. Some, though, joined the crowd because they were hungry and because they were thirsty and entered hoping they'd at least get some water. Others entered because they were forced to enter the place. Still others entered to die there. They knew that the time would come when they would be killed, so they just gave up and entered until the time when they would be killed.

My sister, the last born, was killed there. She was thirteen years old. Her name was Chantal Uwanyiugira. This was on the fifteenth [of April]. She saw people entering and she entered, and the rest of us were immediately separated from her.

People such as yourself who weren't there need to understand that there was total confusion. No control of anything; swarms of people [moving everywhere]. The militia were striking people with machetes and killing them, others were yanking people into the larger crowd; if a person next to you got pulled into the crowd, there was nothing you could do, it was over. It was chaos with people moving everywhere, being beaten, screaming, and crying.

I was in the outer crowd and we continued [on], but then unfortunately we lost direction and we arrived at a roundabout where two roads split off in different directions, and we did not know which road went to Burundi. In the confusion, part of the crowd took one direction and the other part went in the other direction.

My mother and brothers went to the left and I was forced by the crowd, which was being threatened by the militia and gendarmerie, to go to the right. If you stepped in a single direction you could not reverse. You were part of the movement and you are [were] not walking like you do every day, you are being stepped on, moved forward [against your will], and there is nothing you can do to choose which way you will go. And remember, people are crying, traumatized, people are wounded and frightened and . . .

My mother and two brothers who went left continued until, I later discovered, they reached another church, Nyakibanda [Great Seminary]. When my mother reached there she was almost finished; she was tired, angry, and said, "Let me remain. This is enough." My brothers [eighteen years old and twenty-three years old, respectively] entered this place with my mother. Something like three days later the militia attacked and my mother was killed. My brothers, though, fled.

When the militia attacked, my brothers were outside and were taking [collecting] stones to fight the militia with, [the latter of whom] were trying to enter the area. The militia were throwing grenades into the compound. When the grenades began exploding, all the people began fleeing in different directions. Many were killed there, very few survived. We don't know what happened to my mother, how she was killed.

For [those of] us who took a different direction, we walked dozens of kilometers, and fortunately we took the right direction to Burundi. We found a highway, and on the highway there were people traveling from all directions and places [from within Rwanda], and we asked, "Which is the way to Burundi?" and then we followed them. After two hours we came to the border, which was guarded by the Rwandan military and gendarmerie. They told us, "No, you cannot cross!" They gathered us up and forced us to give them everything we had—like sticks, machetes, stones, and [all] potential weapons. Then they pushed us into another area, about two kilometers from the border, further inside Rwanda, to a placed called Nkomero, a small commercial area in Gishavu Commune, Butare Prefecture. And then, immediately, just after thirty minutes, we saw a group of militia, maybe a hundred, coming, singing. I even remember the song they were singing, "Eh Tubatsembatsembe" or "Let Us Slaughter Them Massively." They were moving toward us quickly. We used stones and we pushed them back, and we passed the night there, prepared to fight again if we needed to.

The next morning, at about 9:00 A.M., we saw a military truck full of military people, FAR (Forces armées rwandaises or Rwandan Armed Forces, the Rwandan government army), coming toward us. Immediately, we saw a crowd of Interahamwe coming from a different direction. We said, "It's over!"

Immediately, we began scattering ourselves. And there, again, people were murdered everywhere. We [he and his neighbor] joined a crowd fleeing and we arrived, again, on the border. We didn't pass, because at the border there is a river, Akanyaru River, and there is a bridge and on the bridge there were FAR and gendarmerie.

The people in the crowd threw themselves into the river, and fortunately the river was not too wide, about three meters, or deep, about one and a half meters, and so we were able to get across to Burundi. As we were crossing, people helped one another, pulling people along by their shirts, and others, closer to the bank, grabbed grass [and pulled themselves up]. There were other people who had crossed some hours before who also came down to the river and helped to pull people out of the water and up onto the land.

I threw myself into the river. I was among the last in the crowd and because of all the movement in the water from the hundreds of people, the water was rushing [turbulent] and I got carried down the river. I could swim, but I had a sweater on, which my mother had given me because it had been cold, and because of the water the sweater got heavy so I pulled it off and made it to the bank.

The soldiers and militia on the bridge, they were killing those who attempted to cross the bridge, so all of those who, I guess, feared entering the water, thinking they might drown, tried to cross to Burundi on the bridge. There were about two hundred who crossed in the water and about a thousand who tried to cross on the bridge. Many people who attempted to cross the bridge, if not killed, were pushed back and had to hide in the bush and later many of them were killed. Some people, though, also managed in the chaos and killing to cross the bridge. My two brothers were among those who made it across the bridge.

In Burundi, I went to Bujumbura where my auntie lived. That was in May. My brother, my second oldest brother, joined the RPA (Rwandan Patriotic Army, the military arm of the RPF) after two weeks and I joined. I served for two years and a half. My brother was assigned to a battalion and fought the FAR, French, and Interahamwe in Zone Turquoise [the area established by French troops, ostensibly to help victims but which provided cover for the perpetrators]. I was being trained to protect the cabinet members after the war because we had no police. I was eventually assigned to General Headquarters and the VIP Protection Service.

In August, I completed my training and I was transported to Kigali. Along the way we saw many vehicles on the road returning to Rwanda from Burundi with people who had fled from Rwanda in the fifties, sixties, and seventies. We passed many roadblocks [established] by the RPF, [which] helped to facilitate people [to] reach where they were going.

Kigali was empty when I arrived. In what you could call central Kigali, people began to rebuild their businesses, but there was nobody to buy anything from. Just outside of Kigali you saw houses without doors and windows smeared with blood. The smell was terrible. As a result of the mass graves, you could smell the death.

I got out of the army in October 1996, and I went to Butare to university [the National University of Rwanda (NUR)] in 1997 to study arts and humanities with an option in English Language and Literature. I graduated with a degree in 2003.

In 2000, I had become stabilized. It was the end of my second year of school, and I started asking myself questions: Should I cry the whole night? Should I have a wife? Should I have a child? Should I have ambitions?

In 2000, I returned to my village. My home was not a place I wished to see. I had mixed feelings. I was very angry, very, very angry. And I felt great sorrow. I had fear, too. At that time, [I had] no trust, especially in those people I used to live with, our neighbors.

The place, the first church, my family and I had gone to seek shelter, where the killings took place, had a commemoration in 2000 and I decided to attend the commemoration. Even though I did not want to attend, I decided that I should go and say goodbye to the ones there. No one from my immediate family was killed there, but in Africa those who are your cousins are your brothers and so I decided I needed to go there.

There were many people there, about fifteen thousand—people [Hutu] had to be there, [since the] commemoration was organized by the government, they [Hutu] were forced to come. Every Tutsi—because we [continued to] suffer fresh wounds—were there, too.

This was a very remote place, and the villages were filled [lived in] by people who had committed genocide. The feelings [at the commemoration] were mixed, with high levels of distrust.

The ceremony, with officials, took three hours. The ceremony took place with tight security—even President Kagame [the current president of Rwanda] was there. Testimonies by survivors were given, songs were sung, speeches [were given] by officials, and prayers were said. They also buried the remains of those who were killed in the area. Twenty thousand were buried that day.

I detached myself from where they were burying the bones because I had some feelings—the smell from the bones. I could not be around, if . . . I could not stand it. It made me feel . . . My chest got very tight, like my heart was moved from its place . . .

At that time was when I decided to attend as many commemoration ceremonies as possible because after two hours [following the commemoration] I was glad I had attended the commemoration—I was OK.

At NUR, we had an association of survivors, AERG [Association étudiants et elèves des rescapés du génocide, or Student Association of Genocide Survivors]. AERG brought survivors together to try to understand their programs [problems/issues], and then it would inform the university administrators and the government in order to try to get help for them. At the time, there were many problems such as a lack of housing for students and the fact that students had no place to go on holidays.

After the genocide, in 1997, the first year of university [for the interviewee], I attended a ceremony to bury my father. The burial ceremony was in Ndago, which was something like ten kilometers from my village. There were some mass graves in that area that were very [well] known. There was one very big mass grave where most people were thrown, including my father, I was told. I went there with other people, about a hundred, to bury the bones—actually, the remains of the bodies because parts of the body were missing. For example, a skull was detached from the neck and arms, and legs from the trunk of the body. So, no one really knew if the bodies [skeletons] were their mother or father or brothers. So, when the burial took place for my father, I did not know which bones were his, only that his bones were among the mass of bones in the mass grave.

When people were killed, the killers often took their [the victim's] clothing, shoes, and watches and so the skeletons had no clothing [which may have helped in the identification of the victims].

Some, though, were able to identify their family members, as some of the bodies [skeletons] were still in clothes and had identification cards, which were always encased in plastic. One woman in Kigali I know, for example, was able to identify three of her sons, who had all been dumped in a deep latrine. All had clothes on their skeletons and student identification cards.

This ceremony [his father's, along with others] was organized by local people. Some local people took the initiative to do this on their own. The people in the area collected the bones from the mass grave—which originally was a garbage dump where the killers had dumped many of the bodies—washed them, and laid the bones out. During the ceremony a new grave was dug and the bones were deposited there and covered with cement. The ceremony was very short—the burial, some short prayers, that was all.

I went alone to each of the burials [his father's, mother's, and sister's] because my younger brother was still in secondary school, and I did not want to subject him to such an experience; and as for my other brother, he was still in the military and was deployed a great distance away and I did not want to trouble him.

The first conflict [personal problem] I had after the genocide was a lack of trust. I had to sit in class with Hutus, go to church with Hutus, eat in restaurants with Hutus, and I had a kind of fear that they would do harm to me. I could not separate myself from them. We could not have our own classrooms, and I feared they could do anything to me. So trusting these people was, for me, a problem. Having such fear and suspicion caused me great stress, and I even thought, "Should I quit school?" I mean, we lived among masses of Hutu at school, some ten thousand students. So I had to come to an understanding that not all of them were killers.

I also had the fear that what had happened [the butchery and genocide] could happen again. I had no indications that it could not happen again.

My first year I lived in a dorm with eight students in a room and six of the students were Hutu. The first months—first one to two months—I had great difficulty because not everyone goes to bed at the same time: some at 7:00 P.M., one at 8:00 P.M., another at midnight, some come in drunk, some with a Bible, so every time the door creaked [opened] I woke up to see who it was. It was a very interrupted sleep. I'd sleep for five minutes, wake up for five minutes, and then sleep [for another] five minutes.

No one knew what the others [the Hutu] had done. No one talked about it. People were quiet [private]. People [Hutu who still hated Tutsi] acted contrary to their thoughts. They passed themselves as normal.

In December 2002, I applied for a job with the Kigali City Council to work in the Twinning and Cooperation Department, which established city-to-city twinning. Kigali twinned with seventeen other cities around the world, including: Rome; Pretoria, South Africa; Lusaka; Brussels; a city in China; Mayance in Germany; Quebec; Atlanta; and one town in Malaysia.

I took the exam and I got the highest score—sixteen out of twenty and two others with the highest scores had fifteen and fourteen. The two others were much older, both in their forties. We also had a test on computers and the other two were not capable on computers. I also knew the mayor of Kigali through friends, and he asked the panel [of interviewers] about me. [The mayor had heard about the interviewee from co-workers.] The panel said, "Yes, he's a young man, he has very high scores, knows English and French and has experience on computers." I remained in that job for four years.

For a long time now, I have not been able to understand how people who were killing [relatively recently] could now act like nothing had ever happened—like they didn't hate us, didn't kill us. They act very calculatedly. Some act excessively nice. Some have avoided me. But I cannot understand how they can just walk around and act normal. These people don't attack you, they don't say bad things, but you find out, are told, this one's father is in prison, this one's mother is in prison [on grounds of having allegedly or actually taken part in the genocide]. This one's whole family is in prison!

I cannot understand this! How can this be? And they must have thoughts about me: "Has he forgotten about what happened?" "Has he forgotten us?" and "Has he figured us out?" I was the same way, I did not mention anything. All of us act so calculatedly.

You even knew that some students [at NUR] were suspected of having killed during the genocide because they had been called to appear in front of gacaca. But still, I, we [Tutsi] maintained a distance from such [matters] as we did not want to disturb the interdependence we had on campus [meaning, having to both live together and work together on projects in certain classes].

I started dating my future wife in 2000. I knew her family—her father was a teacher and had been a headmaster, and was active in the Liberal Party, which supported the RPF, like my father. I knew who she was, but had not talked to her [prior to meeting her on campus]. She comes from a very good family.

It was my plan to marry a survivor. I thought I would be comfortable in my home with somebody who I could share the past with. I thought she could help me and I would help her. Of course, there were other aspects that were important, too, that were objective and subjective—that one should be beautiful, intelligent, and nice as well.

Because of the genocide, and because of the terrible things I have come across, the consequences of genocide prevent me from having hope, hope for the future. Here in Africa, people, young people, really, depend on their parents to help [them] in life, with education. And when you have no mother, no father, what do you do? When you have no hope life can be sustained, what do you do? When you have no hope in life, that is death.

After the genocide, one of the things that helped survivors was the fact that a lot of mechanisms were put in place for them. The leadership [within the central government] understood there were lots of problems and tried to develop programs to help us. For example, at school those who did not have a home were given dorms and those without food were given rice and beans. And other survivors who managed to advance [graduate from school and/or do well in business or government] earlier than others helped other survivors. For example, a friend of my father, a priest, came to visit me on campus [at NUR] and he gave me a thousand U.S. dollars. He asked about my family and found out my mother and father and brother and sister had been killed. He asked if I had any problems, and I said, "No, I have no problems." Of course, one has problems, but how do you figure which ones to discuss? And then he asked if I was in need of money and I said yes, and so he wrote a check for four hundred thousand Rwandan francs, which was equal to a thousand U.S. dollars.

The most rewarding aspect of the life in the aftermath is that the victims won over the génocidaires. I don't just mean the victims of 1994, but all the way back to '59, when the seeds of the genocide were planted. I believe that the genocide cannot happen again as the government of [President Paul] Kagame has seen to that. I think they [any Hutu still harboring genocide ideology] know that they are not dealing with simple [naïve or uneducated] people.

Still, no one should have illusions that the genocide ideology has ended. It will take generations to end. We have to address those tendencies in society. Schools and teachers have to have positive curriculums that teach killing is bad, that genocide is wrong.

I'm satisfied with the how the trials of the alleged génocidaires have gone—both classical [national] courts and gacaca. Do you want to know why? You know Hutu leaders and Hutu people have been involved in killing Tutsi for a long time—the sixties, seventies, eighties, nineties, and in 1994 they believed that they could kill everybody, so that no Tutsis would survive. People were even rewarded for killing. But now, at least, the majority of people who killed are known. For example, in gacaca, they made [undertook] something called "Information Collection on Genocide Crimes," and 815,464 were listed by the people themselves in the communes as potential suspects. Ninety percent of these people were tried. Some are in prison, some are in TIG, others will be prosecuted by the Classic Courts [national courts within Rwanda]. The point I am making is that individual responsibility was established. Not 100 percent but if you can list 815, 464, that is an enormous number.

That culture of the sixties, seventies, eighties, nineties, where Hutus could kill Tutsis, that is no longer here. The trials have mobilized the people to the principle that genocide is wrong. And even when gacaca ends that does not mean that those who have not been tried are safe. They can still be arrested and tried.

Individual people [Tutsi] can be killed [by Hutu due to ethnic issues], of course, and there are still indicators of the genocide ideology around. But in relation to our current government, its position, I do not believe genocide is possible. I don't see Hutus developing the plan to pick up machetes and forge a new genocide.

I can see peasants believing that genocide is still possible because they are living in poverty and are surrounded by Hutus who say [threatening and dismissive] things to them. Yes, I can see peasants possibly believing that genocide is possible again. But they don't understand that there are mechanisms in place to prevent genocide from occurring again.

Gacaca is important because we still have victims whose bones are buried in mass graves, and survivors do not know where they are at, and at gacaca they can be told by génocidaires where the bones are buried so they can collect them and bury them with dignity. Also, sometimes those who have murdered a lot of people dissociate from what they did, but if they come to gacaca and confess, then they no longer deny it. They also [provide] important information about why they did this to us. They can tell us why peasants began killing, and they can give us information how this killing came about—who told them to do that, what meetings were held to plan this, what the incentives were to kill. The killers, they know more than us, the victims; they are the ones who did the killing.

Still, it is very hard to know if someone is genuine [vis-à-vis his/her confession and asking for forgiveness at gacaca]. I think the opportunity for perpetrators to confess and ask for forgiveness and then get their sentences cut in half was, partly, a process to get people to confess. The suspects, of course, would be interested in something like that. Some, of course, just confess some of what they did. Some can [and do] distort what they did. And some lie about other people or call survivors liars.

To get a genuine confession is very difficult. During genocide the situation was very complex. Killing could take place in a building with two hundred people. A killer may have just attacked several people out of the two hundred and under very chaotic conditions. Or, he may have thrown in a grenade and killed several people. And those he killed are not around to give testimony. Also, some génocidaires may be in complicity with one another to cover up crimes. So, I think some génocidaires do what I call "lying with accuracy." That is, people come in and say I did this, I did that, but they lie because no one really knows what they did. They give a sense of what was happening during genocide so it sounds real, but it's not. Some people do not tell the truth, not all.

In gacaca there is a sense of justice in that on an individual level a person appears in front of the people [they lived near and who they hurt], and they ask him what did you do? Where were you? At least he must get up and answer a lot of questions. At least there is a sense of holding people responsible for what they did, individual responsibility. They don't get away with it entirely. And at least some people are held responsible, if not all.

There are lots of mechanisms involved to reach reconciliation, not just gacaca. There are, for example: poverty-reduction programs, a reconciliation commission to help bring about reconciliation, and lots of programs at the national and local government levels to bring people together, such as *umuganda* or "common work," during which everyone is expected to take part, and afterward there are meetings to help strengthen peoples' efforts to live together again. *Everyone* is expected to take part in this program.

Gacaca cannot bring about reconciliation on its own; it just contributes. When all of these efforts are brought together and working, then reconciliation can be brought about over time. I think, in general, Rwandan society is moving towards reconciliation. There is, for example, the power sharing in government. Many Hutu are in parliament, many more women are in government, and this shows, suggests, that people should be together.

Still, to some extent there is division between people today—between Hutu and Tutsi. There are some people who are saying: "You came to kill me because I am Tutsi, and you are Hutu" or "You came to kill me because you are Hutu and I am Tutsi so why should I erase that?" And Hutu often say similar things: "You treated my people poorly in the past. Why should I forget that?" But the issue now, for those who wish to have a good future, such divisions, such memories, should be minimized, not suppressed, but what good does it do to make the divisions concrete? They need to be minimized so the historical divisions cannot continue to fester. We need to be proud of being Rwandan, not Hutu, not Tutsi, or as before, "I am a Hutu from the north!"

Still, [on a related note] my wife has been threatened by a person [who was Hutu prior to 1994] who she had been with at secondary school and he now works at a local hotel here in Kigali. He also worked at a school. At the school he was very brutal. He saw her when they were at mass and he would glare at her and she would get scared and leave. This was just two years back. Here [in Rwanda, Kigali] we have an organization that is active in women's rights and I called a legal officer there and they called him and he was kept at a police station for four days. The police told him that what he was doing was harassment and the police told us we should go to court, but he would say, "No, I didn't do anything. I do not even remember [seeing her at church]." Or "My lips were just that way." So, we said, "No, let's wait." After three months he sent someone to see my wife to apologize, saying he did not mean to do anything. So, at least we exposed him and we will see if it's through. He was trying to intimidate her.

The genocide was preventable! Why do I say this? Almost all of the nations that could have stopped the genocide knew that the genocide was orchestrated. All diplomatic circles knew the Hutu were going to kill, and they did nothing. So, around one million people were killed. There are several hundred thousand survivors, including myself. What I wish those countries [that did not attempt to halt the genocide] to consider is the fact that plans to [perpetrate] genocide will succeed unless the nations and states adopt another plan for managing [dealing with] the issue of internal affairs. Unless something profound is changed then their cry of "Never Again" will never be valid.

I have experienced some trauma but it is not bad. When we have commemoration in April, the one image that causes me great grief is what happened to my sister. During commemoration we hear music on the radio, sad songs, and words about genocide, and when I hear the songs I have . . . Once I was driving and when a song came on I went blind for a few seconds and I hit the brakes hard, fearing I would cause an accident and I came back to, but [immediately] I thought that may have been a sign of trauma induced by the memories. What happened to her, my sister, is . . . In my family there were six and the girls were the last born and we loved them so much and she was the last of the girls and we treated her special and when she was killed it was so . . . I was with her when she was killed. Yes, I was with her . . .

I have not sought help for it because it comes irregularly. If it keeps growing, then I will seek help.

My [other] sister lives in Brussels. She had to leave here. She could not live here after what happened. My brother, he is OK.

During commemoration my wife has lots of troubles. She is very, very sad, for sure. She forces herself to get up to work, but she is very unhappy. But look, these stories, these experiences, are part of our life, so we live with them. We force ourselves to go on, but it doesn't mean we aren't sad. We are!

EMMANUEL MURANGIRA

DATES OF INTERVIEWS: January 22, March 29, and April 9, 2008

LOCATIONS OF INTERVIEWS: Murambi/Nyamagabe/Nyamagabe

INTERVIEWER: Samuel Totten

INTERPRETER: Rafiki Ubaldo

LANGUAGE IN WHICH INTERVIEW WAS CONDUCTED: Kinyarwanda

BIRTH DATE OF INTERVIEWEE: September 1957 (interviewee does not know the day)

AGE DURING THE GENOCIDE: Thirty-six years old

PLACE OF BIRTH: Nyamagabe

PLACE OF RESIDENCE DURING THE GENOCIDE: Murambi

ETHNICITY PRIOR TO THE GENOCIDE: Tutsi

NUMBER OF IMMEDIATE FAMILY MEMBERS KILLED IN THE GENOCIDE: Forty-three at Murambi, including all five of his children and his wife

CURRENTLY RESIDES WITH: Wife and a child

On the 7th of April 1994, the bourgmestre, Semakwavu Felicien, and the sector councillors, Munyempara Joseph and Gakwaya Innocent, had a meeting of the commune at Nyamagabe. The meeting started around nine in the morning and at about three in the afternoon it was finished. At the end of the meeting, they came to the market of Nyarusiza. They told the population, "Go and destroy the houses of the Tutsis! Kill them! God has abandoned them!" and "Don't hide any of them [to protect them from harm,] for they have killed the father of the nation [a reference to the shooting down of President Habyarimana's plane on April 6, 1994]. I was there [at the meeting].

They started killing people right away, and they started with the Tutsis doing business in the marketplace. They also began killing cows of Tutsis [as they desired the meat to eat], and destroying and looting the homes of Tutsis.

When my family members saw the killing, they all began running away, in different directions. We all knew we could go to the church, and on my way to the church I met them. I am talking about my larger family, but on the way I was searching for my wife and children as they [his children] were very young.

The Tutsis basically went in two directions—one group headed toward the church in Gikongoro, and another group headed toward the church in Cyanika. You need to realize, this area has one of the greatest number of Tutsis in the country. We went to the church of Gikongoro, and within a day it filled with people. By the 8th, we were about forty thousand.

On the 8th, the préfet of Gikongoro, Bucyibaruta Laurent; the bourg-mestre, Semakwavu Felicien; the commander of Gendarmerie Camp in Gikongoro, Captain Sebuhura; Kamodoka Denis, director of the Kitabi Tea Factory; and Bishop Misago Augustin came to the church in Gikongoro, and they walked around the compound among the refugees [the Tutsi]. At first, we thought such important people were coming to end the violence and to help us to go home.

By the 8th, it was very difficult for people to enter the compound because there were so many people; and yet, it was also difficult for many people to reach the church because of the roadblocks and the killings. Anyone who wanted to pass had to show their I.D. [identification cards denoting whether they were Hutu, Twa, or Tutsi].

There were some people among us, some elders, who complained to the officials that our houses had been destroyed, our cows killed and eaten, and our belongings stolen. They also told the officials that we wished to have justice delivered. The officials said they would solve the problems, and went away. We don't know why they came to the compound and walked around, but I think they were there to evaluate how they would kill us all without leaving any survivors. This was not difficult to figure out because RTLM was sensitizing Hutus to kill Tutsis.

Some of the people in the compound arrived with a little money, and so they sneaked out of the compound to purchase *igikoma* [a liquid porridge made of sorghum flour, water, and sugar] to feed the children. Some Tutsi women who were married to Hutus, and who remained in the village, tried to send us food. They were successful, but they had to sneak it in. In the very early days, people were thinking of the children, and people were still considerate as they thought this all would end shortly. It's also true that the food brought in for children could be eaten by adults, too. So, initially there was enough food.

Women and children stayed inside [of the elementary school on the grounds], and men stayed outside in the open air. This was the rainy period, and when it rained we were out in the open. That was something we had to face.

Eventually, the compound got filthy, and people started to get sick and get diarrhea and die from the diarrhea. Imagine forty thousand people; it smelled horrible and the diarrhea attracted many flies everywhere. No one could wash and people became infested with lice. There was no way we could sleep; we had to protect the compound because the killers kept trying to force their way in, and besides there was no space and it was wet and cold and the rain fell.

On the 11th of April the first attack came [against the compound]. I cannot tell you the number of attackers. It was at night and difficult to see, but maybe about three hundred. They had whistles they were blowing and they were chanting slogans such as "The God of Tutsis is no longer around" and "There is only the God of Hutus remaining!" and yelling, "Make sure no cockroaches escape!"

They had covered themselves with dried banana leaves, which helped them to identify each other so they wouldn't kill each other as they entered the crowd. They carried *pangas* [machete-like tool] and spears and swords and impiri [clubs with nails].

We had only stones to throw at the attackers, and we screamed at them as well, trying to scare them. That night we blocked them successfully.

A week later, on the 16th, the same officials returned, and entered the building owned by the Catholic Church. It was located in the same compound in which we were all gathered. The bishop was in the building so we waited to see the results of the meeting. That meeting lasted more or less three hours. After the meeting, the bishop came out and announced that they decided that we all had to go to Murambi because there was more space there.

The elders among us, and good Christians, told the bishop, "Members of our families have been killed. We have lost everything. Are we going to be safe in Murambi?"

The bishop said, "I'm going to talk to the commander, and he will help you to go to Murambi. He will be sure to see that you are protected." Then he told us that we were to go to Murambi that day.

Tutsis from other communes who were heading to the church were then told to remain in Murambi because even those of us who were in the church compound were going to be moved to Murambi. These people were coming from communes and villages that were eight, nine, and ten kilometers away and were passing by Murambi.

The bishop told us, "Four gendarmes are going to escort you to Murambi." So even though we expected something [an attack], we had to go because they said we had to leave, and that they would protect us there. And so, we all went.

The bishop said he would ask the director of Caritas [a Catholic nongovernmental organization], Madeline Raffin, if she had some food in her stores so she could bring food to Murambi. But, of course, they were lying to us. Later on, we realized that they promised us anything as long as they could get rid of us.

So, we went to Murambi, walking, and it took us about thirty minutes. It was a long queue. So, the night of the 16th we stayed in Murambi with the four gendarmes providing protection.

Once in Murambi, David Havugimana, subpréfet, ordered that the water lines be cut off so we could not get water. And so, the water pipes into Murambi were destroyed. So, there was no water, and the food promised didn't come. Now we are about fifty thousand people because there are still other people coming from other areas to Murambi.

On the morning of 17th of April, the préfet, the bourgmestre, and the commander of Murambi began speaking to the four gendarmes who had spent the night with us. After the meeting, the gendarmes divided people into small groups of fifty or so, and checked to see if anyone had weapons. Even those of us who had sticks had them taken away. People had left home in a hurry and brought nothing with them [thus, few had weapons with them].

Then they told us, "Don't worry, the Hutus in the surrounding area are about to flee, thinking you have weapons and are about to attack them." Later on, we realized they lied about the fear of the Hutu and were checking to make sure we had no weapons, including traditional arms, that could be used when we were attacked. After the gendarmes completed their check for weapons, they left with those others.

We spent the day there, with no water, no food, and spent the night there, too. That night, Hutus in the area—I don't know how many, it was raining and dark and we just heard them screaming and yelling—tried to loot the little we had, but we used stones and managed to keep them out.

Around eight in the morning, the gendarmes and the Interahamwe attacked us. They had massues, machetes, spears, and grenades and Kalashnikovs. We tried to protect ourselves with broken bricks and stones, but they shot and shot.

Women gathered stones and bricks, and we [the men] threw the bricks and stones. This went on from eight in the morning until three in the afternoon. They [the Interahamwe and the gendarmes] killed some of us; I don't know how many, about sixty, and we dug about that many holes and buried them because we feared that dogs would come in and eat the dead bodies. It was not really a ceremony [a funeral], but we dug the holes just so the people could be covered. There were lots of people [still alive] so it was easy to dig that many holes.

On the 19th, the Interahamwe and gendarmes returned in the morning, and this time they were trying to enter the compound. I can't tell how many attackers there were, but, and I may be exaggerating, about two thousand and something.

All of this time we did not have water, and so we had to leave the compound to get water at a well; the strategy of the Interahamwe was to attack people and kill them as they attempted to fetch the water. After two days, people feared fetching the water and quit going there. [Eventually,] even those who still tried to fetch water were prevented from doing so, so they would be forced to die slowly.

Throughout this time, children constantly cried from hunger. And then there were children who were at the stage of asking questions such as, "What are we doing here?" Many parents answered, "We are here because we are Tutsis and the Hutus want to kill us." The children would then ask, "How do you know who is Hutu and who is Tutsi?" But how could we answer such a question when we are only thinking about getting killed.

The other thing I remember about the children is that when some mothers were killed, their children—their babies—would continue to try to breastfeed [by pulling their mother's breasts outside their clothing and sucking on the nipples].

We lived in this situation until the 21st, when a major attack came, this time by soldiers [FAR]. The attack came at three in the morning, and they surrounded the whole school complex [a new school was in the process of being built in Murambi. The complex was to consist of about five long bungalows, with about four or five classrooms to a bungalow]. I have no idea what kind of weapons they had, but they were heavy and strong and made terrible sounds. And they began to shoot inside the compound and throw grenades. This was three in the morning, and we couldn't defend ourselves because the women and girls were still sleeping and so nobody could pile the stones up for the men to throw.

During the attack, we, the men, were running around trying to find stones to throw, and as I was doing this, I was hit by fragments from a grenade that the killers were throwing at us. The fragments hit me in the leg [lower shin area]. [The interviewee pulled up his left pant leg and pointed out a large, deep scarred area where a huge chunk of flesh had been ripped out. The skin appeared to have been badly burned.] I continued to fight on, but [after a while], since we had no weapons, we just lay down and waited for death. You have to imagine, the entire area was surrounded and soldiers were shooting from every angle around the compound and throwing grenades.

There was *no way* to get away. There was *nothing* you could do. We stayed down to try not to be hit, but the bullets were everywhere, and those who tried to get out by climbing the fence were killed by machetes. The shooting and killing went on for a long time.

I got shot in the head about nine in the morning, and from that point on, I could not remember anything. I finally recovered my senses about three in the afternoon, and I found myself naked. I somehow could not believe what was happening. I was somewhat stupid [beside himself and out of his head]. I hid myself under dead persons. Although I did not see anyone trying to escape [because he was under the bodies], I heard many people weeping and crying out due to their injuries and wounds.

That day I saw the apocalypse, the end of the world. God was not there. [Interviewer's note: Up until this point, the interviewee was speaking fairly easily, but as he talked about what he saw that day, he teared up and asked if we could stop and resume the interview the next day. The rest of the interview was put off until a later date.]

———

That day, the préfet, Laurent Bucyibaruta, came to the compound in the same vehicle with the commandant of the military police, Sebuhura, and the bourgmestre of Nyamagabe, Semakwavu Felician, to see how many the Inter-ahamwe had killed the previous day. As they walked around the compound, they pushed and prodded the fallen with their shoes to see if they were really dead. Then they divided the killers into two groups, and had one group remain in Murambi to go around and check to make sure that all those who were down were dead. The other group was sent to the Catholic Church of Cyanika in order to kill the people there, about twenty thousand, who had gathered there [in search of sanctuary].

The rest of the day they spent checking to see who was not dead yet, and killing, killing, killing. They did this until dark. The checking took a long time because to find those who were alive they had to check the thousands [spread across the grounds], and uncover those who were under other bodies.

Within the school, the killers were killing the girls and women with machetes and massues. They tortured them before killing them by slashing them with machetes and hitting them by pounding them with the massues. Also inside the classroom buildings were some men who had attempted to hide, and escape death, by hiding up in the rafters, and when discovered they were shot and killed.

After the préfet and commander came to Murambi, they sent for big machines, Caterpillars [tractors] to come to Murambi to clear away the dead [to push them into huge piles and into mass graves on the grounds of the school compound]. As they cleared the dead they even cleared the injured who had been shot but not killed. As the Caterpillars began their work, they pushed and ran over the injured who had been hiding under dead bodies. As the Caterpillars worked, they ripped the arms and legs of many who were alive. Many who had hidden under bodies or had been injured could not manage to escape in time, or feared getting up because they saw that the Interahamwe were still around.

The Caterpillars, which were driven by the workers with the Ministry of Public Works, all who were Hutu, pushed those who were dead and alive in big holes, and as they did, babies could be heard crying. As soil was being dumped on top of the trenches, the [older but still quite young] children cried out with their hands in the air, begging for rescue, "Please forgive me! I will never again be a Tutsi!"

No one could rescue those children! The natural thing is to rescue babies and children in danger, but in 1994 many people became animals. And, of course, if we [had] tried to jump in the pits, the Caterpillars would either have tried to run over us or we would've been shot and killed.

Those who attempted to flee down into the valley were shot and killed. There were also people [Tutsi] who had hidden outside the compound in the sorghum fields. Many of those had remained outside the compound because when they had first arrived at Murambi they had seen the Inter-ahamwe and didn't wish to enter. Also, the préfet and commander had left Interahamwe to take control of the sorghum fields and to continue the killing process.

I waited until dark and then managed to escape. I can only assume God was helping me, moving my body. It was like I was not there. I somehow managed to get up, leave the compound and head to the bush, the forest, Nzega.

When I escaped, the killers were sharing cow's meat, and so I tried to benefit from their distraction. Also, when I was escaping, I saw some victims who were also trying to escape from the compound but they were heading in the direction of the church [the Catholic Church] of Cyanika, which I believed was a bad idea because people were to be killed there.

Later, I came to understand that the reason why those victims were fleeing toward the church was because the vicar, Niyomugabo, was a Tutsi, and they knew he had a gun and they believed that he would be able to protect them.

It took me about two hours to get from the Murambi compound to the mountain because parts of the path were very steep and very difficult. When I arrived at the mountain, Nzega, I could see that people who were fleeing Murambi to Cyanika Church were continuing to be killed.

The next morning, on the mountain, I was by myself, and I could see people continuing to flee, and I saw them being shot down and killed. There was shooting going on and off all day long.

For four days I was upon the mountain, and I was in great pain and had deep sorrow. I was also thinking, "Why did I survive?" and "Why am I alive?" I was also thinking, "Maybe I should go down to the valley and present myself to the Interahamwe."

The militia who remained at Murambi brought in dogs and went out into the hills with the dogs to track down the survivors, those who were still trying to hide. Around this time, big government buses passed by full of men who had many guns and pangas and other traditional weapons, and I heard them shouting, calling people out from the hills, the mountain, to come and join them [in going to] Nyanza "to kill the *inkotanyi*" [the nickname of the RPF soldiers; but the interviewee insists that the killers were referring to all Tutsi and were suggesting that the RPF was attacking Rwanda and that all Hutu should be involved in the killing of all Tutsi before the RPF arrived].

All four days I was up on the mountain by myself, and during the day I hid myself in the bushes. At night, I began traveling, avoiding the roadblocks established by the Interahamwe. It took me three days to reach Burundi. As I was making my way to Burundi, I saw many persons, maybe over five hundred, who had been killed and were [strewn] about the hills.

At one point, I came to a stream and was going to get a drink of water, but then I saw many dead bodies in the water and so I did not take the water. In the stream, there were about thirty dead people. There were also many babies still on their mothers' backs [wrapped up in a blanketlike pouch, which is the way mothers carry their infants in Rwanda] who were dead and small children [who were dead]. So there were many more than thirty dead.

When I arrived at a border post, the Burundi soldiers saw that I was badly injured and covered in blood, and took me, right away, to a hospital, Kayanza. At the hospital I found other wounded Tutsis who were being cared for there. There were persons from UNHCR [the Office of the UN High Commissioner for Refugees], Médecins sans frontières and the IRC [the International Red Cross] helping the survivors. There, we were provided with all we needed, every kind of assistance—food, medical care, and clothes. Some good Burundians, who were touched by what was happening in Rwanda, also brought food to the hospital. People even told me that when they arrived at the border without clothes, Burundians gave them their own clothes.

At the hospital, they operated on me—when I am not sure—and pulled the bullet from my head. I was at the hospital all the way through July. I did not leave, did not go to a refugee camp. At the hospital, I left the bed on 6th July, after the RPF took Kigali and Butare, and one week later [around the 13th of July] I decided to return to Rwanda, but I knew from Burundian radio that French soldiers were within the Gikongoro, Kisuye, and Cyangugu sectors [the French operation, now infamous for its actions and inactions, was called Operation Turquoise], and I decided to pass through eastern Rwanda and then on to Kigali. Those soldiers [the French] were not in Rwanda to protect us [the Tutsi], but to stop the RPF advance, to protect the Hutu killers, and when they saw it was not possible to stop the RPF, they [the French] encouraged the Hutu killers to flee to the former Zaire [currently the Democratic Republic of the Congo].

We [he, other survivors, and refugees who had left Rwanda at one time or another in 1959, the 1960s, and 1973, as a result of threats and killings by the Hutu], lived in abandoned houses [and other buildings, all on the Rwandan side of the border]. I lived in a school classroom with another person. We, many, many refugees, all cooked our food together. While there, at Bugesera, I suffered great sorrow, loneliness, fear of being killed again, and hunger. Even though UNHCR provided food, it was not enough. They provided us with maize and beans, but the food was not enough to even eat twice a day, so I only ate once.

Some refugees from 1959 went to Murambi to see if they could locate their relatives, but when they couldn't, they knew immediately that they had been killed. They asked the officials and many citizens in the area, "Can you tell us where our relatives are buried [often bodies were tossed in latrines, rivers, or left in fields to rot, and at Murambi thousands were buried in mass graves] so that we can dig them up and bury them with honor [in a single, private plot with a ceremony]?" But they were told, "No people were killed here. Perhaps they were killed fleeing."

The French soldiers and the killers had managed to hide all of the signs of the killings, and had built up the ground [with dirt that was trucked in] and told the people in the area not to tell anyone what had happened there. But some of the refugees remembered that they had left a man in Bugesera from Murambi who had told them all about the killings at Murambi, and so they traveled back to Bugesera to get me and return me to Murambi [to help locate the others' relatives].

When I arrived in Murambi, in September 1995, I found out there was an association called Amagaju. The organization was established by genocide survivors and refugees from 1959, the 1960s, and 1973. The goal of the association was to bury the victims with honor. This organization provided a house for me, as my house had been destroyed. They paid for that house for two years. After two years, the government took over the commemoration of the genocide and began to help the victims.

To live in Murambi without my wife and my five children was . . . it was unbearable [begins crying]. Since 1996, when I was helping people to exhume victims' bones from sites of the mass murder and witnessing again the inhuman ways people were killed, this is when I began to pray. This is when I didn't understand and . . . [continues to cry].

After what happened to me, my wife and five children, and my loss of them, I, to bear to live with this situation, prayed every day, asking God to give me enough force [will] to live. When I prayed, I prayed with other people, and after the praying, there was a kind of hope that we could continue living after what had happened.

I helped ten people to locate their relatives. All of these people were refugees from 1959 who were searching for their relatives. I helped them to locate the bodies [remains]. Often I would ask other people about different incidents [in order to ascertain] where the victims may have been killed or buried. At Murambi, there were four places [mass graves] where the dead were buried by machines [Caterpillar tractors].

There is a problem with how many people were buried at Murambi because the bones of many were destroyed and mixed up [as a result of being moved by the Caterpillars]. The common grave [which contains the bones from the four original mass graves] in front of the memorial contains about forty-five thousand [remains]. In the classrooms [where skeletons of the dead are laid out on low tables and are covered with lime], there are not less than five thousand victims.

Also, there is a Hutu woman who lived near where victims had been buried [an area outside the school compound in Murambi, thus constituting a fifth mass grave site], and she knew where victims were buried. When I approached her, she said, "If I say anything, my husband, my neighbors would kill me, and if I am seen with you I will be killed, too, so let me go and place a sign where the hole is so you will know it. I will place fresh limbs and leaves in the area and that's where you can excavate." There were over thirty-five hundred people in that hole, who had been buried by a bulldozer, then covered up so that all signs [evidence of the mass grave] are gone.

As for my wife and five children, I do not know exactly how they died. The women and children were inside the classrooms. What I do know is that they must have been killed in a very horrible way because the Interahamwe went in the classroom and slashed them with machetes, cutting off limbs and killing them with massues. What is unbearable is the memory of hearing my children [interviewer's note: he said "my children," but must have meant all of the children] and their begging for forgiveness, even though they had nothing to ask forgiveness for.

We [all of the survivors] have the common problem at Murambi, the victims had their clothes and other possessions taken by the killers. Shortly after the victims were killed, the perpetrators took the clothes and washed them in a river so they could use the clothes or sell them. Then the bodies were pushed into the big holes [mass graves], and when they were dug up the bones didn't have clothes and many of the bones were mixed up [commingled], and so we didn't know whose the bones were.

As for the bodies [skeletons] in the classroom [on display in the still unfinished classrooms situated on the compound at Murambi], when the bulldozers pushed the bodies together they pushed them into big piles and those who were below were crushed and mixed up but bodies that were up high—or higher—were not hit with the blade [of the tractors] but only [toppled along] pushing against and hitting other bodies but not being cut up. So those bodies [skeletons] on top were the ones left whole [intact], and were placed in the classrooms.

When I came back to Murambi, I, after having my family killed, asked myself, many times, "Why wasn't I killed?" I often wished I had died and not survived. And for seven years, I didn't believe in life. I often thought of committing suicide, but I didn't [try to].

At a certain moment, however, between 2002 and 2003, I began to think that I was living the way the killers wanted [being depressed and miserable,] and so I decided to make my image [create a way of life] to challenge my killers. And so, eventually, I got married and had a child to show them [the killers] that I was making a life.

Shortly after returning to Murambi I went to cultivate my plot of land, and all of the people there [Hutu] refused to speak to me and even left so they wouldn't have to be around me. They were ashamed of what they did to me and my family, and to see my image [face].

At gacaca, during the phase of collecting information and evidence, and even during gacaca hearings, whenever I provided information about what I had witnessed, the people [Hutu]—especially the relatives of the murderers—shouted, "He's lying! He's lying! He doesn't know!" because no one was supporting me [stepping up and corroborating the validity/truth of his testimony], and so even the judges considered me a liar. I had to testify about what I saw, and the other survivors did not see what I saw because there were so many of us, and we were all in different places [different parts of the compound where tens of thousands had been gathered]. So, of course, we did not see the same thing. But still, they [the alleged perpetrators and their families] all yelled at me, "You're a liar! You were hiding! How could you see me?"

What the government wants with gacaca is to make reconciliation with people, but in some places, in gacaca, there is corruption; and if a person who made genocide [perpetrated genocide or was a génocidaire] and the judge at gacaca are family members, the judge excuses their crimes. Also, in some gacaca [hearings], there are even judges who are génocidaires, and they are judging [grunts contemptuously] those accused of genocide. So you have killers looking at killers. There are many Hutus and few Tutsi in gacaca, and that is bad.

There are génocidaires who ask forgiveness, but then refuse to tell where they buried [the dead]. When they [génocidaires] ask for forgiveness, many ask it in prison but do not ask forgiveness of survivors [that is, face-to-face]. And often those who admit what they did only tell half of what they did, not all.

I have attended many gacacas, but I see many [alleged génocidaires] don't talk the truth. When you are not satisfied at gacaca with what génocidaires are saying, instead of standing up and making accusations in gacaca, you ask gacaca to take down additional information [via a separate interview with those who have specific information vis-à-vis the case], and add it to the [alleged génocidaire's] dossier.

The one man who killed some of my family members admitted his crimes and asked for forgiveness, and was released from prison. Others also confessed and got out, but none of those asked me [personally] for forgiveness. When he asked me for forgiveness, I refused 100 percent to forgive him.

The man who asked for forgiveness was at gacaca; he asked me there. He asked forgiveness just to get out of prison. If he had been asking for forgiveness he would have told the names of the others [the other génocidaires who helped to kill the interviewee's family members and others] so they could be brought to justice. He didn't do that! He was not genuine [in asking for forgiveness].

I said, "I can forgive you, but can you tell us who the others were who killed?" He said, "I didn't know them. They came from other areas and I didn't know them." You cannot believe him.

They [the génocidaires] don't tell the truth—[about] all the things they did, and all that they know. I said nothing [in response to his lie]. But I didn't forgive him. If he [the killer] had given other names, I could've forgiven him; it would have been 100 percent if he had given me the truth. This is the reason [the lack of honesty by the génocidaire] I didn't forgive; there is nothing else [behind the decision not to forgive].

The government tries to provide support to survivors within its possibilities. To continue life until now [has only been possible] because of the government. The government gave me a new house because mine had been destroyed [during the genocide period]. I received it in 2003. People [workers] were paid by the government to build it. There were many houses to build and even today people do not have homes, but I say thank you to the government. We didn't pay for the land, the building [house], or the building of it.

I went for help [psychiatric assistance] in Kigali. But they [psychologists and social workers] don't come to your home. They have not come here to Nyamagabe [Western Province]. But I received training in Kigali [largely supported by World Vision, an international relief organization] to know what to do when we meet trouble in the head. Before that I had no one who helped me, but God did when I suffered and now I have no more [psychological] problems, and I help others.

I suffered [psychological] problems during the burial at Murambi [when his family members' remains were buried in a mass grave], when I saw how they take the bodies [the uncovering of the original mass graves during which the bodies were pushed helter skelter into another mass grave by a bulldozer], where heads were missing, legs and arms were alone [detached from bodies], and seeing all the bodies [skeletons] I felt hopeless. I [began] thinking, "Why didn't I die instead of being here looking at [such] horrible things?" I could not sleep all the night, and I was feeling like I was in the genocide period. When I did fall asleep, in my dream [nightmare] I saw people coming to kill me.

When I saw all those bodies [the skeletons], I felt great anger and sadness. I wished, wanted to find and kill all those génocidaires who killed all those people [including his wife and five children]. But there were very few survivors, Tutsi, left, so I couldn't do it. If there had been more [Tutsi] that also desired to kill the génocidaires, I would have done it!

But now, it's over. It finished [his feelings of deep hatred, anger, and a desire for revenge] in 2000, because I met people with the same problems [those who had also suffered genocide], and we talked about how all of these bad things in life can continue but we should not allow them to do so, and that we, survivors, could not [should not] be like the génocidaires and go kill them. This group was not a counseling group, but survivors who were trying to help other survivors. When there is commemoration time [April through early July of each year], such groups come together. It is in April when we bury bodies [remains]. I don't know why it was finished [his desire for revenge] in 2000. I don't know.

If possible, counseling should be everywhere [be available for everyone in need of it throughout the country] because even now [2008] people have these [psychological] problems. The government has tried to help in the way it could. You see, the last government [under President Juvénal Habyarimana] taught génocidaires how to kill over thirty years, but our government [today] has had only fourteen years and it has done much good. The government has many things to do. There is much to do still, and it is going to take time, a lot of time, to accomplish everything that needs to be done.

When I was alone and had nobody [to be with, to live with], it was very difficult. The government helped me, us, survivors, with life—it has given us houses, paid for education, supported us as it can—it became like my parent.

Something that has helped me is to meet with strangers, not Rwandese, and to talk about my story. It makes me feel better.

What is also good is that I have a wife and I have a new baby [born in March 2008], two children now. They make me feel like a tree with new branches. I feel happy with them [his wife and children], but because I don't live in my village where I was born, I am not satisfied. The Interahamwe destroyed my village, and so we now live in town, [which means] I cannot provide food for my family [which he could do if he lived in his village where his plot of land is located].

Since 1994, no one has tried to hurt me, but in my village, when I cultivated my land, people, at night, pulled up my plants and stole them, and that is a sign they didn't like me. I left the land because I was working for nothing, everything was destroyed.

I live in Rwanda today because I do not have any possibility to live anywhere else. If I could leave, I would leave because I have had many bad things happen to me here. If I had the possibility [the financial means], I would live someplace else. It would be good to get away from where everything bad took place. It would be a break. Rwanda is a good country, so [while] I would live somewhere else, I would visit here.

I feel safe living in Rwanda because there is security [today], and God is with us [him and his family]. Even today, of course, even sitting here, there are people who can come and kill, so insecurity is always here, but [overall] I feel safe.

I cannot sell the land [and thus bring in some badly needed capital] because I make [had] children, and the land is for them. Land is the most important thing in Rwandan culture. Land is heritage. Banks are nothing in Rwandan culture, land is [everything]. Even if you are very rich, you have to have land [to leave] for your children.

I think the people who destroyed my plants are older people, and that those who are born now [in the post-genocide period] will be good and not prevent my children from cultivating the land.

People in my village are ashamed of what they did to me, so they go away from me [avoid him when they see him]. Way in the past there was love between neighbors [in his village], but today there is no love for me. None of my neighbors come to see me or want to be friends.

The genocide ideology is still here, you cannot get away from it. Some of it is in families whose men are in prison for genocide, and so it is in their children. The mother doesn't tell the truth to the child, why his father is in prison; she doesn't tell them he is in prison because he killed during genocide, but she says he is in prison just because he is Hutu.

Before the genocide I was happy. I had my parents, and I had a family [his wife and five children]. I had everything. We had many cows, many plants, coffee, enough food. We were considered rich.

My parents lived near my house, two of my brothers had families, and my other brothers and sisters lived with my parents. All but two died [were murdered] at Murambi; one sister and one brother were murdered elsewhere.

Today, I am not happy. I am sad. I have no cows, I have no job to meet our needs, and the food I need to get for my family is not easy to get [as he has little money]. The house they [the government] gave us has begun to fall apart [part of the wall has fallen down due to water damage as a result of heavy rains], and we have no money to repair it. [All that said], my wife and children help me from feeling sad all the time.

Because all the people were killed [at Murambi] and all their clothes had been taken and buried [in mass graves] and all the bodies broke [were mangled], I did not know which bodies [bones and skeletons] were my wife and children. But I was able to find [detect] the body of my sister. Someone told me, "Come, I will show you where the body of your sister is buried." I thanked him because he had the courage to show me where she was. He also told me who killed my sister. The man who told me was a Hutu, and now the Hutu are angry at him because they didn't want him to talk about it.

The one, Munyadekwa Aaron, who killed my sister, sent some people to me with a message: "Come, let's make some understanding [come to an agreement]," and he offered me corruption [a bribe], but I refused to accept the corruption. I said I would not take money to buy my sister's bones. I told him if he had told me before, honestly, and face-to-face, I would have forgiven him, but not now. [The interviewee began to cry and said, "Pardon me, when I talk about this I become very sad. He left for several minutes and smoked a cigarette by himself, wiping at his tears.]

I judged it [the offer of the bribe] as torture—we survivors are poor and génocidaires know this, and come and say, "Here, take this money and don't say anything." This is torture. Next week we will go to gacaca jurisdiction for this crime. It [the murder] was fourteen years ago, and he won't come and see me [to apologize properly] and he tries to bring me money so I won't take him to gacaca.

When the man [the killer] knew he was to appear before gacaca and that I would testify against him, he tried to corrupt me. For the past fourteen years this killer has been free. His son is the gacaca president, and so gacaca can let him go free or give him TIG [an alternative punishment for people who confess and seek forgiveness for their role in the 1994 genocide]. They [the killer and the president of gacaca] can make corruption [offer various individuals bribes to look the other way and let the killer off] because they are family. There are Tutsi on gacaca [People of Integrity] but they sometimes take corruption, too.

I have no hope he [the killer] will be punished. Not all killers go to prison. Some "become innocent" [are found innocent due to bribes], but they still killed. There are killers who are rich [can bribe members of the gacaca or witnesses who are to appear before gacaca]. There is a proverb in Kinyarwanda that says, "The man who has a branch of a tree cannot be killed by a dog" [laughs bitterly]. It means a rich man cannot be punished because he can make corruption. And if I try to bring in the authorities or others, I could get killed; they could use corruption to hurt my family [pay someone to beat or kill his loved ones]. So . . .

The man who told me where my sister was buried had been a friend of my family. My parents had been his godparents and he had been feeling bad that I had not found my sister, and so he told me about her. Not all Hutu are bad. He was there when she was killed and he tried to stop them from killing her. I don't know why he took all those years to say something, to tell me, but I thanked him for his courage.

When I went to find my sister, the province gave me a car and [some of] my neighbors went with me [to disinter her]. She had a bandana on her head [skull] still, with many colors, yellow, black, green. I knew it was hers, what she wore.

We later buried her at Murambi [Memorial Site]. She was buried in her own box [coffin], but was put in the same area [grave] with thirty-six others. When others are found [discovered at a latter point in time] they will also be buried in the same area, but not in the same box.

I was told about my brother [where he had been killed and disposed of] last week [May 2, 2008]. The man, a Hutu, who told me was working with my brother, who was a chief [boss] on a coffee plantation before genocide, when my brother was killed. The man knew for fourteen years [the exact location of where the interviewee's brother had been killed and disposed of], but he only came to tell me now. Perhaps the man was involved in killing my brother; he didn't say. I didn't ask because you don't ask that. This is [the time] to find my brother; it will come later [a discussion and examination of the evidence to determine whether the man was involved in the murder of his brother].

Next week I am going to get [disinter] my brother. He's at Mudasomwa. The man who told me about my brother said he was with him when he was killed. He told me the persons who killed my brother, Munyanderkwe Arraon and M'Bogroye Viauney. I know these two. They were our neighbors in the village where we were born. One has been in prison for others he killed [during the genocide].

———

[Interviewer's note: The interviewee spends almost every single day of his life now acting as a guide at the Murambi Genocide Memorial Site. In the museum at the memorial site, one entire room is filled with life-size photographs of his family members as they appeared before the genocide. When asked how he can remain at the memorial site day in and day out and how he can stand to see their faces filled with joy in such a setting, he responded as follows]: I cannot miss being with my family. I have been with those bones for many years, fourteen, and it's like a habit. Those bones are like my neighbors. The photographs of my family . . . I wish I had the photographs of all my family members—mother, father, brothers, and sisters—it would be better for me. They [the photographs] remind me of mine [his family]. It helps me to remember the good things they did for me. Also, for example, if you give me a photograph, it will help me to remember you, and I can show it to my friends and tell them about you.

KWIBUKA

DATES OF INTERVIEWS: May 10, 11, 13, and 15, 2008

LOCATION OF INTERVIEWS: The Centre for Conflict Management, National University of Rwanda, Butare

INTERVIEWER: Samuel Totten

INTERPRETER: Not needed

LANGUAGE IN WHICH INTERVIEW WAS CONDUCTED: English

BIRTH DATE OF INTERVIEWEE: July 17, 1985

AGE DURING THE GENOCIDE: Nine years old

PLACE OF BIRTH: Kibungo Prefecture, Rusumo District, Secteur Nyamugali

PLACE OF RESIDENCE DURING THE GENOCIDE: Kibungo Prefecture, Rusumo District, Secteur Nyamugali

ETHNICITY PRIOR TO THE GENOCIDE: Tutsi

NUMBER OF IMMEDIATE FAMILY MEMBERS KILLED IN THE GENOCIDE: "Ten to eleven members of my immediate family, and my other [family members, extended family], in Bunyambiriri, the mountain near Mranga, about twenty to thirty. I am not sure of the exact number because we never visited them and so I did not know them that well, but some have told me the number was twenty to thirty. As for why I said ten to eleven members of my immediate family were killed, I do not know what happened to my father as he left to join the RPF and 'disappeared.' It is possible that he was killed by the extremists on his way to join the force."

CURRENTLY RESIDES WITH: Mother, two sisters

I first experienced the ideology of genocide in 1992. It was when I first entered school. That's when they [the teachers and school administrator] asked my ethnicity. We were made to stand up, and say what our parents were [Tutsi, Hutu, or Twa].

I knew we were Tutsi, but I did not know the deep meaning of it. My parents didn't even like to talk about it.

Children I played with called me names [because he was Tutsi]. They heard information from their parents and other people. They knew it [that his family was Tutsi] even more than I knew. At our school, in my class, in year one, there were three or four who were Tutsi out of a class of twenty children.

When we played football, they [the Hutu children] would say, "We are not putting you on our team." The first [several] times they would say it was because I was Tutsi, but later they would not say it [meaning, they would not give the reason] because we, I, knew what they meant.

Other times, there were to be two captains of two teams choosing sides, and one would choose and then the other would choose, and I would never be chosen; not because I could not play but because of the ideology, the hate they felt [for Tutsi].

In Kibungo, where we lived, it was near Tanzania, near there was a national park and a river, River Kagera. Many people, Hutu, were brought to cultivate land near us so they would have good land to work. Many of these people were brought from Gikongoro and Ruhengeri. In Gikongoro, the land was not so good for cultivation and in Ruhengeri there were too many people, too many for all to have good cultivation [an opportunity to farm successfully]. They were people favored by the government. They would be given land—and even cows—so they would have manure to cultivate with.

I was intelligent and a good student, and the teacher, who was male, appreciated me. But after he was made the headmaster of our school [and the times changed], he became more concerned with political issues, and began to be hard on me because I was Tutsi.

In January or February 1994, at the beginning of the second term, I was late to class. I lived a long way from school, about four kilometers. Generally, it would take me between thirty and forty minutes [walking] to get to school. The usual punishment for being late to class was that you were made to stand in front of the class and explain why you were late. Or, you could be stopped before you entered class and you would be hit with a small stick three for four times on the legs. It was not hard, but it stung and we were little so it hurt. Or, you could be forced to get on your knees and use your knees to walk into the class to your seat. Many were late for different reasons, but even if children came in late together it didn't mean we would be punished together [that is, it didn't mean the same punishments were meted out to all of the students for, generally, Hutu were treated less severely than Tutsi]. But when I was late, I was told by the headmaster to go to his office. He told me, "You're late again! Your being late disgusts me," and he took me by the neck and hit me and knocked me down. I ran out, crying, because it was more than I was expecting. It was a very harsh punishment, and not like what most of the other students received. When I got home, I told my parents, "I am not going back," and my parents did not force me to go back because they knew what the situation was like—the genocide ideology.

I was the oldest child, and none of my other sisters and brothers were in school yet. When I refused to go back to school, our neighbor, a Tutsi, who had two girls at the school, feared what might happen to them so he told them not to return to school, and so they didn't.

From those days, I just stayed home bringing the cows to get fed [in the pasture], guarding them, and taking them home [at night]. But then, on April 6, [1994], the president's plane was shot down. We didn't hear about it that night because we didn't have a radio in our house. In the morning, when we went outside, everyone was talking about how the president had been killed. The tension was great. As the tension increased, our father told us to be careful and to remain at home. I was the only one who could leave, to take the cows to give them grasses, and then I would stay with them [the cows].

The week before the president's plane was shot, my father was harassed in the streets by local Hutu. He was accused of taking information [being a spy] to the army outside [the Rwandan Patriotic Front, which was based in Uganda and had attacked Rwanda in October 1990]. He took the threat very serious[ly], and was even angry. He told my mom that he must go. Two days later, he left home. Our mom didn't tell us where he went. After the RPF stopped the genocide, our mom told us our father had gone to join the RPF and he may be on his way home. We, the children, had no idea where he went because he used to go to the border [between Rwanda and Tanzania] to make some trade and business so he used to be gone for one week, two weeks. But then the genocide began, and I . . . by then I did not even think about my parents because I was on my own [concerned with his own problems].

I have no idea what happened to my father. We don't know if he ever made it to the RPF or was killed in battle. I even went to the Ministry of Defense [to inquire about him], but they had no information about him.

The most shocking thing is that I don't know where he died. I cannot go there to dignify him [properly bury his remains], to serve him as a son. Often I think his bones [remains] may be in the forest, that . . . [throat catching, eyes welling].

After our neighbor told us the father of the nation [President Juvénal Habyarimana] had died, some people, Interahamwe, who were young, in their twenties, and very powerful, came up to where I was with our cows and took a stick and hit our bull to separate it from the other cows. I had seen some of them before; they were always around, but I didn't know them, did not know their names. Then they tied a rope to a stick, made a loop with the rope and when the bull stepped into the loop, they pulled on the rope and pushed the bull over. As they were doing this, I stood up and shouted at them, but one came over and grabbed me, hard, and said, "We can kill you before we kill the cow." When he went back to the bull, I took the two other cows and left right away. By then, the others had taken a machete and had sliced open the bull's neck and began skinning it.

When I arrived home, my mother told me to take our cows to our neighbor, a Tutsi, because he was a man and he could protect our cows. After I took our cows to the man, I met those people who killed our cows; it was like they were following me because they wanted the other cows. When I met them again they asked where the cows were. I refused to say. I liked those cows so much.

So the men grabbed me and forced me to sit with a group of people who were gathered together. In the group, the people were mixed: men, women, children, boys and girls. There were about ten to twenty.

All these people [those who had been forced to gather in a bunch] were next to, beside, a roadblock where everyone's identities were being searched. Some were arrested [pulled aside] because of what they were [their identity cards identified them as Tutsi]. Those at the roadblock [manning it] were strong boys, Interahamwe. I say boys because they were not married yet. Some had taken banana beer and some had cannabis, and they were very aggressive. Some had sticks, some had clubs. They grabbed me and forced me [to join] the group.

By chance, my friend, the headmaster's son, saw me. The headmaster had a small boutique [tiny open-air stand] where he sold salt, rice, sugar, things for simple use, that his wife and even some of his children operated. He called me, but those at the roadblock would not let me go. But then the boy left to go convince his father to get them to let me go, and the headmaster came to where I was and called my name and signaled to me. They [the Interahamwe] had refused to let me to go see my friend, but they could not refuse his father's, the headmaster's, request to see me. They did obey him, and let me go. Right away, I went to hide myself. I went to hide near my friend's house. I stayed there for about six hours, and then my friend came and told me that I should go because they could no longer help because it was very dangerous there, near the roadblock. He was a really good a friend, and truly concerned about my safety.

So I left. I decided to return to my house to see if there was anybody there. I discovered that our house had been destroyed, burned. Because our house was built of bricks, the whole house could not be burned down but

the roof and doors were destroyed and so was the little house [hut] where
we cooked.

As I was thinking, "Maybe I could hide near here," some friends of our
family appeared who were also looking for a place to hide so we decided to go
and hide together.

We were thinking, "Perhaps we could go to Tanzania." This was about six
in the evening. So we set out for Tanzania, which—the border at the River
Kagera—was about three to four hours [on foot] away. On the way, we came
across many roadblocks. We could hear the killers at the roadblocks whistling
[shrill whistles to catch the attention of other killers], and shouting, "Let's kill
them!" And we could hear shouting and crying, so we knew when we were
approaching the roadblocks.

At one point, when we heard the whistles and shouting, we stopped and
found an empty house from where people had fled and we hid in it. There
were six of them [those he was traveling with], a whole family—a mother, a
father, and four children. We planned to hide in this one house until we heard
no noise and the people had left the roadblock, but that didn't happen because
when we entered the house we were very hungry—it was the second day I had
not eaten—so the man and his eldest son and I decided we would go outside
to find something to eat.

For some reason, the Interahamwe at the roadblock went to the house,
discovered the rest [of the people—the mother and three children—who had
remained in the house] and killed them. For me, I don't even know why the
man [the father of the family] asked me to go with him to locate food because
I was very young, but . . . we went and cut down some bananas and we also
got some beans out of a field.

Returning to the house, I was carrying the bananas on my head, and I was
the one who went in [the house] first, and when I saw that they had been
killed I was shaken . . . stunned, and the bananas fell from my head and I just
keep looking in shock. The father came running and yelling to get away so
we would . . . didn't . . . have to keep looking at. . . . The children had been hit
and cut on the necks and heads, and the mother had been raped. There was
blood everywhere. The woman was sliced upon; it was as if they [the killers]
had sharpened a lot of sticks and even. . . . It was *horrible*. The man [father]
even told us—me and his son—to leave so we didn't have to look, but I saw
everything with my eyes.

But it didn't end there because they [the killers] were not very far [away] and
they came again, and when they did, we—me and the son were outside—ran.
They didn't have much interest in the children [the interviewee, at the time,
was nine years old and the man's son was about eleven years old] so they

entered the house and they took the man. He was crying for his wife and his children and they took him away.

We, the boy and me, didn't run very far because we were waiting for the man [the boy's father]. So we could hear and see what was taking place. They took the man and forced him to dig a hole, and even while he was digging he was being beaten. They cut him with the machete [the interviewee began crying and couldn't go on for several minutes], and that's how he was killed. They cut off his head with the machete.

The son and I were the only ones left, and we continued on together. He knew how to swim, but I did not [could not] swim, and when we arrived at the river he wanted to just throw himself [jump] into the river but he feared I couldn't make it, so he stayed. We sat there the whole day [trying to figure out what to do]. As other people [Tutsi in flight] arrived, they told us that the RPF had taken the region.

Many people died at the border areas. They either jumped into the river and couldn't swim and died or waited by the riverbank, as we did, but were discovered by the killers and killed. [The interviewee broke down crying again and wept for five to ten minutes, still speaking but wiping away tears that continued to flow.] Many people fleeing [from inland Rwanda toward Tanzania] found the border, but among those fleeing were many who were murdered at the roadblocks.

We left our hiding place, and, as we ran, I was shot in the leg [the left calf] by an arrow from a bow and arrow. [He lifts his pant leg and shows the wound, the size of a silver dollar, which is a mass of twisted flesh.] There was a big hole and later a RPF doctor sewed it up. For a long time I had much pain in the leg and my leg was numb. Even now, even after taking so much medicine, it gets numb and I cannot run fast. I used to enjoy sports, but I can't, even now, play sports.

When I was hit, I fell down crying, but I could see them [the killers] running after me. The other boy threw himself into the water and I never saw him again. I don't know what happened to him. It is possible he was met on the other side by killers who had fled from [the] RPF into Tanzania . . . or maybe, he fled into the forest, into the national park and lived there, or he may have been killed by a wild animal.

I pulled the arrow from my leg and then I threw myself in the water. I decided I would rather die by water [drown] because I didn't want to be sliced with a machete. I had seen that happen to so many people, and. . . . So I threw myself in the water and I sinked [sunk] and drinked [swallowed] so much water, but somehow I came up. I was carried far down the river and went under again and again and came up near the riverbank, on the Rwandan side. There were many crocodiles in the water, but I still made it to the bank. I don't know how.

When I reached the bank I just sat there; it was muddy. It was as if I was unconscious [in shock]. It was like I was dead; that's what I thought. I just stayed there; I couldn't even [didn't have the strength emotionally to] be afraid. I didn't even think about being killed by those [killers] fleeing or coming out of the woods. When you are in a bad situation you often, a person has a lot of fear, but other times when you have suffered so much you do not have fear. Sometimes it is even an advantage to die, to be killed, because you feel you are already dead. And [besides,] I had no hope I would live.

The RPF came from [inside] Rwanda and that is how I was saved. My leg was so swollen I could not move. It would not move, and they took and gave me medication. They put bandages on my leg. The RPF had a group who could continue battles, and others who could help the injured, and I was transported by those who helped the injured. I was taken to a RPF camp. They made a bed [stretcher] out of two long tree branches and grass, and they carried me to their camp. The camp was about two kilometers from the river, a place called Kagasa.

After two days I met my family in the camp, my mother and my two sisters. Before I only had one sister, but my mother had been pregnant and had had my little sister. She [the new baby sister], we called her Akayezu [a little one for Jesus].

When my mother saw me she was so happy because she thought I had been killed when I took the cows because that was the last time she had seen me. So, yes, she was very, very happy. And even though she had suffered, she was the one who started caring . . . taking care of my leg.

We stayed in that camp for two and a half to three months. There were very few military [soldiers] in the camps, some doctors, not even real doctors, just those with a little training, and not many Tutsis [civilians], maybe between 250 and 400.

Then we went back to our village. We had to walk back. I carried our few things—our mats for sleeping—on my head, and my mother carried my baby sister and even my little sister carried her mat.

When we were coming back to where we used to live, we came across many corpses of people who had been killed, mostly at roadblocks. Many who had been killed were piled up beside the roadblocks, off to the side. The region had a very terrible smell because the corpses were beginning to deteriorate [decompose] and the smell was very bad.

When the killers were fleeing they had no hope of returning, so as they left or passed a house they would pull off roofs, doors, and take everything inside the houses. So, all of the houses were just frames, bare.

You could not find any domestic animals—large animals such as cows, or goats. But dogs were there in big numbers because they ate people's flesh. Many were fat. If a person was asleep they often tried to eat them. The dogs would also roar at you as you passed by, and you were not safe to be near them. No one wanted to be near those dogs because they were disgusted that the dogs had been eating the corpses. When we returned home, we didn't find the flesh of the bodies [of the victims], but only the bones.

On our way we often could not find any water, because we would find corpses in the wells and there was no rain because July is the sunny time [summer] here and there is no rain so it was very, very difficult. [During the genocide] many people hid by or near wells so that at least they would have water, but killers caught many Tutsi near wells and killed them and then threw their corpses in the wells. The bodies were thrown in to poison the water so others [Tutsi] couldn't drink the water or if they did they would get ill or die.

People, corpses were even thrown into latrines, dead and alive. I [have] one friend, who now is studying in China, whose uncle was killed. His neck was sliced [slit open] with a machete, [along with] many other family members, and they were thrown in the latrine, but they [the killers] let the children live and so they were forced to remain where their uncle was in the latrine.

Many, many bodies were thrown in latrines and when we were returning— on the way back to our village—we could smell where corpses had been thrown in latrines because the smell was very different from the way latrines usually smell. The RPF even put out orders that no one was to use latrines where bodies were and that people should dig new latrines. That way, later, the remains could be retrieved from the latrines.

When we reached home we found everything destroyed. While we were still in the camp, the UNHCR gave us sheeting to build shelters [lean-tos] and we brought that sheeting to our land and lived under those [lean-tos] until 1996. Once we returned, I began working right away, cultivating. Even my little sister worked, staying at home [versus attending school], preparing porridge for the family. Shortly, though, we returned to school.

Then in 1996, another NGO [nongovernmental organization], LWF [Lutheran World Federation], built a house for us made out of bricks with a roof of iron sheets [most likely corrugated tin]. Every house had a toilet about three meters from the house, and we also used a general well [to obtain water for drinking, cooking, and washing]. There was no electricity.

In October and November the new government called all the children to return to school. Returning to school was very painful for me [shaking his head at the thought of it] with all the problems I had—my leg [the pain and numbness] and all the responsibilities I had at home. My mother had to assume the responsibilities of my father, and so I had to do all the cultivating [growing and harvesting crops], fetching water, fetching wood, all the work because the others [other children] were very young. And so I was often late to school, but my teachers knew my position.

I was late every day. From an early age I took on many responsibilities that even many other children couldn't do [because of the difficulty of the tasks]. I had to work hard because my sisters were now my burden. I had to help them.

When I studied, I often wondered if the hard work was worth it because I had so many responsibilities. I didn't know if I could succeed or go to university, but I decided I would try to do my best, do everything I could to succeed and then if I failed it wasn't because I didn't try but because I just ...

In 2004, the year I was supposed to take the national examination [for entrance to a university], my mum was very, very sick, and she spent two months in the hospital. [Interviewer's note: His mother was raped during the genocide by a family friend, a Hutu, who was hiding her from the killers. As a result of being raped, she contracted HIV/AIDS.] In addition to caring for her and doing work at home, I had the obligation to study hard to pass my exams. So I would spend a week helping my mum and another week working all day and half the night to see if I could achieve good marks [rankings]. It [all of the responsibility, obligations, and hard work] has helped me now as I have a spirit [to work hard and to prevail].

I did very well on my [national] exams, and I was given a national scholarship to attend the National University of Rwanda [NUR], the main university in the country. When I told my mother she was very, very happy.

When I first arrived at NUR in 2006 I had to study English, and so although I am in my second year I am but a freshman. I study law, and chose it because I believe, unlike other jobs in Rwanda where you need to know someone to get a good job, in law you are evaluated based on your merit.

Even as a student I am still responsible for my family. My sisters see me as their father—even though my closest sister [in age] is just two years younger—and count on me to care for them, to provide for them.

After the genocide, the first years after the genocide, I was terrified to go to school fearing that those who wanted me killed would harm me. But at school no one bothered me.

Where my mother lives [which is in a different village from where they lived prior to and during the genocide], many have helped her, have been very kind to her and even children have helped fetch water for her.

As for me, what I've tried to do, from very early on, as a young child, was close my eyes and force myself to focus on the future [and not dwell on the past]. At school, I do not worry whether a person has a family member in prison or that they [he or she] might want to harm me. I do not think most go around with the genocide ideology and still want to kill.

As for Hutu students at NUR, I think many carry shame in their hearts for what their fathers did. They have the shame with them every day. For example, I was visiting some friends in their room and we were all just joking around. Then, seriously, one of my friends said, "What my father did was shameful. He did unbelievable things and if you cannot forgive me I understand. But I am shamed, and now my father is in prison and I just try to help my mother and younger brothers and sisters."

As he spoke, I began thinking, "What is the difference between us? Yes, his father harmed Tutsi, wanted to kill us and did, but he, my friend, he is in school and, like me, he has many obligations. Just like I go to the village to help my mum when she's sick, he may go to his village to help his brothers or sisters when they are sick. So what is the difference between us?"

I don't go around hating everyone, I can't do that. I judge people individually. I don't judge them on the actions of their fathers. Also, I believe if a person [the children of killers] has the opportunity to do a good thing for someone and has to choose between [doing so] for [one of] two people, I believe he [the children of killers] will do it for me to show me how much he has learned from the mistakes of his relatives.

I have no worry that someone will come back and harm me today. I have my two hands, and I can stop him. He can try to cut my neck, but I believe I can stop him. *But*, I cannot say I have total security. For example, if I go one day to testify [in gacaca] there might be those who will wish to harm me. But if I say I don't have security, don't feel safe, I will be disregarding the effort of the government to provide security.

When I first arrived at NUR I was given a place to stay, a place with another survivor and I was fine. I knew if I went out at night I could come across those [former extremist Hutu] who might want to harm me, so I didn't go out at night. Also, there is silence that speaks. You can see someone who is silent, but has bad ideas [feelings] for you. And you can see that. And if someone laughs but keeps [his] teeth closed [clenched], you know he's angry and there is a problem [over your background]. Or, there are those that just laugh at nothing [and are uncomfortable being in one's presence].

If I return to our village where our house was destroyed, it can [could be] very bad for me. If I returned to cultivate our land it could be dangerous because there are people who still live there, next to our house, who have family members in prison for killing [during the genocide].

So security is still an issue. For example, Karim John, who wrote and sang songs about the genocide and who had been a [RPF] soldier and had been protected by the government, was found murdered along the Nyabarongo River. He had been beaten [about] his head. It was so terrible I can't say the words. And when I think he can be murdered, a former soldier who is being protected by the government, and then think about myself, I worry greatly about security.

I tell my mother when she wants to return to our land to cultivate she must take workers from her new village in order to protect her. I tell her not to go alone, and I tell her she must return before the sun sets otherwise she will not be secure. I think if she goes there by herself to negotiate with those who still live there, I might even hear that she has been killed.

I am not saying the government does not try to protect survivors, it does. It does a lot, but it cannot protect everybody everywhere.

Not only security is an issue, but ongoing trauma from the genocide. My youngest sister used to suffer from trauma, but is better today. Generally, in Rwanda those who suffer trauma receive counseling by talking about their problems and are told how to cope. They do not receive medication unless the trauma is bad [at that moment], and then they receive an injection that puts them to sleep.

In 2003, the first time she suffered trauma, she was at school. There was a conference and a person was brought to testify [about the genocide], and after she returned to the dormitory she began crying and screaming some words—that she was going to be killed. They moved her into another room to try to calm her, but it did no good. She had to spend a month at the hospital. Actually, three weeks at the hospital and one week at home.

Then, when my sister was in her first years of secondary [school], mostly senior two, she [again] suffered trauma [pronounced attacks of trauma]. She would start to recall the past, to relive what she had gone through. My sister called out my father's name, and screamed they [extremist Hutu] were going to kill her. It's like the present has changed into the past and what she sees [in her mind] becomes real, like she is living it all over again.

It happens to many. For example, in 2004, the tenth year of the commemoration, there was a big meeting at the stadium [in Kigali] and many suffered trauma. Poems [about the genocide were read], songs [were sung about the genocide], and scholars visited and spoke [about the genocide], and many survivors were crying and screaming. You could even hear people who suffered trauma at that time crying out, "They are coming!" and "They are trying to kill me!" and "They have machetes!"

Also, there are cases where some see others suffering and when they try to comfort them they then begin to suffer trauma themselves.

Sometimes I suffer trauma, but I tell myself I have no right to suffer such troubles. I tell myself I must remain without trauma so I am able to help others who suffer, especially my mum and sisters.

I cannot listen to the poems and songs on the radio [about genocide or the genocidal period] because it makes me so sad. I must. . . . Perhaps I may suffer it [trauma] later . . . years from now. I have read about Holocaust survivors who did not suffer trauma until many years after the Holocaust, and possibly that is what will happen to me. I may need to pray that it doesn't happen to me. I just try to read about trauma and how to help myself [cope] with it so I can just cure myself.

I, myself, personally went to Kaduha, where my father's family used to live for a ceremony and proper burial in 1998. My grandfather and grand-mother, my two uncles, and their families were all buried there at that time. We were even told how they were killed. People who survived gave the testimony. An aunt who survived gave testimony and told how all [the interviewee's grandfather, grandmother, uncles, and their families] were killed together.

At the ceremony, one grave was dug and all the bones of the family were put in that grave. It is very difficult to know which bones are which persons so all those bones were put together.

We buried them quietly and with dignity, but since we did not have the means to arrange for a nice memorial site, later the remains were dug up by the state [the government of Rwanda] and reburied at an official, formal memorial site, the Kaduha Memorial Center, with the remains of many, many other persons. This is what's done in Rwanda with the remains of the genocide victims. At the memorial centers, a nice site is created but all of the remains of hundreds, even thousands, are buried together. Some sites have more than one hundred thousand [remains interred]. The site in Kigali, Gisozi Memorial Center, has two hundred thousand remains buried there. In Kibeho, there are about twenty thousand, and in Murambi I think there are about fifty thousand.

Every year there is a ceremony there, at the Kaduha Memorial Center, on 21 May, and I go there. The date is the date on which the people in that area were murdered. At Kaduha Memorial Center there are [the remains of] between ten and twenty thousand. I am not sure of the exact number.

When there is a commemoration everyone in the area must be there—even the families of killers who are in prison—because it is a national policy. There are the victims there who may now live in Kigali, Butare, or other places, and then there are guests, such as military and government officials, police, NGOs, journalists, and others who may be interested in the ceremony. So many people are there; thousands of people.

Generally, we go to the memorial site at night [the night before], and we listen to testimony. There is also time for remembering, when people, survivors, get up and remember their relatives [who were murdered], and during this time they speak directly to their relatives, to remember them, to dignify them [speak about their merits], to talk about them and how they helped you [in life]. The [formal] ceremony is the next morning.

Me, I have not given testimony yet. It is not time yet. I will, but I wish to give my testimony when I will be charging someone. Once the killers are arrested and in prison then I believe I will give testimony. I will do it because it is an obligation, and it [may help] to calm my soul.

I think that the government has tried to help survivors. For example, the government is trying to build houses for widows. The government has developed a fund, FARG [Victims of Genocide Fund] to help survivors to go to university.

So, the government tries [to help survivors], but it needs help. For example, here at the university [National University of Rwanda], where students have volunteered to build houses for survivors, the houses are not constructed very well. There are instances where entrepreneurs have helped with such projects by providing supplies, but there are times when they failed to provide enough cement to make sure the houses are strong. So, that's not the government's fault.

I can also say that the government does not provide enough money to build strong houses that last for a long time. The houses for the survivors are built of soil bricks [bricks made from soil and straw] and not hard [kiln-fired, professionally manufactured] bricks. So, when the rain comes, it immediately begins to destroy the soil bricks.

Every student who has a national scholarship gets twenty-five thousand Rwandan francs [roughly US$50] for lodging and food. I always take half of that and send it to my mother and sister so they have enough [to cover the cost of food and other basic needs].

My friends who I live with know my situation and don't make me pay for lodging, which is the amount I send home. As for food, I have less, but do what I must.

Recently, the government changed the regulations for scholarships, saying that so many students are in need of help that from 2008 we now have to pay back the scholarship once we graduate. So now it's more of a loan than a scholarship. So, now I am thinking, "How do I pay that amount of money since I have a younger sister who is in senior twelve [and ready to go to university,] and I must pay for her university and there is also my youngest sister in senior one who will also go to university?"

The government has also helped to establish commemoration [ceremonies] for the lost ones. It is also helping those who have contracted HIV/AIDS by providing them with free medication. They also provide protection for survivors, showing no one can hurt survivors and get away with it. The government is also helping survivors go to [the] hospital if they need to, by providing them with a health card [health insurance coverage].

Before 2004, though, my mother did not get the chance to get the antiretroviral medication [for HIV/AIDS, which she contracted as a result of having been raped during the genocide], and thus she became very sick. At any time I was prepared to hear the worst news [i.e., that she had died of AIDS]. In cooperation with the government, the Clinton Foundation began giving free antiretroviral medication to those in need and since then my mother's health has greatly improved. But my mother still suffers from illness due to her weaknesses from AIDS.

After the genocide, once I was older, my mum told me what happened to her, where she went to hide, and the fact that the man, a family friend, raped her. Today she takes antiretroviral AIDS medication. I know she can be sick—very sick—at any time, so I always return home to check on her. Even today [some fourteen years after the genocide], I feel she can . . . might not be with me [could die at any time].

The most tragic moment of my life, actually there have been a whole series of tragic events, but one of the most tragic was when my mother told me the truth about what happened to her [how she was raped and contracted AIDS]. It was terrible to hear! Out of everyone, I want my mum to have a good life. . . . When she told me that, I was very, very sad and depressed.

Many women who went into hiding were raped. Many of those [friends and neighbors who were Hutu], who could protect them [girls and women] and give them a place to hide often turned on them and raped them. Sometimes they even demanded that women allow themselves to be raped as the price, the cost, for being hidden.

I've told my mother that whenever she is suffering to call me immediately, and that I will return home to care for her. My sisters live far way and are in secondary school and can't go to her, but since I am at the university I have flexibility so I can take my books and study there while caring for her.

I think the government is trying to help survivors who need counseling, but I do not think it can be said, at this point, that survivors are satisfied with the support they receive. Those who need counseling can go to hospitals and present their card from FARG and get counseling, but those who need transport cannot reach counselors. They live too far from counselors, and do not have enough [money] even to take simple buses. There is also the problem of [a lack of] information. Many in rural areas do not know how to get help—when, where, or how.

Also, there are not enough counselors available. There is now a department at NUR called clinical psychology and one at a university in Kibungo called Unatek, and every year these two universities do not graduate more than a hundred students and that is for a population of 9.2 million people. Also, of those hundred, many might not even serve [choose to work with] survivors, but find other jobs. Also, they are not well trained. They are trained for two or three weeks, and they do not have the knowledge to really help survivors.

As for gacaca, what our government has decided is to try is do good for the whole community, for the whole nation. All I know is that there are some places [in the country] where you find very, very, very few survivors, and in such places I think traditional gacacas should not be held there because the majority [Hutu] are sitting on the gacaca and the majority finds the person [alleged génocidaire] innocent and he is freed. There are some regions where no survivors exist, and thus no one exists to tell the truth. In places like that I think gacaca is impossible.

Another challenge in gacaca has to do with the judges, those persons of integrity. Many, if not most, have never even studied law. Also, there are some areas where judges themselves have been found to have committed crimes during genocide.

Another challenge is that there are those who are tired of telling their stories, because they have been asked to do it over and over again. And there are the women who have been raped and cannot [due to utter humiliation] go there [gacaca hearings] and say they have been raped; and if a woman cannot [does not] stand [testify] to say she was raped, then, according to gacaca, that rape didn't happen. So, that is another challenge.

When you combine all of these realities, you discover that the level of the truth is impossible [to ascertain in a lot of cases]. I'm not saying that the courts [gacaca] are useless, but they are missing some essential parts. They are likely to resolve the country's problems, but the level of justice is not as great as we [survivors] wish.

If someone [a loved one] was killed and the killer simply says, "I am sorry" and asks for forgiveness because it's a policy, what does it mean to ask for forgiveness? You are not giving the one who was killed any value. Real forgiveness requires steps. To forgive you have to prepare it. First, you must make sure that those who were killed are given the dignity they deserve. Those who have been killed must be acknowledged as having been innocent by the killers, meaning they did nothing to be killed over [for]. Second, the one who harmed you [and/or your loved one(s)] must sincerely come and ask you for forgiveness for what he did. In *gacaca*, it is easier to ask for forgiveness in general than to come and ask forgiveness face-to-face with the one you offended. Third, it is only time for survivors to forgive once the offender has shown that he has learned from his errors, his mistakes. Then you forgive. This is totally different from where you are forgiving to help a person [the killer] get out of prison. [Interviewer's note: If a génocidaire freely admits his/her crimes and asks for forgiveness in a manner that is genuine, then he/she earns the right to have his/her prison sentence cut in half.]

Another thing: gacaca could help [bring about potential healing and reconciliation] if survivors see that it is a real solution, truly effective. After a killer gets out he goes on to live his life, but he should be required to provide reparations to help change the survivors' lives; to at least give them, for example, some metal [for a roof] to keep out the cold, to do something to make the survivors' lives better.

Survivors need to be mobilized [prepared] to have confidence in gacaca, to believe it leads to true justice. Those getting out of prison must be mobilized [taught] how to conduct themselves when living with survivors. For example, there's the problem in Gikongoro where those getting out of prison have killed survivors.

In many cases, when prisoners get out of prison the first thing their families do is make [host] a party; so, even before going to see survivors, they have a party. Even before going to speak with those they harmed or to try to reconcile with the survivors, they celebrate. So, while the survivors may have been invited to the party, how can they even go? And while they [the freed prisoners] make their party, they drink beer and when they drink beer they begin to say things that might shock the survivor and then a survivor may think, "Why did I ever forgive the person?" And when the survivors don't go to the party, the former prisoners and their families may think, "Well, they don't want to reconcile," and so the two—the former prisoners and survivors—maintain their separate lives and continue as they were, unreconciled.

As for people around the world and the genocide, it happened in front of their eyes, but they were inactive. They had the possibility of stopping it, but they didn't. Most of their representatives were either in this country, Rwanda, or nearby, and understood what was taking place. For example, people in the U.S. and Europe were watching the World Cup and if they only could have taken one minute and really thought about the fact that Rwandans were being killed then maybe they could have influenced their governments to take some action.

I think they [people from around the world] could now be active in helping us with the consequences we are facing; not only for us but other countries where people are suffering. I think today even when people hear about atrocities taking place they are still inactive. When the problem is for others, other people, in other places, people often think there is no problem.

The ones who suffered—especially the children, who are now grown up—most of them do not have a bright future. Maybe if people around the world could help those young ones have a better future, it could help the future of our country. Many have had no help because they have no parents and no education and are now parents themselves and need help. I am suffering, but there are many in this country who are suffering even more than me. There are many children who have to raise themselves and their brothers and sisters, and have given up their own dreams, their opportunities to go to school. All of these people face consequences that they did not bring [upon] themselves. People around the world who don't look beyond their own lives, their own countries, have no idea what people are still suffering here as a result of the genocide.

Today, I can't say I'm not happy because the great gift in this world is to be alive. I am happy because I still have a few of my family members alive with me. [Note from interviewer: On March 10, 2010, the interviewee sent the following e-mail: "Hello Sam, I'm sad to inform you that my only remaining parent, my best friend and best advisor, my mother, has passed away. It is so sad. We poured on her health care almost everything we had, God wanted her more than we did. I think I'm a good example of people who have truly witnessed the bad taste of this world. I'm glad that you still remember me. This shows how people like you are good friends, and only God will repay you for the efforts you do to remember the Forgotten."] There are others who are all alone, but God has given me some of my family to be with. It is true, I have lost many relatives, and my life is not as it could be if I would be with them, but at least I have received this chance to survive. I could have been killed by others, been killed at the roadblock or drowned in the river.

EMMANUEL MUHINDA

DATE OF INTERVIEW: May 31, 2008

LOCATION OF INTERVIEW: Iris Hotel, Kigali

INTERVIEWER: Samuel Totten

INTERPRETER: Angelique Mukamurenzi (a third-year journalism
    student at the National University of Rwanda and a survivor
    of the 1994 Rwandan genocide)

LANGUAGE IN WHICH INTERVIEW WAS CONDUCTED:
    Kinyarwanda

BIRTH DATE OF INTERVIEWEE: 1985

AGE DURING THE GENOCIDE: Nine years old

PLACE OF BIRTH: Nyamata-Bugesera

PLACE OF RESIDENCE DURING THE GENOCIDE: Ntarama-
    Nyamata

ETHNICITY PRIOR TO THE GENOCIDE: Tutsi

NUMBER OF IMMEDIATE FAMILY MEMBERS KILLED IN THE
    GENOCIDE: Nine

CURRENTLY RESIDES WITH: No one

In our village, we had a good relationship with people, Tutsi and Hutu. But leaders from the high [national] government brought disputes to the local government, and caused problems for both Tutsi and Hutu. They [national government leaders] wanted to differentiate [between groups of] people in school. When I started primary one, in September 1992, teachers asked us: "How many Tutsi are in this class?" and "How many Hutu?" When I first started school I did not know if I was Tutsi or Hutu. So when we were first told to stand up if we were Tutsi, I stood up. And when we were asked if we were Hutu, I stood up again. The teacher told me to sit down, that I was not Hutu, but Tutsi.

At first, when we were young, we were told to stand, but later, when we were older, they [the teachers] began to teach us history about it [the relationship between the Tutsi and Hutu]. I even remember teachers saying the RPF were enemies of our country. They even took us, all the students, brought us all together, to sing songs against the RPF. We, the Tutsi students, were brought there by force, and we didn't like it. We [his family] even had family members in RPF, my uncles.

I went home and asked my parents what I was because I was curious, and they told me Tutsi. But they didn't tell me what that meant. They didn't talk to us [the young children] about this. There were eight of us [children]. I was the last. The eldest was twenty-two.

What I remember about school in 1993 is that the teachers started to teach the difference between Hutu and Tutsi. They taught us that Hutu are cultivators, tough and strong, and Tutsi are tall and raise cows and lazy and don't like working. After talking to us about the differences between Hutu and Tutsi, they told us about how the Tutsi took over the government of the country many years before and how they colonized Hutu.

What the teachers were saying made me want to know more about Rwandan history. So, I began to ask other people, such as my grandfather, about our history. He told me that the government [under the Tutsi] was not bad to Hutu. He said that many Hutu were servants for Tutsi, but many others were our neighbors. My grandfather also told me that what showed Tutsi were not selfish was that there were some Hutu who were leaders who governed in some districts [during Tutsi rule]. [Interviewer's note: What the grandfather presented was a highly sanitized and one-sided view of the relationship between the Tutsi and Hutu. In fact, throughout the colonial period the Hutu were treated as second-class citizens. Furthermore, "Since the Tutsi were the 'natural-born chiefs' they [were] given priority in education. . . . To obtain any kind of post-secondary education, the Hutu had no choice but to become theology students at the Kabgayi and Nyikibanda seminaries. After graduation they tended to experience difficulties in finding employment corresponding to their level of education and often became embittered and frustrated, something which was to play an important role in the 1959 upheaval" (Prunier 1997, 33). Finally, in fact, the vast majority of those holding administrative positions were Tutsi.]

My parents and brothers and sisters, all of us, listened to RTLM all the day, and what I remember most is how RTLM said that the enemy of the country is Tutsi. They also said they would bring back Tutsis to their origins, where they came from. This was said by [Leon] Mugesera, a minister [a notorious propagandist], on the radio, and it became a slogan of Hutu Power. [Interviewer's note: The interpreter said the interviewee meant that the commentators were suggesting that Tutsi were not from Rwanda but from Abyssinia (Ethiopia), and that they would be returned via the Nyabarongo River: "To send someone by river means you kill the people and throw them in the river" (and they will float out of the country).]

Even though I was young, such words made me think how the situation had gone wrong and what the consequences would be as a result of such comments.

Nyamata is near Kigali, and it was easy to see what was happening at the airport because at night it is easier to see a long ways. When the plane [of Rwandan President Juvénal Habyarimana] crashed we could see the flames and smoke and we heard guns shooting.

When we saw the flames, our town became silent. After that day [April 6, 1994], the genocide started in our village [on April 7]. Before the genocide began, our village, the people, gathered in groups, Tutsi in one group, Hutu in another. After we separated, we, the Tutsi, went to the Ntarama Church. We became refugees.

The church was around four kilometers from our village. We arrived there in the afternoon, around two o'clock.

We walked with masses of people from our village and other villages. Many hundreds, more than ten thousand, fled to the church. People stayed in the church, behind the church, around the church.

We considered the church . . . a place . . . to be safe, a place where people can't kill you. When we arrived, we stayed outside the church, but at night we, the young people and the old people, went inside the church to sleep. The mature people [adults who were not elderly] slept outside the church.

That afternoon we didn't have anything to do so many of us prayed. The work was to pray only. That first day we didn't have a problem, but the second day a group of Hutu came to kill us. They came in the morning of 8 April, around nine. Before they—the Hutu, the Interahamwe, many were dressed in uniforms the colors of the MRND, and they used the MRND flag to fabricate their uniforms—reached the church, some of our group began to fight them, trying to protect the rest of us. Some men used their traditional weapons [bows and arrows, lances, machetes], but the Hutus had modern weapons, such as SMGs [short machine guns], pistols, and traditional weapons such as machetes and impiri, because they were supported by the government. During that attack I could see what was happening as it was only about thirty meters from the church. Thousands of Hutus, many thousands, attacked. The attack went on for five hours and many people, Tutsi, were killed because we only had traditional weapons.

During the entire attack I was outside the church. In the church there were many, many people and there was no place for us to stay. Many people were killed who were not fighting, because when a gun is used the bullets can go very far. So even children were killed, and mothers and . . .

The fighting was like a suicide. Even though many Tutsi were killed, they kept fighting, fighting. They were very passionate. Even when only a few men were left, they kept fighting. It was like a suicide.

The people, Tutsi, who were killed, we buried them. Around one thousand people were killed. We didn't use good graves, single graves, they were more like symbols of graves. Those families who lost many people made a group grave. Some families, though, if they lost one or two, they made single graves.

Those who were wounded, we put traditional medicine on them. Even those with machete cuts, deep cuts, we used plants [as compresses]. At that time you could not go to the hospital.

It was very difficult to bury all of the people, but all of us [the Tutsi] helped the others bury the dead. In our family, there were two people who died. My grandmother and grandfather were shot by someone with a gun. We buried them both together. We put them together because there was not much room, the dead were so many. It was easier to make one big grave.

That night there was no attack. But that night, unlike the first day when we were not ready for the attack . . . , we were prepared.

On the radio, RTLM, we heard that the government was encouraging people to come and kill the Tutsi gathered at that church. They were calling people from Gisenyi and Ruhengeri, and Byumba because there were many Interahamwe who had been trained in that area by Rwandan and French troops. It took them [the Hutu extremists] about four days to reach our area.

The second attack came on 9 April, at nine in the morning. Nine o'clock was the time work always started before genocide and so every day, like work, they came at around nine. [Interviewers' note: In fact, the extremist leaders referred to the killing during the genocide as "work," and encouraged, over RTLM, all Hutu to go out and complete the "work" that had to be done.] This attack, the second attack, on the church, lasted for about two hours. The Interahamwe were very few this time because I think they [other Interahamwe] had a fear because the Tutsi had fought back, hard, and they [the Interahamwe] knew if they returned to fight they could be killed. During this attack not more than possibly ten persons [Tutsi] were killed.

The next day there was no attack; there was no attack until 11 April. It was the biggest attack; it was very, very terrible. It was the day many people were killed in the Ntarama church. During that attack, there came many, many

Interahamwe; thousands, over ten thousand. They used buses—government buses, private buses—[and] military trucks to transport Interahamwe to the church. Not only Interahamwe, but there were also military [personnel] in military uniforms, especially the Presidential Guard.

Many people feared what was [about] to happen, and they tried to enter the church. As for me, since I didn't have enough force [strength] to enter [push his way through the crowd and into] the church, I stayed outside the church, behind it.

When the attack began, they [the killers] began to shoot at the windows of the church. They were using SMGs, grenades, and pistols. [As] they attacked the church, they killed people outside the church, and as they threw grenades and shot bullets into the church, people inside the church were killed, too. The sound of weapons was very loud and everywhere.

Before the Interahamwe entered the church they began to check on the ground to make sure all of the people [sprawled out, wounded or murdered] had died. One person they found who had not been killed was a woman who was pregnant, and they grabbed her and began to terrorize her. They began to ask her for money, but she didn't have enough [to satisfy them] and they pulled her clothes off and said they wanted to see how Tutsi children looked when they are still in the mother. They took the mother and cut her [sliced her open]. She fell down and the baby [fetus] fell outside of her. That mother screamed until she died.

At some point I fell down and I stayed down. I felt as if I was dead, and they [the killers] considered me dead. At that time I didn't know . . . feel . . . didn't know if I was alive or dead.

Once they destroyed the windows, they began to enter the church. After about five minutes, I opened my eyes and could see what was going on.

The people who were in the church had been singing since the beginning of the attack and were still singing, singing for God, the Christian music sung in church. [Interviewer's note: The interviewer, Samuel Totten, asked the interviewee the name of the song that was being sung, but the latter said he could not recall the title of it. Totten asked him if he remembered how the song went—the words or the tune—and the interviewee said yes, he remembered the tune. He hummed the song. It was "Onward, Christian Soldiers."] In my mind, they thought they were going to die, and that is why they sang that song. Their voices were very loud.

As soon as the Interahamwe got in the church, they took their machetes and impiri and began beating and cutting and killing the people. As the people were being killed they never stopped singing. The singing did not stop until they cut [slashed and killed] the last one.

After killing them, there was no sound. All screaming stopped. There was silence. Even the Interahamwe who had been singing songs during the killing came out of the church silent.

At that church, I didn't think that were was anyone else alive. Only me. But around six [P.M.] a few survivors came out of the church, not more than twenty persons, but out of those persons many had been cut [sliced and hacked] by Interahamwe, and others had other injuries and were covered by blood from those who had fallen on them and been killed. That day they [the killers] did not return.

Many, many people were killed that day. When you include the people on the ground [outside the church] and inside [the church], there were about five thousand who were killed.

After the killing ended, the other survivors and I went to Cyugaro Primary School, near that church, and we spent many days there, from 11 April through 23 April. During that period the killers attacked again and again and again. There were many attacks, but what I can say is that there were four terrible attacks.

During the first attack, they [Hutu hordes] shot at us but mainly came to steal our domestic animals: our cows, goats, and hens. That attack, which started in the morning around nine o'clock until about twelve [noon]—about thirty-five people were killed. There were so few—out of three thousand [Tutsi]—because they attacked in order to steal our animals. They stole around fifty cows and three hundred goats and hens. I don't know the number. They mainly killed the people who were near the animals.

I think one strategy they had with that first attack was to take our animals and starve us because without our animals we would have nothing to cook and we would have to go far away to get food and then [we] could be killed.

The next attack came from two sides—one attack came from Rugunga and the other attack came from Kibungo. The Cyugaro Primary School is between Kibungo and Rugunga. So, they [groups from each village] attacked us at the same time. The attack from Rugunga came a few minutes before the attack from Kibungo. There was a person who was called Ngango, a rich man from Rugunga and head of Interahamwe, and he had a grenade and when he was about to throw it, some of us decided to defend against the attack with lances. As he started to throw the grenade, they threw their lances at him. The grenade he threw killed many, about ten, people, but one of the lances hit him in the chest and it killed him. When he fell, all the killers fled because their chief was down.

But after some minutes, about five minutes, the attack from Kibungo came. They started shooting at us, and we defended. During the battle, they [the killers] killed about forty persons [Tutsi], but out of about five hundred attackers only about five were killed. The attack lasted for about one hour.

The third attack was on 19 April. On that day there were two attacks. The first one came around twelve [noon]. There were Interahamwe and three soldiers. As they attacked, there were about thirty men among us who were very, very strong [tough], and they began to defend our group. They decided to first kill soldiers because the soldiers had weapons, guns [versus traditional weapons such as machetes, lances, impiri]. But during these attacks on the military, they [the thirty men] lost about twenty-five. The five who remained killed one soldier, and the other killers, when the soldier was killed, fled. That day about fifteen Interahamwe were killed, along with that one soldier.

Later that day, about two to two and a half hours later, the killers attacked again. That attack was made up of Interahamwe from Gisenyi, Ruhengeri, and Byumba, plus soldiers who arrived on three big military buses. They came with many, many people, thousands. After about ten minutes they began shooting us, using pangas to cut us; and because we didn't have the [strong] force [that they had had at the beginning of the day, since the twenty strongest Tutsi men were killed that morning], some of us began to run, and as we did many were killed. As many people were killed that day as in the church.

After that attack—there were about ten thousand of us before that attack—and after that day there were about four thousand because about six thousand were killed. That was a terrible, terrible day. That day is the day I remember the most because most of my family I lost on that day.

When the attack came into the classrooms, I fled and left my mother and grandparents in that class. They threw a grenade at my mother and that grenade cut [off] her arm and leg. My grandmother, they cut [hacked up] with a panga and killed her and [they killed] my grandfather with an impiri. I fled but not far, about one kilometer. I ran with many other people who were also fleeing. After the attack I returned to the primary school. I returned almost right away as soon as the attackers left. I fled that day because I had a pain [fear] in my heart. Never before that day have I [experienced] such a fear.

I returned to the school to see my mother, how she was. I saw her with my grandfather and grandmother, both [of whom] had been killed. I put them in a grave.

My mum was not good [was missing an arm and a leg] and could not move, and I found and put traditional medicine [a type of grass used as a compress] on her legs. When I went among the other people, I found my brother, the eldest, the first born; they had cut [hacked] him on the leg and face and the lips and had killed him. I lost many members of my family, but I couldn't find them all among the dead. Everyone—my father, brothers, sisters—were all killed there, all except my mum.

The day after, 20 April, another attack was made. It was more of an attack to see how many we were [and how strong the Tutsi remained]. When they attacked, I took my mother to the bananas [the banana grove] to hide her and placed banana limbs and branches over her. After the attack, which lasted about three hours, I took my mum back to the primary [school].

The next day there was no attack, but on 22 April came the terrible attack. During that attack my uncle asked me to bring my mommy to a [nearby] garage. That man, that rich man, Ngango, owned many garages. My uncle said if we took my mum to that garage no one would even know if anyone was there. After taking her to that garage, my uncle asked me to go because it was a very small garage and there were many other people there, including his wife and children. The garage, though, was attacked by Interahamwe. They killed all the people—about nine persons—in that garage, including my mum. When I returned I found them all dead. . . . From that period, I was alone. I existed as one person in the family.

After that attack, many people decided to leave the primary [school]. So, many of us went to hide in the papyrus. There were two sections of papyrus, one in Kayenzi and another in Cyugaro. First, we went to hide in the papyrus near Kayenzi and we stayed there for four days. Then we went to hide in the papyrus at Cyugaro, and we stayed there from 26 April to 14 May. In Kayenzi papyrus, which was short, the attackers could see us, it was between two hills, and the Interahamwe attacked us from each hillside. One group of Interahamwe entered the papyrus while other Interahamwe guarded the other areas. Those who entered the papyrus would collect [round up] people and kill them and, with the directions from the Interahamwe on the hills, continue and collect other groups and kill them. That way they killed many people, about two hundred.

After that, we decided to leave that papyrus and go to the Cyugaro papyrus, which was about two kilometers away—not far because Cyugaro papyrus was a continuation of the Kayenzi papyrus. We spent many days there. During that period there were many other attacks.

I remember one day [when the] Interahamwe came with soldiers. They knew we had one gun we took from the soldier we had killed, and also, it was not easy to enter that papyrus at Cyugaro because it was very, very strong and there were trees in there and so they were nervous about entering. So they used their guns to shoot us, the big guns, RPGs [rocket-propelled grenades], killing some of us, while others entered the strong papyrus along the river.

After shooting at [into] the papyrus, they [the Interahamwe and soldiers] entered the papyrus and killed children and old people.

From that day on, they [the Interahamwe] came each day to attack us and kill us because they knew we were weak. In that papyrus we had a radio and we listened to the radio about [how] the war between the government forces and the RPF [was going]. We got information about the location of the RPF, and [how far it had advanced into Rwanda], and from that we got a sense of hope that we would be helped.

The attacks by the Interahamwe and soldiers continued, but they weren't as strong as the first ones. Even though the attacks were not strong, there were many other problems; some of us had been cut [slashed] by Interahamwe, we didn't have enough food for all of the people, there was no place to sleep—some of us had to sleep in the water, some on the papyrus—and there were no toilets, so there were diseases.

After 11 May the attacks stopped. But we didn't have enough information why the attacks stopped. Later, we heard that Gako Barracks, near Nyamata town, those barracks [of] the government, [had] left because the RPF had attacked the barracks. When the military fled so did Interahamwe and others.

Even when the RPF came to the papyrus we didn't come out because they couldn't communicate with us [as those in hiding had to be quiet so they wouldn't be detected and shot at by the Rwandan army and/or Interahamwe], and we refused to come out when army soldiers were near. On 13 May, the RPF came and surrounded us—not to see us but to search for Interahamwe. When some people, four persons, went to find some food, one of them was caught by the RPF. That was on the 15th.

The RPF told the person who they were, and brought some RPF from our village [individuals from the village who were members of the RPF, for the purpose of proving that the soldiers were telling the truth about being RPF]. After meeting with those RPF from our village, they [the four individuals] came and told us the RPF were there. Many of us did not believe the four; we said it must be a trick. So, they tried to convince us they really were RPF and they told us that they even saw RPF from our village. But we kept arguing with them, but finally they convinced us. We all feared that it was a trick, but what convinced us that they were RPF was when those RPF from our village came into the papyrus.

They [the RPF] told us to come with them, to leave the papyrus, and to go to Nyamata Town. Before we reached Nyamata Town, we met with RPF leaders at the Pentecostal church, which is between Ntarama and Nyamata. Those RPF were led by a general named Ibingira Fred. He told us about the liberation of Rwanda, and tried to give us hope to live. He said, "No one again will be killed by Interahamwe." He asked us to go to Nyamata Town because in Nyamata Town it was easy to control the security.

We reached Nyamata Town around 6:00 in the evening. Where we slept they [the RPF] placed troops.

After that day, some NGOs [nongovernmental organizations], including Doctors Without Borders, came to the area and began to treat some people. The RPF also provided food and clothes for all the people, began to open some houses for living, and took orphans to orphanages. Basically, they were trying to help us begin life again, with enough food, security, and a place to sleep.

In May, they took many of us to an orphanage in Nyamata, and I remained there for around six months. During that period, if people—an uncle, aunt, older sister, older brother, [former] neighbor—came to stay [remain in the area], they could help an orphan and then the orphan went with them to live.

After six months I went to live with our [former] neighbors—all were children from about nineteen years to seventeen years to sixteen years—in Nyamata Town. I lived with them from January 1995 to 1999. From 1999, I began to live alone because the family I was living with left to live in Italy with an auntie.

Two months after the genocide I returned to my village, Rusekera, and when I reached there I found our houses destroyed. In the streets grass was growing. Domestic animals had become wild, including dogs and cats. For example, when I met [came across] some dogs they tried to attack me because they had been eating people, and they wanted to eat me. I also saw sorghum that was ready for gathering [harvesting], but there was no one to gather it.

When I reached our house, I remembered [it brought back a flood of memories] our family. Nothing was left. Everything had been taken, stolen or destroyed. I felt so bad. It was very, very difficult to see. . . . I remembered many things, who had been in the house, where people slept, what we did there [very quiet, sad, looking at ground, tears flowing].

I was never able to bury any of my family in proper [single] graves. After genocide the government gathered the remains and buried them in mass graves [not desiring to talk about this, the interviewee looks down at the ground, is quiet, extremely sad].

The worst aspect of my life since the genocide is that I have no one left in my family. No permanent place to live, and it is very difficult psychologically and that makes life very difficult because you don't have any stability in your life.

I have aunts and uncles and cousins, but I don't live with them. Here in Rwanda it is not easy to seek help from others [not even relatives] because even they have difficulty satisfying [meeting] their needs [such as food, clothing, and shelter], and they have children with needs.

For myself, I don't go to gacaca [on a regular basis] because I don't want to hear those who come and tell gacaca they had nothing to do with the killing of my relatives even though many saw them doing the killing. They come and stand in gacaca and do not relate the truth.

At gacaca I met the man who destroyed our house. Neighbors said that he destroyed the house, but he refused to admit it. Gacaca gave me other appointments to meet with him, but he left, went away. Before the decision was made to have him pay me [make restitution] for the house, he fled to, I think, the DRC [Democratic Republic of the Congo]. When someone goes to the DRC it is impossible to bring him back to gacaca.

Many who killed people or destroyed someone's home do not tell the truth. Some gacaca in other villages work well, but in our village it does not work [laughing bitterly] so well. Some do not accept responsibility for their actions.

If someone comes to gacaca and tells the truth about what he did and asks [for] forgiveness, I can forgive him. Even if a person doesn't tell me 100 percent what he did, I could even forgive him. No matter what he says, he cannot bring my mum, my father, my brothers and sisters back. Even if he pays me for the destroyed house, he cannot bring my mum, my father, my brother and sisters back. So, why should I not forgive? If I hold in the anger, if I hate, if I want revenge, this is what causes people trauma. They don't go on with life, they suffer over everything that happened.

I think our government has tried to support survivors, but I think that because of all the survivors' problems, the government has not been able to support them 100 percent. So our government chooses to help those who show they can perform. An example is those who get help from the government to study. Our government supports [provides funds for attendance at a university] those students who earn a certain amount of points [certain scores on the national examination], but if a person does not have those points [scores], possibly, in a survivor's case because he has no one to support him [at home or to guide him during his secondary studies], the government will not provide money to attend university.

I think the government has tried to help people who suffer trauma, but I don't think it's enough because many people still suffer trauma. The counselors are not 100 percent good because they are given two weeks' or three weeks' training and then [are] sent out to the field and it is not enough to help people. For example, I have a cousin who suffered trauma and still does. From senior four, or since 2004, she has suffered greatly. During the genocide, they [the killers] cut [slashed] her head. She doesn't have a great life; it's a bad life. She screams, has terrible headaches, most of the time. She tries to go to school, but [always] returns home; it is impossible for her to make it through an entire school year. Impossible.

We've tried to help her, but she is still suffering today. She tried to go [to school], but after two or three weeks she had to return home because of the trauma. Sometimes the government tried to help her and sent her a counselor and she got well, but then she became sick again. She suffers from trauma every day, all day.

I don't feel well 100 percent living in Rwanda. When I meet a killer, I do not feel well, and if I return to my village I do not feel well because I remember so many things [about life in the past and the killing]. I feel safe in Rwanda. I can go to school and. . . . Before genocide very few Tutsi were on our campus [the National University of Rwanda in Butare].

But I don't let people know about my past. Now, today, I like to have a closed life because in African society some might not feel good [toward you or treat you well] if you're not in their program [similar to them]. That's why I like to be closed in my life. Even though our government stopped the genocide, there are some [Hutu] who still have genocide ideology, and so it is not safe to let them know about your past. I don't like [having] much contact with them [Hutu].

EDITH MUHOZA*

DATE OF INTERVIEW: June 5, 2008

LOCATION OF INTERVIEW: Dian Fossey Lodge, Gisenyi

INTERVIEWER: Samuel Totten

INTERPRETER: Angelique Mukamurenzi

LANGUAGE IN WHICH INTERVIEW WAS CONDUCTED:
Kinyarwanda

BIRTH DATE OF INTERVIEWEE: July 2, 1973

AGE DURING THE GENOCIDE: Twenty-one years old

PLACE OF RESIDENCE DURING THE GENOCIDE: Busasamana-
Gisenyi

ETHNICITY PRIOR TO THE GENOCIDE: Tutsi

NUMBER OF IMMEDIATE FAMILY MEMBERS KILLED IN THE
GENOCIDE: Two

CURRENTLY RESIDES WITH: Older sister

*COMMENT BY INTERVIEWEE: "It's not good to put [include] my
[real] name because the people who helped save me would
not be happy to see my testimony. They would not be happy
because [while] they might have hidden me [they may have]
killed other Tutsi and might want you [the world] to forget
about them and just remember what they did for me. For
example, when survivors gave testimony about what happened
[at gacaca] it was better to give it in secret because if you gave
it in the open you could be killed for giving it."

Here, in 1990, in Gisenyi Town, there was a military group called Zoulou,
a government military group from Mutara [which was a province near
Uganda]. The Zoulou were the ones who fought the RPF there, and when
they returned to Gisenyi they were feeling very confident. They came to
Gisenyi to disturb the Tutsi. At this time, when Hutu neighbors told us,
"The Zoulu will come today," we went to hide in the bush. Others went to

hide in the Catholic church. Sometimes they just told us that [the Zoulou were coming] as a lie so we would go hide and they [the local Hutu] could loot our homes.

When the Zoulou *did come*—when it was not a lie—they would loot our houses, as did our Hutu neighbors. The Zoulou also beat Tutsi if they found them at their homes and had not gone to hide with others. [As for] those Tutsi who were sellers [sold goods in small kiosks], the Zoulou would take their stock. They would break into the stores and take the stock.

At this time, our neighbors called us [all the Tutsi] *ibyitso* [in Kinyar-wanda, *ibyitso* means "accomplice" or "traitor"], which meant that Tutsi were suspected of having communications [or were collaborating] with the RPF. Someone who was called ibyitso, that person was arrested and put in prison.

A cousin of mine, a man, was called an ibyitso by a neighbor and he was arrested. He was kept in jail for one week. Some strange white people [most likely they were international human rights activists] went to the jail, and prisoners, including my cousin, told them they were in jail for nothing, and those white people went to the national government and asked the leaders to let those prisoners out.

In 1991, many political parties began [were formed]. Two of the parties were MRND and CDR [Coalition pour la défense de la république, or the Coalition for the Defense of the Republic, which was the hard-line, Hutu nationalist political party that was virulently anti-Tutsi and, at times, worked with MRND]. Those two political parties were for Hutu. Here in Gisenyi Town they had more power than other parties. When those parties had meetings or rallies Tutsi could not pass in the street. When they had rallies they also, often, rioted and terrorized people, and Tutsi would seek refuge.

In the middle of the year, the CDR came to our house and took everybody [the interviewee and her two older sisters and a younger brother] except my father, who was ill, out of the house and told us they were taking us to prison. By chance, as we walked to the prison we passed a local leader, a Hutu, and he asked where they were taking us. They told him, and he asked for our release and the CDR let us return to our home. We had done nothing! They arrested us because we were Tutsi.

The situation remained the same until 1993. Beginning in December 1993, CDR began checking people's identification cards. They asked for identification cards at roadblocks, and when they stopped you they often arrested you if you were Tutsi—disturbing us, making life inconvenient, difficult.

In December, the CDR rioted and when I reached the border [the Rwandan-Congo border, which is about fifteen minutes by automobile from Ginseyi Town], on my way to secondary school—I was attending school in the Congo because it was cheaper there—at the border they asked me for my identity card and my student card. They kept me there for three hours as they looked at my cards.

The security [situation; meaning, one's safety] in January, February, and late March 1994 was very difficult; it was very dangerous for Tutsis. The roadblocks continued in existence. They were run by MRND and CDR, but CDR was the most dangerous.

On the 7th of April, I found out that the president's plane had crashed. I was coming from the bathroom, at the employees' house where I was living with three other employees, two men and one woman. Each of us had our own bedroom, at Busasamana Commune, about four hours on foot from Gisenyi Town. As I came out of the bathroom, one of the men said, "Do you know what has happened?" This was about six thirty in the morning, and I said, "What?" And he said, "I heard on the radio that the president was killed and we shouldn't go to work." So, we stayed at that house for three days, until the 10th April. No one was outside!

Between us, we did not have the same ethnic background—the two men were Hutu and the other lady was Tutsi, but those men were good with us. They did not bring problems.

On 9 April, Interahamwe came to the house at three in the afternoon. There were about ten people, men and women, and some military [personnel]. Only the military—four [individuals]—came into the house, the others stayed outside. When we heard they were coming, we, the other woman and I, hid under the bed. The two men warned us they [the soldiers] were coming.

The military banged on the doors and yelled, "You two Tutsi come out!" The military even looked under the beds. When they saw us, we crawled out, and they took us into the living room. They moved all of the furniture out of the way and put two chairs in the center of the room, and made us sit down and told us, "Pray your last prayer."

After we prayed, they told us, "We're going to kill you!"

We apologized, and we told them we didn't know about what had happened [meaning the shooting down of the president's plane]. They said they could not forgive us, and that they had already killed many people at the Catholic church in Busasamana and Mudende University near Busasamana. People outside the house were screaming, "Bring them outside and we will kill them!"

Three of the soldiers were willing to pardon us, but the fourth had a Tutsi girlfriend at the university who had been killed. He had found her half alive and killed her to avoid having her suffer [anymore than she already had], and that was why he was very angry and was not about to let us go. The three soldiers were ready to allow us to go because the two men [who resided in the employees' house] were begging them to let us go, but the fourth soldier was angry. The signal that showed us he could not let us go was that he shot [rounds off] from his rifle into the wall. When he shot the wall it scared me so much that I ran and grabbed another soldier, who shoved me away from him. So hard he ripped my blouse. They then pushed me back on the chair on which I had been sitting. Two of the soldiers went outside with the two men who lived in the house with us, and when they [all four men] came back in the house, the soldier who shot the wall said, "If you don't kill them, I will!"

The two men and two soldiers [all of whom had gone outside and returned] came over to us, and one said, "People who are being killed are not being buried, but what can help you is that we will bury you." One of the soldiers cocked his rifle [placed a round in the chamber] and we were ready to be killed, but one soldier said, looking up [as if at God], "I put my knife in sheath." In Kinyarwanda that means "It is the end of fighting, killing people." Then he said, "My mission was to kill you, but I am not going to kill you. It's your luck."

We were very happy, and we went to hug him but he shoved us away and said, "Even if I don't kill you, you will be killed by others." Immediately after he said that, I began to think, "What will happen tomorrow?" This all went on between three in the afternoon and seven in the evening.

We asked the two men [who lived in the same house with the women], "What do you think? That we leave, and return to our house in Gisenyi?" They told us, "Let us go out and see what the situation is, and then we will tell you what you can do."

When they came back, they told us it was not possible to pass the night in the house because it was too dangerous for them. They said, "What we can do for you is hide you at the hospital." The hospital was near the house so we went to the hospital because the doctors there were friends of those two men. We stayed at the hospital for two days. During those two days the two men tried to find a way to help us reach the Congo.

The first attempt they tried to take us to the Congo did not succeed. It did not succeed because the soldier who had agreed to protect us and take us to the Congo really intended to shoot us when we approached the border, but other soldiers, who knew this soldier and were friends of the two men in our house, found out [about the one soldier's plan] and told the men and the men told us.

But then a problem erupted when one of the two men at the house decided to move out. Then, the man who stayed started to feel hopeless because he feared that others [Hutu] might begin to think that he was helping us, hiding us [at the hospital]. The man who stayed said there was nothing else he could do to help us and that the situation was hopeless. He then said, "If people find out that I am protecting you, it will bring me problems."

We told him: "You've helped us for a long time, and if you can do anything for us now it is that you kill us yourself. Instead of disturbing you [causing him problems], you can kill us."

The man said, "If I kill you, everything we've done will be worth nothing. Maybe the reason you are still alive is because of the Lord. . . . Maybe God has a mission for you." Then he went back to find his friend to see if they could find a way to bring us to the Congo. He went and reached the roadblock where the soldiers were, and told them that we were hopeless and had asked him to kill us. The soldiers returned with the man to the hospital, and when we saw them we told them, "As we are the last to be killed maybe it will bring you problems." One of the soldiers said, "We've already got a problem!"

Other soldiers began asking the soldier we were talking with, "Why haven't those girls been killed?" Those soldiers said that if the soldier we were talking with didn't kill us then their advice for the troops looking for us would be to shoot us themselves in order to save us from being killed [by the Interahamwe] with impiri and machetes.

Shortly after that was said, a group of Interahamwe approached the soldiers and greeted everyone. One asked me and my friend our names. We told him, Edith and Jeanne. Then he asked for our identity cards. Because the soldiers told us not to give our identity cards to anyone else again, we gave him our student cards. He [the Interahamwe], though, refused to take it. He insisted on seeing our identity cards.

He then asked us what we were doing at the hospital, and we answered that we were there to see people we knew who were sick. He asked us how long we had been there, at the hospital visiting, and we told him that we had been there for two hours. We were lying to save ourselves. He told us that we were lying because he had come to the hospital with information [about how long the two women had been at the hospital]. He said, "If you've visited for two hours then that is enough!" and he told us to leave. We refused to go out, telling him our visit was not over. He said, "So you refuse to leave?" and he went outside.

The Interahamwe outside began yelling, "If you refuse to leave we will enter the hospital by force."

The two soldiers, the friends of our friend, went outside and told the Interahamwe to get away if they didn't want to be shot. The soldiers also told the Interahamwe, "If those girls are still alive it's because we know when we will kill them."

The Interahamwe present [in the room in the hospital] refused to leave, and one told us, "If you are not killed today I know tomorrow you will not be saved."

We, my friend and I, told the military [the soldiers], "The Interahamwe said we will not be safe tomorrow, so if you cannot bring us to the Congo, try to do something else for us." All of this had begun at six in the evening and went to about eight in the evening.

That night the soldiers took us back to the employees' house. We took our bags, and we went with two soldiers, the man who lived with us before, and a man who had studied with my oldest sister. The friend of my sister said he would bring us to his house before we left for the Congo because his house was near the Congo.

On the way to the man's house he kept stopping and talking to people in the street, and the soldiers wanted to know what he was talking about but he wouldn't say. When we reached the man's house, the soldiers said they wanted to go in the house to make sure it was safe, but the man refused to allow them to do so because, he said, everyone was already asleep. When he said we could enter, the soldiers said they would stand guard outside the house. The man [the owner of the house] refused to allow them to do so. It was then that the soldiers decided it was better if we returned to our house, but we told the soldiers we didn't think that was a good idea and we would rather go into the forest. The soldiers agreed and took us to the forest. There, one soldier stayed with us while the other went to his post. As we sat there we could hear guns and bombs. The soldier said he could not stay there if the fighting continued nearby because he did not want to get caught by inkotanyi and said we could go with him or remain.

Because we didn't know the forest, we said we would go with the soldier. By chance, the noise of the bombings didn't occur again [for several hours], not until midnight. So we remained in the forest and by that time the other soldier returned to be with us. From two in the morning we began—the soldiers and the man and us—walking toward the Rwandan/Congo border. The soldiers searched for a way so we would not come into contact with Interahamwe or other soldiers. From the forest to the border was four hours on foot.

When we reached the border the soldiers said they could not go into the Congo because they were not allowed to do so. They said goodbye to us and gave us two thousand Rwandan francs. They advised us to rip up our identity cards because we didn't know who we would come across. They also advised us not to tell anyone that we were refugees because they could kill us. We started walking, but the soldiers advised us not to go where there were no roads or streets. So, we started walking and we walked and walked. From six in the morning to eleven in the morning we did not meet anyone in the street. Where we were was deserted.

The first person we saw was a woman in the distance. She was near a fork in the road, and we were going to take the road the woman was not standing along but the woman called to us. We didn't go to her so the woman sent her child to us. The child came to us and said, "Please, my mother sent me to ask you to come and meet her because she wants to talk to you."

My friend urged me," Don't go there! She could kill us!"

I told my friend, "We don't know where we are going. Let's go see what the woman wants to tell us."

When we reached the woman, she told us that where we were going would take us to a roadblock of the Interahamwe. She said that the road wound back into Rwanda. The woman said the road that we, Jeanne and [I], were going to take was one where the Interahamwe had already killed a woman and her child. We said thank you to God because maybe it was God who sent us this woman.

The woman obliged her child to take our bags and to take us to the true border leading into the Congo. The child brought us to the border and the Congolese received us. They wrote our names in their book, and because we passed a long time without eating and drinking they gave us rice and sugarcane. After four hours they brought a car and took us to a refugee camp with other Tutsi—this was about 20 April. We stayed in the camp one day.

Jeanne had friends who lived in the Congo, and those friends had an uncle in the Congo whose wife was a seamstress and had sewn clothes for Jeanne. When they received us, they told us not to return to the camp. So we stayed with this family all of the month of May through 20 June.

By then [June 20th], I had found my oldest sister who married a stranger [someone not Rwandese], a French[man], and had been living in the Congo. Our neighbors [next to the seamstress's family] told me where she [her sister] lived. So around 20 June, Jeanne and I went to live with my oldest sister. We stayed there until the RPF took Rwanda in July. We returned to Gisenyi at the end of July. We, Jeanne and I, walked back.

There were many bodies in the streets as we returned to Gisenyi. There were hundreds of bodies. They were on the side of the road. To make the town, Gisenyi, safe, the Red Cross and other volunteers took the responsibility of removing the bodies from the street so cars could pass in the street without running over them.

When we reached our [her family's] house, it was destroyed, burned, but the walls were still standing. In the house was a person who had been burned [either to death or after he/she had been murdered]. I didn't know who he was.

I found one cousin alive. By genocide [before the outset of genocide] my father and mother had died. One sister and one brother were killed during genocide. My sister was killed in Kigali and my brother was also killed in Kigali. We never found out where they were killed exactly, and so we were never able to give them a decent burial. One sister was in Gikongoro Province and survived. She was at Murambi.

During commemoration days [April through July of every year], especially hearing the songs they play on the radio, I suffer trauma. It's not easy to explain how I feel, but I am usually [on a day-to-day basis throughout the year] sociable with others, but during commemoration days I am not. I feel changes in me. I feel sadness in my heart, and I don't feel like talking and just want to be alone. It helps to ease the sadness by praying.

After genocide I have [found] that I do not want to talk to Hutu neighbors [in the village where she had lived with her family prior to the genocide] or have a relationship with them. To meet them in the village is a problem for me. To see them, challenges my heart, to see a Hutu makes me angry. I cannot greet them. I pass them and do not say anything, don't look at them. They can pass by me and not say anything either.

Some Hutu neighbors disturbed my older brother. When he passed the children of one Hutu family they insulted him by making noises, saying [derogatory] things about him. Their mother, when she saw my brother, would spit on the ground and at his feet. After this, the woman was arrested because she had sent the Interahamwe to kill my brother. She was in prison for about five years for trying to have him killed. She's now free again.

I feel safe in Rwanda today, but not 100 percent. I can only talk to Tutsis. What I was [her ethnicity, Tutsi] during genocide, what happened to me [during the genocide], where I was . . . , now, I only feel comfortable, safe, talking about such information to Tutsis. I cannot tell everything to him [former Hutu] because I'd be afraid of him [what the person might be thinking or his/her reactions].

I say I feel safe in Rwanda today, but not 100 percent because, for example, when I return to my village and meet a [former] génocidaire I fear he might kill me. I cannot go back to my village during the night because I could meet people who wanted to kill me during the genocide and they might do something bad to me. No one knows what they might do. They could make [throw] rocks [stone her or her house]. And if they gave me a job in the village, I would not go there because I would not have security [safety] there.

I can go to any other village in Rwanda and feel safe, but not my village. So

I think there is at least partly reconciliation. Security [safety] where you lived during genocide is not easy.

As for gacaca, I think gacaca can help survivors because it helps them to know who killed your relatives. If you know who killed your relatives, they can be judged. Gacaca can also help survivors know where their family members were killed and dumped so they [the survivors] can get the bones and give them a decent burial.

Gacaca also can tell us who burned houses so they can pay for the houses they destroyed. [That said, while] some have the possibility [means] to pay, others don't.

Some in gacaca come and say what they did and ask for forgiveness, but others either don't tell the truth or only provide a partial view of the truth. Some do not ask for forgiveness or, if they do, not in a genuine way. Gacaca helps survivors to forgive génocidaires *if* the killers are honest and genuine in saying they are sorry when they ask for forgiveness.

In those cases where génocidaires have killed and they go to gacaca and confess and ask for forgiveness in a genuine way, I think it's fair for gacaca to reduce their sentence by half. But, if they [the génocidaires] tortured someone during genocide they shouldn't get out. That is different. It should not happen. This aspect of the law is bad [where those who tortured their victims are allowed to have their sentences cut in half if they confess and ask forgiveness, even if in a genuine fashion].

I think gacaca will help [bring about] reconciliation. I think genocide ideology has decreased, especially when pre-1994 is compared with today. People [former Hutu and Tutsi] are marrying today. People [former Hutu and Tutsi] are working side-by-side today and there is no problem. That shows that there is reconciliation. In the military, today, there are ex-FAR.

The government has helped survivors a lot. I can give an example from my own life. It has helped me to stay at the university [L'Université libre de kigali], and to finish my studies. It also helped support me when I was writing my thesis. It also helps with health; it gives us [free] health insurance. Because our home was destroyed, the government has helped to rebuild it. A good house.

Before genocide it was not possible for many Tutsi to have a place in school [to matriculate at the secondary or university levels]. Before genocide my auntie went to the hospital in Kigali and she stayed a whole month without a doctor. Just because she was Tutsi. That would not happen today to Tutsi or Hutu.

Also, to go someplace in Rwanda before genocide it was very difficult because there were many roadblocks in the street. But today, you can go anywhere, freely.

The one thing the government could do to help us [survivors] is to find jobs. I think it [government assistance with finding jobs for survivors] will come.

Even though today it is difficult to get a job, notices are published about jobs [openings], and you can get an application, apply, and take exams. Before genocide Tutsi couldn't get jobs because they didn't know [were not informed] about them. In the military, there was only one ethnicity, Hutu, but now any ethnicity can enter the military. Before, officers in the military couldn't marry Tutsi girls, but today an officer can have Hutu wives, Twa wives, Tutsi, any wife they want. Before genocide, in classes [at school] they asked our ethnicity, ethnic backgrounds, made Tutsi stand up on their side, made Hutu stand up on their side, but now there is no such problem. [Interviewer's note: In actuality, over the past decade, Rwandan authorities have uncovered numerous instances where "genocide ideology" is purportedly still prevalent in some classrooms and schools; situations where Tutsi, in general, are mocked and accused of being troublemakers and bad for Rwandan society, and where individual students, in particular, are singled out as Tutsi and ill-treated. Such incidents occasionally take place despite the fact that the Rwandan government has banned individuals from considering, and referring to, themselves as Tutsi, Hutu, or Twa; rather, all citizens have been instructed to consider themselves Rwandans and only Rwandans. Before genocide everyone had to have identity cards, Tutsi, Hutu, and Twa, but now identity cards have nothing about a person's ethnicity.]

I think, though, up until now there are not enough counselors to help survivors with trauma. If a survivor needs a counselor they often have to go very far [away]. I think the country does not have enough [trauma counselors] because it is poor and the provinces do not have enough funds to hire all the counselors needed.

During commemoration [of the genocide, an annual event between April and early July], my sister, she has changes. She doesn't travel there [their village, where the killings of their family members took place] to take part because it could cause her greater trauma. It could make her head as if she is back in the genocide. My sister has never returned to Murambi. She told me what she saw there was horrible and if she returned there it would be too difficult, it might bring back all the memories, make her be in genocide again [have flashbacks]. I go to commemoration in Gisenyi, but it is not easy. I feel great sadness in my heart. I miss my relatives . . . so much. In my heart I am very sad. I cannot have happiness in my heart.

RUBERWA

DATE OF INTERVIEW: October 6, 2008

LOCATION OF INTERVIEW: Mont Huye Hotel, Butare Town

INTERVIEWER: Rafiki Ubaldo

INTERPRETER: Not needed

LANGUAGE IN WHICH INTERVIEW WAS CONDUCTED:
Kinyarwanda

BIRTH DATE OF INTERVIEWEE: May 15, 1981

AGE DURING THE GENOCIDE: Thirteen years old

PLACE OF RESIDENCE DURING THE GENOCIDE: Kibilizi, Gisagara
Commune, Butare Prefecture

ETHNICITY PRIOR TO THE GENOCIDE: Tutsi

NUMBER OF IMMEDIATE FAMILY MEMBERS KILLED IN THE
GENOCIDE: Interviewee shook his head and refused to say.

CURRENTLY RESIDES WITH: Three sisters

On 9 April 1994, in the evening when I was coming back from the grazing fields, I found the whole family gathered in our kitchen. This was the first time in my life that I saw my father sitting in the kitchen. I [had] never seen it before. In our tradition, adult men do not sit in the kitchen. The kitchen is only for women and children. Three days earlier, the presidential airplane had crashed in Kigali.

As a child, I used to joke a lot, especially when my father was at home. So, when I saw everyone gathered around the kitchen fire, especially both my parents and my ten brothers and sisters, I said: "Look at all your heads as the flames shed light on them. Imagine one cutting them off and throwing them away and all of them reaching the valley rolling like balls. I wonder which one would be the first to get there?" I was simply joking around, of course, but my mother got angry and said I should not talk like that. My father said: "Please let him joke; maybe he is God's Messenger." I did not pay attention to what was being said, and I went on and said, "Imagine all your hands in that fire!"

While I was joking this way, my parents were already engaged in a discussion about what was happening in the country. They were saying that the complicated situation in the country was the same as what happened in 1959 when there were troubles in the country and they had ended after a while, and that this, in 1994, was going to happen the same way. After a while we left the kitchen and went to sit in the living room in the big house. Discussion went on until a wild cat passed by making strange sounds. My mother said: "This is not good, when wild cats come by homes it is a bad sign. It predicts chaos and ruin." I understood it as if she meant that our house was going to be destroyed.

By this time, there were fierce Interahamwe in our neighbourhood, and we knew they were going to target our family. Soon after the crash of the president's airplane they had started to throw stones on the roof of our [Tutsi] houses. Some cows in our herd were also attacked in the grazing field, and my father knew that since then we could not sleep inside our home because it would have been easy for them [the Interahamwe] to come and kill us all. Actually, this was already happening; other Tutsi families in our commune had been attacked and beaten in their homes.

My father told us we had to leave our home and go hide at our Hutu neighbours. So some of us went to our closest neighbour thought to be Hutu. But this family was not originally from our commune, and it seemed as if they had changed their identity cards when they came to our area. We only learnt the situation that evening as we arrived when they told us it was now known they were Tutsi, and because of that they were very afraid like any other Tutsi family in the area.

So, we went to another Hutu family who were our friends. We thought they would hide us; but when we got there, after they welcomed us in the living room, the man in the family said he was all of a sudden missing five hundred Rwandan francs that he left on the table in the living room. He accused us of stealing the money, but that was not true. My father realized we would not be safe there since the missing money story was an alibi to call Interahamwe to kill us.

My father then decided we should leave the area and seek refuge at the [family] home of our mother. Because my mother was Hutu, it was easy to be safe at her parents' house if we could walk the distance between the two areas without being caught by Interahamwe. I remember it was around three in the morning of 9 April when we left our village of Kibilizi and headed toward Tumba where mother's family lived.

When we crossed the bridge between the two different villages my father said: "Goodbye now. I am going back home. Keep going until you get there and do not worry about me. I know how I will make it."

After we arrived at our grandparents' place, we stayed there together for five days. Even though there was fear in the country and in our area in particular, killings did not intensify in the first five days we spent there. After those five days my mother, my young brother, and my youngest sister went back home to help my father because he could not take care of the cattle and other family activities alone. I stayed there with my elder sister and my two young sisters who survived with me, and are living with me today.

After a few days, killings started on a large scale, everywhere, in Tumba, and in Kibilizi, at our place of birth. Tutsis got killed, houses burnt, cattle slaughtered, and women raped. Those of my [extended] family took separate directions [meaning, took different sides], and my sisters were raped. One of my maternal cousins, who was Interahamwe, raped my elder sister.

I stayed inside the house with my two young sisters. One day after the killings intensified, my young brother, he was seven years old at the time, joined us after he separated from the rest of the members of the family back home. I asked him how he found his way, and he told me he kept walking, alone, the whole night without knowing where to go and in the morning, he, by chance, saw a big sign indicating the directions toward Tumba and Rango and he kept walking until he could recognize the way to our grandparents. He also knew we were there, and he thought that, if lucky, he would find us alive.

We stayed there, and lived with our grandparents. There was not enough food, but our maternal aunt did her best to feed us. At night, we slept in her room as it made us feel safer, but during the day we stayed inside the yard but never together as I did not want our presence to be noticed by neighbours.

I did not know where my other siblings and parents were, and one of my younger sisters kept asking me why we were living at a place other than home. She wondered where our parents were and our other brothers and sisters, and I kept telling her: "Do not worry, they will come very soon."

After a couple of days, my aunt chased us away saying we were too big a danger, that people will sooner or later know she is hiding Tutsi. So, we went to live at our uncle's home, and I begged him to let us live in the kitchen, as he did not want to let us in. We did not receive food there; instead, we kept going back and forth to our aunt's place to ask for food.

One day, during this time, I saw our cousin who was a fierce Interahamwe attacking the home of Safari, a Tutsi neighbour. Safari tried to run away, but my cousin ran after him and he beat him with a massue.

I realized our cousin would kill us, too, if he could. So, I rushed back to my uncle's home where we were hiding in the kitchen. But our uncle came in and angrily told us, "Go away, otherwise they will come to kill you and my kids might be killed as well."

I went into the house without my uncle's permission and grabbed clothes of his kids [who were] our age, and my sisters and I wore those in order to appear as my uncle's kids so that when the killers came for us they would confuse us with our cousins.

No one came to kill us that day, and we went to hide outside in sorghum fields. We lived that way for a while, hiding outside and secretly coming back to the kitchen at uncle's place in the night. We had no food; we simply chewed sorghum plants in order to squeeze out the sugar liquid that would help us fool our stomachs.

On 27 April 1994, my mother arrived at my uncle's house. She was very dirty and wore banana leaves, as those who helped her escape told her to wear dry banana leaves so that she looked like an Interahamwe. [Interviewer's note: To wear dry banana leaves was common among Interahamwe in different parts of the country. It helped them identify each other during attacks on the Tutsi, and helped them from mistakenly killing one another.] Some Interahamwe in the rural areas wore banana leaves when they went to kill. When she came, we heard her as we were not hiding far from the house, and we ran to her. When she saw us she cried, and my young brothers and sisters cried too, but I did not cry. She related how some of our relatives were killed at the Akanyaru River [near the border with Burundi], and how others [women and girls] had been raped.

She said my elder brother was thrown in Akanyaru River, with his hands tied in the back to prevent him [from] trying to swim and escape. She said she saw it herself, and she cried recounting the story.

She told me that my death was soon coming as the Interahamwe promised there would be no Tutsi males spared. My mother said she believed my father was still alive because killers had not managed to find him. And so, we believed he was still alive because mother said so.

We stayed in the area for a while. My sisters stayed with my mother since Tutsi females were not such a target for the killers as Tutsi males were. [Interviewer's note: Since Rwanda is culturally a patrilineal society, killing Tutsi males effectively meant that one was preventing Tutsi posterity.] My younger brother and I went into hiding in the fields and came back in the evening to eat what my mother had found for us during the day. Sometimes we stayed in the kitchen in order to escape the cold we faced in the open, but we stayed without our uncle's noticing because he did not like us there.

One night, while my brother and I slept in the kitchen, my father came and shouted at the window of the room where my mother slept. I concluded he had been in the surroundings for a while because he could not have known where my mother went and where she was sleeping [without having been told by someone]. I overheard my mother waking up, and heard them as they whispered. I moved closer, and overheard my father whispering that the killings were many and very terrible.

On 22 May 1994, my uncle and my cousins went to loot the belongings of Safari, the Tutsi I mentioned earlier. I was hiding, and as my uncle passed by I overheard him telling my cousins to go and find me and bring me home because he feared the Interahamwe were going to search the whole area that day and they would find me and kill me. He wanted to protect us at his home. This was very good for my younger brother because he was exhausted, and he had started to lose strength and felt very sick in the fields. Even though he was sick, I had no other option other than to keep him with me.

A little later, I gathered that my uncle had plotted with the Interahamwe from Kibilizi, where we had come from, to place us in a spot so when they came for us it would be easy to find us. So my cousins came and told me to go home, which I did as I was not yet aware of what was changing in my uncle's attitude. When I reached my uncle's house, uncle ordered me to sit down and help others peel beans they had just looted from Safari's fields.

An inner voice kept telling that I should leave. It kept coming. So I stood up and said I wanted to leave, but my uncle got angry and said: "They will kill you on your way to nowhere. And I do not want to lose time going to fetch your dead body to bring it back and bury it. I told you I will protect you here and no one will kill you in my presence." After a minute or two, the same inner voice urged me to leave again, and this time I got worried about my younger, sick brother who could not leave with me because by this time he could not even walk. So, I knew I had to leave alone. I stood up again and wanted to leave, but my uncle said: "Look, take that small casserole and peel enough beans to fill it." I later realized he wanted me to stay there until the Interahamwe had arrived.

I accepted to stay and fill the casserole with peeled beans, but after a while I saw that it was not happening quickly. It was getting late and something was telling me to leave immediately. I looked around and saw that everyone was busy peeling beans, and I took the small casserole and went close to the bigger container where they were putting all the peeled beans and quickly took some to fill my casserole. I said: "Look, your job is done. Can I leave now?" No one realized what I did, and they gave up and there [were] no more questions.

I stood up and started to walk out of the compound, but just a couple of steps away I saw my other uncle coming toward me. I realized he was kind of surprised, uneasy, uncomfortable, afraid, and puzzled.

I asked him, "What is wrong, uncle?"

He replied: "Your relatives are coming to fetch you."

As I looked behind him, I saw a group of Interahamwe coming from a bit far and I recognized one of them. He was from Kibilizi, where we come from. His nickname was Gasongo. He had a hammer, and he was dragging my elder sister, the one who I said was raped by my cousin [the Interahamwe]. As Gasongo walked up, he said, "The first RPF accomplice is found."

The group of these Interahamwe were heading toward the sorghum fields, and I got afraid. My father was hiding there. I knew it because the night [before] when he came, I overheard him telling my mother that none of his friends was willing to hide him and he did not know where to go. My mother told him she could not hide him in the house because it was very dangerous as Interahamwe came to search the house frequently thinking she was hiding Tutsis. Then she told him: "Remember, you said yourself that the plan is that there will be no Tutsi spared in Rwanda. Our Hutu friends have refused to help you. Please, be brave and go to the *gendarmerie* [police] at Tumba, and ask them to shoot you. I do not want to see when they cut you into pieces with a machete."

My father tried to go to the police many times, but failed to report himself because of fear. He kept coming back, and so I knew he was hiding in the sorghum field close to us. But we would not dare to go where he was hiding because our uncles and cousins were not supposed to know he was around. But when the Interahamwe [from the outside] came, I realized that it was known that my uncles did not like to kill us themselves. They connived with the Interahamwe from our place of birth to come and convince us to return home where they would kill us. At this time, my father, one of my elder brothers, my younger brother, and I were still alive. Of course, I only mention the male members of my family here since we were the most wanted.

So, when I recognized these Interahamwe, I quickly saw that it was our end. And so, I asked my uncle: "Could you please hide me? See, they are coming to kill us."

He said he had no place to hide me, and he urged me to leave him. He ordered me not to go to his house as he pretended it would mean danger to his kids as well.

I also thought about my father in the sorghum. I wanted to warn him. So, I took a different direction to the fields and started to look for my father. I was not the only one searching for him. When the Interahamwe could not find him in the houses of my mother's relatives, they had started to search

around in the banana plantations and in the sorghum fields. I only realized
we were many looking for my father when he heard me approaching him. He
whispered to me and told me to stay where I was as a means to tell me he saw
me. He also heard the Interahamwe approaching him, and he stood up and
ran in their direction and said: "Here I am."

I saw his back, and I realized he heard me and wanted to save me as they
were going to catch both of us if we reunited in the hiding place. I saw them
taking my father away, and I ran away in fear for my life and I never saw my
father again.

While running, I met my younger sister. I actually passed her as I was
running like a madman. I was afraid. But I heard her voice, and I rushed back
to her. She told me that when my mother saw the Interahamwe coming she told
the kids to run and hide. My sister was too young to know why to hide and she
was just there on the way, in the open, where anyone could have seen her.

I spent the night outside, and in the morning, early morning around 4:00
A.M., I headed toward the house where my mother was living. On the way, I
met my maternal aunt and she said: "Where are you going now? What are you
coming to do? Your father is dead by now, your brother, too. And Majyambere
[the interviewee's uncle] said he will tie you on the bike and take you back
home at Kibilizi and deliver you to them [the Interahamwe]."

I got afraid. I was so desperate. I did not know what to do. I climbed a big
avocado tree that was near the way and stayed there all day long hoping that
no one would discover I was there. In the night I went to see my mother. When
she saw me she cried, and said: "Son, where are you going? They [the members
of their immediate family] are all dead, and they [the Interahamwe] will come
back to get you."

Later on, people told my mother that my father managed to pay for two
bullets: one for him and another one for my elder brother. My father was shot
dead, but my elder brother did not collapse on the spot after the shooting. He
struggled with death and tried to stand up, and as he did the Interahamwe
threw him in a big hole, alive. For some strange reason I thought that is how
I was going to be killed.

I went back to hide in the fields and there I met Babina, the only son of
Safari, the Tutsi I mentioned earlier. All the rest of that family [had been]
exterminated already. Babina was my age. We both thought that one day very
soon we would be killed. . . . Babina became my best friend of all, and I do not
think I will have any other friend like him. We spent all our days squeezing
juice from sorghum plants.

Once it got dark each evening, we went to eat some food at my mother's
place. Babina would sit by the avocado tree, monitoring the area, and I would

sneak in the kitchen and fetch food, come back quickly, and then we vanished into nature again.

On those days when we were exhausted, we both went to the kitchen and while one of us would stay awake, the other would sleep and vice versa. This was good because we could rest at the same time we ensured that we were safe. If someone showed up, the one awake would wake up the other and we run would away. Also, at four in the morning we would wake up and leave the place before anyone would notice us in the surroundings. No one knew that we sometimes spent the night in that kitchen. No one except my mother.

However, someone knew we were in the area. It was my cousin, the one who kept looking for the place where I was hiding. One day he saw us in the sorghum fields, and he said: "Your days are numbered."

My mother begged him not to kill me without informing her first. She wanted to know his timing, and then she would tell me what to do. She told him: "Do not kill my son without telling me in advance. I would like to pay you so that you kill him in a nice way instead of your uncles delivering him to the Interahamwe in Kibilizi."

One night, 18 May 1994, around eight in the evening, Babina was sitting by the avocado tree monitoring the situation while I collected food for us, and I heard him crying, calling my name. I left everything, ran out and saw my cousin dragging Babina by the neck. I followed them but [at] a distance so that my cousin did not see me. [Eventually] he threw Babina in a big hole.

Babina kept calling me, but I could not do anything to save him. He called me until he died, probably of exhaustion and hunger. From that evening on, I stayed alone, and I was so desperate. I wanted to die more than I wanted to live, but I kept hiding. Even so, I was worried that the owners of different sorghum fields would come to harvest and find me there. Maybe they would not have killed me, but for sure they would have called for help, alerting everyone that they saw an inyenzi.

Sometimes I felt extremely lonely and afraid. To ease my loneliness, I would find a jerry can and go to fetch water so that I could see people. No one paid attention. To them I was just another kid going to fetch water. This I did over and over, and in the evenings I returned to my mother's place to see if there was something to eat.

One day, I do not remember the date, I went to fetch water in Rango. It was where I went in order to ease my loneliness. A young boy who saw me at my uncle's place before the killings, asked, "You, where are you from?"

I replied that I was from the village, and that my family just moved there. He said: "You are a cockroach!"

He tackled me and dragged me along, and told other kids that they needed to squeeze my nose and check if there was a bone. He said if they found there wasn't, they would assume I was a Tutsi, and then they would take me to an Interahamwe called Juvénal and he would kill me. They dragged me to the nearby forest and they squeezed my nose very hard; they also bit me, threw water on me, and cut my shirt into pieces. In the middle of all that I begged them not to take me to Juvénal, the Interahamwe. The whole time they kept asking me if I was a cockroach, and I consistently denied that I was. A woman passed by and urged the boys to leave me alone, and they released me but they kept the jerry can.

I never went back to fetch water. Instead, I started to walk from one sorghum field to another, and I mostly spent the days in the plantation of my uncle. I was thinking to myself, "If someone comes here and finds me in my uncle's property, I will say that he sent me to work for him, keeping birds away from the sorghum almost ready for harvest, and they will walk away and leave me in peace."

So that is how I spent days in the sorghum fields of my uncle. That was my self-assigned activity, living out there without doing anything. The whole time I kept reciting the rosary. When the genocide broke I had just received confirmation at the Catholic Church, and so reciting the rosary kept me busy, and praying helped me in defying death.

Still, I ended up waiting for the day the Interahamwe from Kibilizi would come to get me. After all, my friends and most of my relatives were dead by now. I thought staying alive in a world where I would live with the Interahamwe was worse than suffering a short moment while being killed. At least, I thought, I would not suffer anymore afterward. But, I did worry about the method that the killers might use to finish me off. I did not want to be killed with a machete. I was terrified by the idea. I wanted to be hit, *hard*, with a club. I imagined that its bumpy lower part once heavily applied on my head would produce such a shock that I would not resist, that death would be immediate, and that way I would not suffer [prolonged agony]. I compared a nice death to a shot at the hospital. All the times my mother took me to the health center for vaccinations when I was small she told me the shot is slightly painful but it helps to avoid potential epidemic diseases that would affect one's life for a long time. If the vaccine killed diseases, a shot that would kill a person without giving him pain would be the best.

At one point, I was so hungry I could not resist anymore, and I simply walked home to my mother in daylight, in the morning, and without hiding. When she saw me, she, in an urgent voice, told me: "Go inside and find food, eat quickly and leave this place. I am going outside to see if someone passes around, and if there is something suspicious I will let you know. But be quick." I sat down to eat *ubugali* [a local dish made of cassava flour boiled and mixed in very hot water and eaten while still warm. It is basically a cassava porridge], but all of a sudden I heard the sound of boots outside, like it was a big group of people marching toward the house. My mother came in quickly, very terrified, and said: "My son, you have been hiding for nothing! They are coming to kill you now! Let me hide you somewhere here in the house." I struggled to get out of the house as she was blocking me at the main door and pushed her [aside]. She grabbed my shirt, but I quickly took off the shirt and it remained in her hands. I broke for the yard, disappearing into the banana plantation.

This was when I noticed how this life of hiding and constant fear damaged me. I ran away from my mother around eleven o'clock in the morning, and lost my senses once in the banana plantations. I recovered my senses around six o'clock in the evening and I saw I still had in my right hand the very first portion of food I was about to eat in the morning when they came to kill me. I thought it was a gift from God. I ate what was in my hand, and I felt good.

The following day, I met Kararama, one of my cousins, on the road to the Akanyaru River, and when I saw him I thought he wanted to kill me, [so] I ran to the forest nearby. He ran after me, and I was so weak that I could not escape. When he reached me, he stopped me. I was too tired to ask for forgiveness, and cried. He did not have any bad plans for me. He instead wanted to let me know that the people I heard the previous day were the Interahamwe in exercise as they were about to receive weapons from the government. He told me that my mother was very sad that I left in great fear, and she wanted to send me the message that the Interahamwe were not coming for me. That is why she told Kararama that if he saw me he should inform me [of such]. He told me I should go back and see my mother, but I hesitated. I asked him to go and bring me food, and when he left I immediately left that place as I was not sure if he would not come back with killers. I do not know if he came back.

In June, a date [the exact day] I do not remember, but I do remember very well that by that time there was [only] a tiny number of Tutsi still alive, [and] meetings were [being] organized by local authorities to apparently pacify the region. But it was a trick to make the few remaining Tutsi come out of their hiding places. It was a way to facilitate the killings. My mother later told me she received a message that the Interahamwe from back home [their village] wanted me found, and that "they want to kill you themselves on a Friday when they come to receive the prize at the stadium in Butare Town for having killed the biggest number of Tutsis in the area. People said that this Friday killings will be called 'THE GRAND FINALE.'"

When my mother told me this it was a Wednesday around ten o'clock in the evening, and it was very quiet around her home. She told me: "My son, listen to me now. You are my child, like your elder brother, like your young brother, like your sister, killed in the church of Mugombwa with her husband and children. I just heard Kanyabashi, the bourgmestre, say that not a single Tutsi male will stay alive in this country of Rwanda. You have been hiding for so long. The Interahamwe said they are coming to kill you this Friday. If they do not find you, they said they will kill your sisters. And even after that they will keep searching for you. And even if the Interahamwe from Kibilizi do not kill you, some others will kill you. What do you think? How long are you going to hide? Please do accept to die. Where you will be going is not a bad place, your father is there, your siblings are there in big numbers. Please do not give me unnecessary headaches. I no longer have empathy; it dried out of me by now. Do you see your brother around? Where is he?"

So, I went to the other kitchen where I slept, off and on, and I kept thinking about what my mother said, and I suddenly started to think about my friend Babina. I started to think there is another better world than this one, a place where all those who are unjustly killed go. That night I accepted death, but I kept being worried about what they [would] use to kill me. The following day I stopped hiding, and I stayed there at my mother's home. I was already dead. I did not think about anything nor listen to anyone. I was somewhere else.

My mother took me by the hand and brought me inside the house and gave me food. I kept food in my hand unable to eat. My mother started to feed me. I could open my mouth, but could not chew or swallow. There was no saliva in my mouth. I could not talk and my teeth could not move. On Friday, I woke up and when my mother saw me she got afraid to see me because she thought I was dead [had been killed] during the night. She gave me a hundred Rwandan francs and said: "Look, go and buy whatever you would like to eat. I have nothing else to do, because they will kill you today. Goodbye." I took the money and went to sit outside the compound waiting for the killers. I forgot I had the money in my hands. I did not have any energy left. Around 9:00 A.M. I was still there. My sisters were locked in the house with my mother. One of my uncles arrived there very early to tell my mother that I should not disappear because it would mean that everyone else among my remaining sisters would be killed if the killers missed [could not locate] me.

I stayed there waiting, and around 10:00 A.M. a crowd of people came by, singing and shouting a lot. These were the Interahamwe. They stopped, realizing I was there waiting for them, and they said they were first going to the meeting at Huye Stadium to receive their prize for having killed many people and after that they would come and pick me up. I was not afraid

because I had lost any sense of fear. When they were heading toward the
town of Butare, the wife of my uncle told me to run away. Maybe she felt
sorry for me. I do not know. For a reason I do not understand, I ran away. I
kept running without knowing where to go. I kept running and once close
to the Akanyaru River, I met refugees from Bugesera who were running
away as the fighting between the army [FAR] and the RPF was intensifying
in the region. I followed them.

We went to Musange. It is in the former commune of Gishamvu, here in
Butare. A woman noticed me and asked me where I was coming from. I kept
silent. She saw I was very tired, and she said that it was obvious I had not eaten
in days. She gave me a boiled liquid of sorghum flour.

After a week, I saw my mother there. They [his mother and sisters] also
came to Musange fleeing the war. My uncles were there too. The nice woman
told my mother how they met me, and my mother told them that they also
came fleeing the war and that we had lost each other. I did not say anything.
My mother gave me a big bag to carry and we headed to Gikongoro.

On the way to Gikongoro we stopped close to Gasarenda, a market
town that is near Gikongoro. We came across people, including the same
killers from Kibilizi at my home. The same killers who came to kill me
the other Friday. They were there with their children. They also fled the
war between the Rwandan army and the RPF. The children, most of them
were of my age, went to tell their parents that they saw me. Their parents
did not pay a lot of attention as everyone was finding [figuring out] where
and how to pass the night. The children came back to stare at me, and they
gathered stones and threw them at me. After people organized themselves
and found where to stay, the killers from Kibilizi came to kill me. My uncle
took a *madras* [basically, a blanket] and covered me. He told them: "No
one will take him from here now. Right now we are all refugees. Those that
we have killed we have killed and that is enough now. I hope they could
be resuscitated and we can show them alive. I am afraid we are going to
heavily pay for their deaths." The killers left. In the morning my uncle told
me: "Wake up, and go all the way to Gasarenda. Once there, wait for us and
we will join you. Otherwise, when they come back to kill you, I will not be
able to resist."

On the way to Gasarenda, a car passed me transporting the very Interahamwe from Kibilizi, and they saw me again and shouted: "There he is! There
he is!" I ran back in the crowd in order to see if I could meet my mother's
family. I did, and we continued to Gasarenda together.

Now the dilemma for me was that I was heading to the same place as my
killers, and I did not know how to survive this time. I wanted to go back,

but I did not know the way back. It was also difficult because everyone who attempted to go back was killed, because the Interahamwe said all those going back into the RPF-controlled zone were joining the inyenzi.

We went to the refugee camp of Gisunzu, a hill dominating the town of Gasarenda. There, my mother sent me to collect food at UNHCR [Office of the United Nations High Commissioner for Refugees], but it was dangerous because the killers regularly came there to get food as well.

One day, I met kids who knew me. One of them was Mbarushimana. This kid went to tell other kids, and I got afraid and ran away. I did not bring food back, and my mother got angry. I did not care. I ignored her as I was ignoring everything that I did not want to hear. Sometimes I just did what they wanted me to do without saying a word. Other times I just ignored my mother and my uncles.

We lived in the camp until the day my mother and I planned to escape the camp. We left the camp, and once at Ndago in Nyaruguru we met a woman that the Interahamwe had hacked with a machete. Her neck was terribly cut. The killers wanted to punish her because she wanted to go back home to join the cockroaches [the RPF].

When the genocide ended we were at Gikongoro. This was in July 1994. At that time, we went back home, and on the way we met a woman who was bleeding at the neck. She was cut with a machete after she was caught in someone else's fields trying to loot food to cook.

Once in Matyazo, I met some young Tutsi men who returned from Burundi, probably former refugees, and they ran after me as they wanted to kill me, claiming I was a small Interahamwe.

Once home at Kibilizi, we found everything destroyed. No house, no plants in the fields. The house was totally destroyed.

I started to ask how my relatives were killed. I already knew from my mother that [my sister], her husband, and their three children were killed at the church of Mugombwa. The new information I learnt was that they were all killed with machetes. My brother Mathias was thrown in Akanyaru River after they tied his hands in the back. My other brother Abraham was shot and beaten with a massue, and thrown in a[n] [outside] latrine before dying. When they dumped him in the latrine he was still alive. Abraham was with my father when he bought bullets for both of them to be killed in a nicer way. I do not know how my sister Odette was killed. So far I have been able to give Abraham and my father a decent burial.

I was lucky, however, [to discover that] my elder brother, the firstborn in the family, survived, contrary to what we thought. It means that I found a brother and a new parent, as in such a situation he was going to take care of me and other family members that survived. He had opened a boutique [a small store to sell basic goods], and he asked me to work for him. He instructed my mother and my sisters to go back home and work in the fields. They temporarily lived in a house of some Hutus who fled. But this life did not last long because in 1995 my elder brother got married and I went back to primary school.

I finished primary school with the best grades [out of the entire class], and I was sent to Groupe scolaire officiel de butare, one of the best secondary schools in the country. Everything we had by then—like the insurance money of my father and the money in my father's bank account before the genocide—was in the hands of my elder brother. He promised that he would pay school fees for me, and that he would build a new house for my mother. But when I went to senior two at secondary school, my brother and the rest of the family separated because he was saying he would not be able to pay my school[ing] any longer and by then he had not built a house for my mother.

From that time on, I took the responsibility to take care of my family. One thing I did was to ask for a certificate attesting that I am an orphan of the genocide. This helped me during studies because FARG came later and paid for me.

In the meantime, the Hutus returned from Congo [where they had fled to at the end of the genocide out of fear of being killed by the RPF], and they wanted their houses back. It meant we started moving from one house to another, occupying those that were still empty waiting for their owners [to return].

My mother begged neighbors to build a house for her, so *umuganda* [community work] built a house for us. My mother bought the construction material and umuganda built it. In 2000, however, the house fell apart as it was not well built.

We were lucky because at that time I finished my secondary studies, and I quickly applied for a job as a primary school teacher. With the money I earned I had the house rebuilt. Through today, we still have a bad relationship with my elder brother.

Because of many problems, I started to lack the ability to sleep at night. This went on for a year, and I developed a complex, complicated sickness. I could not sleep; on the contrary, I developed bad thoughts [had nightmares] all the time. Most of the time, I saw myself with people I know are dead and I was very terrified because I knew those people died a long time ago.

Remember, those who killed us were still there [in the village], and they did not want us alive back then—and they do not wish to see us now. For example, the house the community work built for us, it was wrongly built and I believe it was done intentionally. And I know this because when it fell down they even said they knew it was going to happen.

At my job, I was mobbed, and those who know I know [that they] attempted to kill me in 1994 kept circulating bad stories that I beat Hutu children at school. They wanted me sacked. I was not. But I was given a disciplinary punishment, and transferred to another school.

I kept struggling with the issue of finding a decent home for us. In the meantime, I got the opportunity to go for further studies at NUR [National University of Rwanda]. But, at the same time, my mental condition was dramatically taking grave proportions.

I started to visit doctors, but it worried me that they could not see [figure out] what my real illness was. I had stomachaches, my intestines were in constant pain, and I started to experience painful muscle contractions all the time. I also had pain in all joints of my skeleton, and I started to experience high blood pressure. I lost weight in a scary way, and I could only sleep for two hours at night. During those two hours of deep sleep I often woke up in pain after terrible nightmares. Most of the time I dreamed of being killed. At times, I would see a cow with human legs killing me. I had a lot of dreams like that, and they always terrified me. Every morning I wondered where and how I could find a doctor to treat me. In order to get distracted, I listened to the radio all the time as it kept me company. My sisters were at school. Who else could I have talked to?

I visited all possible hospitals, and doctors used all possible machines available in Rwanda but no one could find out what my illness was. I then turned to traditional medicine. Some people exercised witchcraft on me, each in their ways and their expertise. I went to more than twenty sorcerers, and every time I paid a lot of money. The last ones I visited are called the Abarungi. They are from Uganda, and they claim to be in touch with very powerful spirits.

My sickness worsened, and in 2005 I took the decision to suspend my studies. In 2006, a former classmate, a girl with whom I studied, she was then at KIST [Kigali Institute for Science and Technology], helped me to meet with psychologists, and it was easy for them to see that my sickness was psychological and that it was a direct consequence of the genocide. From that time, I take medicine and I regularly get psychological counseling. I came back to the university in 2007, and every night before going to bed I take medicine. So, I would say I have lived and am still living through the consequences of the genocide because I am sick and I have to pay for the drugs and they are expensive and I do not have an income to pay for all those things. I am also responsible for a family of four people that I have not chosen to be responsible for [but is obligated to care for].

When you look at me, you cannot really fool me that you do not see signs of poverty on my face. My family is poor, too. And I am frustrated about this because I am not a lazy person and I am not less intelligent either. I feel like I hate myself, and I feel I am not a free individual. I think the society judges me in a negative way.

From 1996 to today, I have been in conflict with my elder brother, and I think he is partly responsible for my sickness. I hate his wife because I imagine that she has changed him. I hate everything that is or might sound Hutu. I hate Hutu and especially those from Kibilizi, where I come from. I hate everyone who looks like a Hutu. And it makes me sad because my mother is Hutu. I hate every man of my father's generation. When I meet people and I think they are the age of my father, I do not want to look at them or say hello to them. Why should I say hello? After all, they could not be my father. Because of all these behaviors, people in the society do not feel comfortable with me. I think they hate me, and it is perfectly OK with me because I want to be alone as it makes things easier for me. It helps me to control my illness.

People in my neighborhood would like to consider me very young, but it does not work that way for me. I want them to see me as a grown up, responsible for a family, like my father. But they do not, and it complicates the relationship between me and them. So, I am not welcome in my neighborhood. I have tried to change things with the help of the counselors but I have failed.

The most challenging part of my post-genocide life is to fight against humiliation and poverty. People will not see me as someone who grew up in a stable family, as it was for me before the genocide. People see my problems today, and do not see that I came from a good family before the genocide. I am alone and without any relevant social references.

Regarding justice in Rwanda, the gacaca trials are more political than anything else. They do not really help the survivors of genocide. It is very simple to understand what happens during the trials. The killer is there to defend himself and is supported by his family, but the killed are not there! It means that the killer says whatever he wants to say. The gacaca trials should at least try to find compensation for survivors.

As far as I am concerned, the government has helped me because I am at school and FARG pays for me and everything is OK at school. However, I live in extreme poverty, and I have to find a home for my family. Who will help me to solve those problems? Now I am living with a terrible illness, and it is not an accident that I have it. It is clearly a consequence of the genocide—something I did not initiate or sympathize with. It targeted me!

The Rwandan government should help me and many others with similar hardships cope with our difficult lives. Just as Japan helps the victims of the bombings of Hiroshima and Nagasaki. Now I am mentally handicapped and my future is not clear.

Going to school has improved my life, but I am still uncertain about life. I am facing a lot of problems. Additionally, those who killed our beloved ones are still around and they are still killing survivors. It means that a day, an hour that I do not know of, I may be killed. Do you think that I am particularly thrilled that those who killed are enjoying better lives than me? This is the reason I would like to live other than in this country; because I do not feel peace in me.

The Rwandan government should provide us with compensation for the genocide that was committed against us. But, I would, ironically, say that it is too late for the government anyway. The day they will decide to compensate us very few will still be still alive as we are dying slow by slow from natural death and sickness resulting from the genocide. And assassinations will soon finish us.

There is also that anxiety that some leaders in the current government are accused of genocide; take the example of the minister of defense or the speaker of the parliament. [Interviewer's note: At the time of this interview, the speaker of the Rwandan parliament was Alfred Mukezamfura from the Parti démocrate centriste. Different media outlets in Rwanda have alleged he may have taken part in the genocide, a charge he has denied. As for the minister of defense, General Marcel Gatsinzi, before joining the new Rwandan army after the genocide, he was a high-ranking military officer in FAR.] In the eyes of the survivors, it looks like the government is minimizing the genocide.

As for the foreign countries that abandoned us during the genocide, they should be more active in rebuilding Rwanda and care more about lives of genocide survivors in particular. For example, because of the genocide, my life has changed its direction; I live with a sickness that will never heal because of the genocide. I face constant problems in my daily life and these are the consequences of the genocide. I live in constant sorrow because of the genocide. That is why what happened to me should be told to other people in the world so that genocide does not happen again in other parts of the world.

During the genocide, my brother, the one still alive, and with whom I have family issues, was hacked in his head with a machete. I think he is deranged, even though he seems not to be aware of it. One of my sisters, the last born in the family, is now traumatized. She was doing well before, but in 2007 she started to traumatize [experience trauma] once people began talking about what happened in the genocide.

I can live with all this because I also hear about other people with terrible stories, and realize I am not the only one with problems. But I will not forget what happened in the genocide; not even for a single day because its consequences are enormous and they have seriously impacted our lives in a negative manner. That is why I consider it a duty to spread the message about the genocide that happened here so that it does not happen again anywhere else in the world.

In Rwanda, there is still an attitude of genocide. And I think had not it been for the fear of strict security by the current government, the génocidaires would have restarted the killings again.

Another problem that is widespread in the country are the popular questions in gacaca: "You, the witness accusing me of killing Tutsis, how did you survive? Why didn't I kill you?" Most of the time it is a sign that all that is lacking is the opportunity to finish you off.

During local elections for local leaders a considerable number of people are still looking for Hutu candidates. It does not matter if there is a Tutsi with serious [considerable] community-planning experience or ideas; they just want to rally for a Hutu, even if he will not be able to serve the community!

Before the genocide I was a very happy child. Today, I am simply unhappy, totally unhappy. My heart is sour. Laughing and joking I do not do. I do not have means to afford what I think is enjoyable and nice for me. At my age, young people go to dance at nightclubs here in Butare, but I cannot do that because I have to take drugs and go to bed, and I have to save the little money I can find for family matters. Furthermore, the drugs I am taking are strong. I am always tired, with constant headaches. Do not forget, I have to take care of my mother and my sisters, and then there is the tough work of being a student requiring me to use my head that is not healthy at all.

In a perfect world, I am supposed to respect the advices [sic] of doctors. They told me I should go to bed early, avoid noisy and crowded places, sleep in a quiet place, and avoid any other stressing [stressful] activity. This is simply impossible because at NUR I have to live with other students in the student room [dorm], I have to study until late if I want to make good grades, and I have to solve family problems. My life is useless.

Sometimes I nourish high hopes that the future will be better; but because of my sickness and tough drugs, I sometimes think that one day these drugs will be inefficient and I will sink in my sickness, as it was the case before I started treatment. Also, when it happens that I get stressed for a short moment, the consequence is that I have to take some three days to rest and recover. I frequently wonder how and where I will live without encountering stressful events and situations, keeping in mind that the older one gets, the more responsibilities in life [one has]. My life will not be easy. Imagine if I am lucky and finish my studies; how will I handle a job? And my wife and kids, if I am to ever start my own family? I think that the best for me would be to have my own family because that would absolutely make me happy. All in all, I have problems, but I think I try to be positive and work hard. Chances for a better life for me stand at 50 percent now.

The most challenging memory for me is the day when my father stood up in the sorghum fields as a means to protect me. Had he kept quiet, the killers would have discovered both of us. But my father stood up and they took him away and I clearly saw he wanted to protect me. I would like to see him again and tell him his gesture saved me. I do not tell such things to my mother and my sisters because it would discourage them. On the contrary, I have to show them that everything positive is possible, that our lives will get better. But it costs me a lot of energy because at the same time I have to deal with the deep sorrow in my heart.

ANGELIQUE ISIMBI

DATES OF INTERVIEWS: May 3 and 4, 2008

LOCATION OF INTERVIEWS: Center for Conflict Management,
National University of Rwanda, Butare

INTERVIEWER: Samuel Totten

INTERPRETER: Angelique Mukamurenzi

LANGUAGE IN WHICH INTERVIEW WAS CONDUCTED:
Kinyarwanda

BIRTH DATE OF INTERVIEWEE: December 20, 1987

AGE DURING THE GENOCIDE: Ten years old

PLACE OF BIRTH: Nyanza

PLACE OF RESIDENCE DURING THE GENOCIDE: Ntyazo in
Nyanza

ETHNICITY PRIOR TO THE GENOCIDE: Tutsi

NUMBER OF IMMEDIATE FAMILY MEMBERS KILLED IN THE
GENOCIDE: About twenty

CURRENTLY RESIDES WITH: Aunt

In 1990, when the war [following the invasion into Rwanda by the Rwandan
Patriotic Force] started, people [Hutu neighbors] began to insult our family
and other Tutsi families in our village. There were many families of Tutsis in
our village, and they were all insulted.

The Hutus also hit Tutsis, only the men. Both my father and uncles and
brothers were attacked, hit at this time. They [the Hutu] hit them with
branches [long, thin branches with leaves that served as whips] from the trees.
I saw this happen. I was six years old. Our father told us to pray to God to help
us with our difficulties.

The Hutus would meet the Tutsis outside [of the latter's homes], often at
the bar [often a single room in a roughshod wooden building with a dirt or
concrete floor] and start talking to them, calling them inyenzi, which at the

time referred to the enemy of the country, to those who lived outside the country and was [sic] considered the enemy by the Habyarimana government. And then, they would beat them. This happened from 1990 until [the] genocide. This happened about two times a month in our village.

When I saw this happening [to her father], I was afraid and cried. Our mother took us [all the children] into the house, and closed the door. There were ten of us [siblings]. I was in the middle—and my brothers and sisters were crying, too. Some of my older brothers saw this [the beating of their father] and tried to help my father, but they were also beaten, so badly.

In about August 1993, they [two communal policemen] threatened to kill my oldest brother. They said he was joining the inkotanyi. But he didn't belong to the RPF and didn't want to join; they [the policemen] were lying. They beat him with a rifle on his head and beat him on his shoulders and back; they beat him so much and said they were going to kill him. They screamed at him [as they beat him]. This happened in his house.

My brother apologized and asked for forgiveness, and so they didn't kill him. He was apologizing for nothing [just to placate his attackers], but he had no choice. After beating him, they left him. My brother had to go to a doctor.

They [the Hutu], at this time, were creating lists of people to kill. I knew this [was happening] because it [the topic of the lists] was talked about at home. Our neighbors would come over and talk to my mother and father about such lists. We [her siblings] would hear this because we were with our mommy. Sometimes I was afraid when I heard this, but more [often] I was not because I did not think such things could happen. I did not know about genocide and that genocide could happen. I did not know about the world [that such atrocities could and did take place in the world].

My parents discussed going to Burundi, but decided not to do so. They thought about Burundi because it was near [closer, for example, than Uganda, which was another logical option for Tutsi fleeing the violence in Rwanda].

In school, we, the Tutsis, were told to stand up [and indicate] to our neighbors [fellow students, who were Hutu] that we were Tutsi. My teacher, a woman, who was Hutu, wanted us to know who was Tutsi and who was Hutu. The teacher didn't like us as [much as she did] the others [who were Hutu]. She said, "These Tutsi are inyenzi! They are not good!" The Hutu children would laugh at us, and we [the Tutsi] would get angry. I didn't know what inyenzi meant—I was only ten years old—but it made me feel bad because the teacher was saying we were different from them [the Hutu children], and it felt like she was insulting us and the Hutu children were laughing at us.

My sister, an older sister who was fourteen years old, had a man teacher, a Hutu, and he hit her and two others girls [solely because] they were Tutsis.

They [the girls], like my sister, were Tutsi. They were the only Tutsi in the class, out of about fifty.

The teacher said my elder sister looked like King Rudahigwa, a Tutsi, [who was] king during the colonial period. All kings were Tutsi. And so he was saying all Tutsi looked like the kings from the colonial period, and he added that the current government [the Habyarimana regime] didn't like Tutsis. When he said such things he hit them. He would hit them with his hand and branches [thin, long branches which he would use as a whip] from a tree, and he also spit in their faces. He did this in front of the whole class.

Because my sister was treated this way, she left the class [meaning, she quit school]. All [three girls] left class [quit school]. They all left at different times. My sister left in April 1993.

My parents told her to go back to school, but my sister refused because her teacher hated her. So, they let her stay at home. I, though, stayed in school until April 1994.

I remember, on Radio Rwanda, hearing the names of suspected inkotanyi being read—those in Butare and eleven students from Nyanza. Leon Mugesera, an Interahamwe, was on Radio Rwanda, in about April 1993, and said there were Nyanza secondary [level] students who were suspects [allegedly supporters of the RPF]. [Interviewer's note: In June 2005, in a unanimous decision, the Supreme Court of Canada ruled 8–0 that evidence supported claims that Leon Mugesera incited genocide in Rwanda. The court determined that Mugesera's speech before about one thousand people included language inciting racial hatred. In part, he said, "We the people are obliged to take responsibility ourselves and wipe out this scum," and that they should "kill Tutsis and dump their bodies into the rivers of Rwanda."]

Sometimes, at home, we listened to RTLM. It was a new station and we listened to it. We were in the countryside, and we had nothing else to do [for entertainment] so we listened to the radio. They [some of the disk jockeys and reporters] said they would kill the inyenzi. The music was good, but I didn't like the radio station [the hateful messages about Tutsi that it broadcast].

On April 6 [1994], we were listening to the radio in the evening, and the radio [abruptly] went off [the air]. When it did not come back on we went to bed. In the morning we heard the president had been killed. Other people heard about his death during the night, but we didn't. In the morning we heard about it on the radio. My parents told us, the children, "There is going to be a war." The radio ordered everyone, all Rwandans, to remain at home, not to go anywhere.

From the 7th [of April], nobody [neither inside their home nor any Tutsi in their village] stayed in his bed. We all went outside at night into the forest [but returned to their homes during daylight hours believing they would not be attacked during the day]. We did that because they [the Interahamwe], who had been training to kill people, came in the night and took people away to kill them. We spent all the night sitting and standing. You cannot sleep when you have problems like this.

Around 14 April, the army [FAR] arrived and stayed [in the vicinity of their village]. People [some Tutsi who had seen the soldiers arrive] came in the morning and told us that the soldiers were coming to kill us [all Tutsi], and so we fled. We left our house that day, and went into the forest. From that time we did not return to our house, not even during the daytime.

That day [the 14th] our home was destroyed. [Hutu] neighbors destroyed our home. They pulled our home apart, taking off the roof, the doors, windows, everything.

When we heard that they [the Hutu] were coming to kill us, we left without eating [their evening meal, which they were in the process of cooking], and we ran toward Isonga, a nearby hill about one kilometer away. We ran because Hutus, our neighbors and Interahamwe, were throwing rocks at us and our [Tutsi] neighbors and were hitting people [Tutsi] with machetes and ubuhiri, and were killing as many as they could. We, all of us, our family and about ten [other] families [all Tutsi]—over one hundred people—ran toward Isonga. Many houses were being destroyed, and the Hutus were making fire on the houses [burning them to the ground].

Many people were going there [Isonga], and we wished to join them. There were many, many people, so many, thousands, perhaps ten thousand.

All of our family members made it safely [to Isonga], but three people among us were killed. They were behind all of us, and got caught and were killed with machetes. A woman, a child, and a man [were killed]. The man was very old and the woman was sick and the child was about five years [old] and with its mommy.

There was no food or water; there was nothing there, [except some] people with their cows and goats. People were killing goats to eat. We only had cows, so we purchased goat meat to cook ourselves. We would put it in water and boil it.

We stayed there from 14 April to 28 April. During the time, the Interahamwe attacked us on about 16 April, and almost all of the men [Tutsi] fought them off.

We had no defense [weapons] against the attack. We used only stones. The women and children helped to gather the stones, but only the men and older boys threw the stones, fought. The Interahamwe came from everywhere [all directions]. They had weapons, machetes and ubuhiri, but very few Tutsis were killed by Interahamwe because we were many and they were few. And the Interahamwe did not have guns.

But when the military came, on 27 April, many Tutsi were killed. Many people were being hit by the big guns and fell [either wounded or dead]. So many were being killed, even members of my family. Out of the [approximately] ten thousand people who were on that hill, only one hundred survived. People were being killed by guns and machetes. Those who were not killed ran out and [attempted to] escape [on] 28 April.

The battle lasted from about 16 of April to 27 of April. On 28 April, at about three in the afternoon, the military arrived and they brought the big gun. [Interviewer's note: The interviewee did not know what type of weapon the military had. Among the many weapons the Rwandan military had at its disposal were the following: Kalashnikovs, G3s, and a limited number of 81mm mortars, 83mm Blindicide rocket launchers, 57mm antitank guns, among others.] They started killing us with those guns. The Interahamwe went outside, and when people [Tutsi] tried to escape the big guns, they chopped them with the machete.

Because I had such fear of being found by the killers I made myself not to cry. Tears were coming, but I did not run out [from her hiding place in the bush] or cry out because I couldn't [otherwise she could have been killed]. When you see something bad, people dying, your heart becomes as a stone because you fear you will be killed so you must be hard [stoic and quiet so as not to reveal oneself to the killers].

Those who escaped from those big guns were killed by machete. Many people were shot by the military in the head, chest, stomach, and leg, and those wounded but who kept running were killed by machete and so were others who were not shot.

When those big guns finished, the Interahamwe came and finished those who had fallen [were badly wounded] and babies [who may or may not have been wounded] next to their mothers.

Over two hundred, maybe three hundred, people were fallen [dead or wounded] in front of me. I could see from where I was hiding. These were the number in the clearing, but there were many others in the brush who had been caught and killed by machete.

Around six at night, about ten [Tutsi survivors] came out of the bushes, and when others saw them they joined them. They thought it was safe to come out because the military and Interahamwe were not there.

When I thought it was safe, I also joined the group. I followed those who were escaping and left the hill with them. As we moved toward the river more and more people joined us until there were about fifty. Among the fifty were my older brothers, two uncles, an older sister, a cousin, and an aunt. All the night, from six [P.M.], until five in the morning it took us to reach the Akanyaru River. At five [in the morning], Interahamwe saw us.

Between 15 April to 27 April, all of my brothers and sisters and mommy and father remained alive. This was also true of my uncles' families and my grandparents. But on 28 April that changed. They all died [were murdered] from 28 April. Many were killed on that hill, and many who left for Burundi on that day were killed in Akanyaru River [the river bordering Rwanda and Burundi].

My mommy, on 28 April, didn't run like others and soldiers came and put a knife in her chest. She was with a baby [carrying her newborn infant], and she could not run. The baby, they killed him also, the same way, with the knife. Also, my grandmother, my father's mother, was killed that day, at the same time and the same way as my mother. They were together. The wife of my oldest brother was also killed, and also her baby. I was running but I was near them when they were caught, and I saw them . . . [being] killed.

My father was running away, too, but I didn't see where he went. I was told [later, following the genocide] by a survivor, who was with him, that he [the interviewee's father] was caught by the Interahamwe and [they] took him back to our village and beat him with ubuhiri. They beat him to death. They found him hiding in the forest and took him to the village to kill him. They brought back to the village all those they caught and killed them there. Only three of my brothers and sisters [out of nine], four including me, survived. Three of us are girls and one a boy. The boy is older than me, and the girls are younger than me.

We traveled through the night, but we did not go by road, but up and down the hills and forests. The older people helped me, a child, with the walk.

We came to the river, Akanyaru, at five in the morning. On the way we passed by people who had been killed by the Interahamwe. Many, many people! About three hundred people. Some were half alive, but we couldn't take them with us. There was not the possibility. There were those who had been hit with machetes and ubuhiri and their heads were half off [necks badly sliced], and there was nothing we could do for them.

We could not rest because we had to get to Burundi before it was day. I walked the entire way. A child could walk from here [Butare] to Kigali [a two-and-a-half-hour drive by automobile, up and down hills] during war, genocide.

When we got to the river it was still dark, but the moon was shining and it gave light. The river was big, very big, about five hundred meters [wide]. It is so big [that] to get from Rwanda to Burundi, you use a boat [a canoe].

When we just about reached the river, an Interahamwe along the river saw us and made a sound with his mouth, warning the others. The others, about one hundred, quickly, in about two minutes, made a circle around us and attacked. They [the Interahamwe] were all ages, about fifteen years to forty years. Most were between twenty and thirty years [old].

The Interhamwe had machetes, ubuhiri, and bows and arrows, and they forced us to take all of our clothes off. All clothes! They did this so they could take the clothes to their own families at home. Then they tied our hands behind our back. We could not resist because we were outnumbered, and we had no weapons and they did. Then they began killing, with the machete and ubuhiri, by hitting people in the head and necks and throwing people in the river.

I was the last one attacked and I was hit in the head with an ubuhiri [she has a huge indentation on her forehead over which is a large chunk of scar tissue], and the top of my head was cut [sliced open]. When I was hit, I was near the river and I fell in the river and the river carried me and I was tossed [about] and pulled under the water.

I cannot swim, and water was going in my mouth and nose. As soon as I was thrown in the water, Burundian soldiers were getting in the water to help. Only two of us, one other child and me, were saved by the Burundian soldiers. By the time they reached me, I had been pulled down the river only about three or four meters. I believe I would have died if the Burundian soldiers had not pulled me out of the water.

When the soldiers pulled me from the water I was half alive. My head was injured and I almost died [drowned] in the water, and I could not think or talk for about thirty minutes. I was in great pain and I wanted no one to touch my head. The Burundian soldiers had no medicine [or bandages]. Also, my head was bleeding a lot, and I had much blood on my face. All I had was my hand to cover my head [wound].

The Interhamwe began attacking the Burundian soldiers using the bows and arrows. The Burundians shot at the Interahamwe with big guns [possibly automatic weapons] to make the Interahamwe scared, to go away.

Finally, when I could, I began talking to the other survivors that the Burundian soldiers had saved. There were others, beside us [she and the other girl], they saved earlier, and they took us away from the river [somewhat inland, between five and ten kilometers away]. All of the other people [about forty-eight] were killed or drowned in the river. Many other people were also in the water [swirling around]; many were taken by the river.

The Burundian soldiers came back later that day, about three in the afternoon, and they took me to a *centre de santé* [typically, small, poorly equipped clinic with minimally trained staff in Rwanda and Burundi] where they had my head cleaned and stitched up. After I had my head sewn, they took me right back to the camp where all of the survivors were staying.

Three days later they brought me to the hospital in Kirundo District. My face was all swollen, puffy. I could not even see out of my eyes, and I was suffering terribly. This time they took me to a proper hospital with greater capacity and better doctors. At the hospital they injected me with a serum and they made some cover for my head. I stayed there April to August. All that time I didn't get better. My face was so swollen I could not see and the pain did not get less. They had to cut my head up [open] and pull the scalp apart to help me. I was there by myself the whole time

In August [1994], I was taken by a Burundian woman to a refugee camp in Burundi where there were about two hundred refugees. In December [1994] we, the refugees, began, in small groups, walking to the Burundi/Rwanda border. We walked from three at night to eleven in the morning before we reached Rwanda, at Bugesera. We walked across the border, and [once] in Rwanda we walked to the town center in Bugesera. There, we moved into houses that were not occupied.

From December to August [1995], we, about two hundred refugees, stayed in Bugesera. I lived with another survivor, a girl, in a small house. We got food from soldiers who helped us. For all those months we did nothing.

In August [1995], a Rwandan soldier came to our house in Bugesera and took us to an orphanage [Ja Rwanda] in Kiyovu, which was once a French school [located in Kigali]. I stayed there four years, until September 1999. There were about four hundred orphans at the orphanage, boys and girls, from one month to eight years. A French man operated the school, with other adults, mostly Rwandans, who provided supervision. Some French came for short periods, and then would return [to Europe].

At the orphanage they provided us with everything. The adults were good [to us]. We went to school there, and it was safe.

My brother and sisters asked the military if they would help them try to find [out] if there were any other survivors in [our] family, and they agreed and found my aunt in 1996. My aunt brought my brother and sisters to live with her in Nyanza. That's when my aunt began looking for more of our relatives and found me in 1999. I finally moved [into] my aunt's home in 1999 and was reunited with my brother and sisters.

As for gacaca, I think there are some trials that are well done and some that are not well done. For example, in my own sector there are some men who confessed [to] their crimes, and they were given small judgments [sentences] that are not appropriate to their crimes.

Before gacaca courts, the judges ask the man, the criminal, to confess his crimes, and some do not—many do not—want to admit their sins. And when there is little evidence presented [or available for the People of Integrity to consider and weigh], they are given small judgments [sentences] for their crimes.

Personally, there is the case of the killer of my mother. He was charged by many persons of being her killer. Despite the evidence and proof provided by neighbors of his guilt, he kept denying his responsibility and he was released from prison. He had been in prison since 1995 as an alleged génocidaire. At the time, he was suspected of having killed many people. He was released in 2007.

I feel great sorrow about what happened [at gacaca, over how the man was released and not held accountable for the murder of her mother]. Even if they chose to release him [which gacaca did do], I wish he would have, could have, been made to inform me where he had thrown my mother's and my little sister's dead bodies. It also makes me feel I've failed to provide them [her mother and little sister] with a burial with dignity.

For sure, the man [the murderer of her mother] has given corruption [provided bribes] to the panel of judges [the so-called People of Integrity who preside over gacaca hearings]. From information I received from other persons, I believe they [the People of Integrity] were given corruption. I, of course, could not go and track down or observe such corruption [being handed out].

Some of those judges are closer to the killer than they are to me; they may even be related to the killer, and so there was nothing I could do [to convince them of the need to heed the evidence against the alleged murderer].

Yes, there is a way to protest this [sort of injustice at the hands of gacaca] as at the district level there is a person in charge of gacaca trials, but the problem [is that] I was studying, completing my studies at secondary level, at the time, so I could not, and did not, have the time to make an appeal in time, and there are time limits to making an appeal. If you do not do it within a certain period of time, then it is too late. And I was late.

My brother complained to the district level, but members of the killer's family told the same official that my brother was lying. What might have happened, but I don't know [for sure], is that others who provided testimony about the killer could have been corrupted [talked into accepting bribes] by the killer or killer's family to change their stories. I do not know.

The killer's mother is Tutsi, his father is Hutu. The survivors, Tutsis, who first said the killer did kill my mother are the killer's mother's relatives, and they, later, became corrupted by the killer [as a result of being bribed], and changed their testimony.

I am very, very unhappy about this [situation]. He [the killer] is not free because he confessed or asked for forgiveness from his heart. I could have forgiven him if he had confessed and asked for forgiveness, but he didn't. Because I am a Christian and in the Bible it says I should forgive, forgive others their sins, I do so.

I am also unhappy they [the killer, his family and friends] say I am a liar. Most[ly], though, I am unhappy over the death [murder] of my mother. Also, as I said, he [the killer] never showed us where he threw [dumped] my mother and my baby sister. Also, this man was to have killed my brother's wife and baby, and he was not held responsible for those deaths either, and never said where he threw them.

This man now lives back in my village where I was born, Nyanza. He lives about one kilometer from my house. I see him every day. He says nothing to me. When he meets me, he runs quickly.

It is very difficult living like this. When I see him it is very, very difficult and what I fear most is that he may kill me.

I believe the government has done what it could to help survivors. The government is now working on getting us [survivors] houses and there will be no charge. The government, through FARG, pays for all children of survivors to go to school [secondary and primary]. But, attendance [obtaining a scholarship] to university is based on scores; you need to have a certain score to [qualify] for funds from FARG and the government.

The most positive aspect of my life today is that I finished secondary school. For many years I wished to complete secondary school and now I have done so. I was twenty-two years when I finished.

[One of the] most difficult aspects of completing secondary school is that I had a problem, no possibility to purchase all things I needed for school. FARG gives you money for school fees, gives you notebooks, pens, but does not give you [a] bus ticket to get to school or personal supplies such as toothpaste, deodorant, body lotions, feminine supplies.

When I was suffering psychological problems because of genocide, life at school was very difficult because it prevented me from going to school—sometimes for one week at a time. In April [during the national genocide commemoration period], I would be away from school for even more than one week. Sometimes up to two weeks. In April it rains much and in April during the genocide it rained on us. [The rain brings back sharp and painful memories of the genocide period, which is compounded by the many ceremonies during April's month of commemoration.]

In April, skeletons [of survivors] are brought to commemoration sites and buried, and it is talked about how these people [whose remains are being buried] died and when I see and hear this I feel very unhappy in my heart. When I meet anyone who made genocide [was involved in its perpetration] I think [fear] he can kill me.

I am most sad on 28 and 29 April because that was when I had the greatest sadness, difficulties. That is when I suffer most.

I need to be on the path to university so I can reach the level to get a better job, but it [the government] is very selective of who they help [as it is based on marks and scores on national examinations]. Survivors study under different circumstances [some are orphans, some young people head households, some are from impoverished families] so it is not just. They [the government] should be able to take all who wish to go to university.

Before the genocide I did not worry about someone coming into my house and killing me. Today, because other genocide survivors have been killed, I worry that I, too, could be killed like that, that someone could enter my house and kill me.

Before the genocide we closed our doors at night, but didn't lock them. Today, we close our doors and secure them strongly because we fear the killers of the genocide who are now out of prison.

My older brother was told by the killer of our mother that we [Hutu and Tutsi] will always be together in the country. The word that was used in Kinyarwanda, "Tuzarubanmo," means, "Even though we are enemies you cannot do anything to me." It's a threat that they are free to do anything they wish to us and we cannot stop them.

Every Tutsi receives [threatening] notes from former extremists and their families. When you are sleeping they come in the night and they put letters under your door. A message I received under my door was, "We will show you." In Kinyarwanda, this phrase, "We will show you" translates into: "Because you are supported by [Rwandan President Paul] Kagame's government, if it ends, we will show you!" which means, "We will kill you!"

In 2003, during the first week of April, my house was stoned [had rocks thrown at it]. They were thrown at the house for about one hour. It was about one in the morning. I was with two others in the house, my older sister and my younger sister. We began screaming and called for our neighbors to come and help us, but nobody came to help. They [those who were doing the stoning] threw the rocks at the door and the roof. I feared that they [the attackers] were going to kill us. My sisters, too, thought the genocide was starting again.

This [the stoning] was done for a full week, except they [the attackers] would jump [skip] one day and do it the next. Each time it happened [the stoning on the different nights of the week] I feared there was a war, the beginning of a new war.

During that week we were so afraid, so scared that we left that village, Nyanza, and house, and moved to Butare Town. We left because we had no peace there.

Where we live now, we have security. Patrols come in the night and provide security. All citizens pay for these patrols, Tutsi and Hutu.

This message I received came after [Paul] Kagame was elected [president of Rwanda]. It was left under my door. Since it was left in the middle of the night I do not know, exactly, who left it. I received it about five years ago [July 2003].

When I picked the letter up and read it, I felt, thought, another genocide could happen. I took the letter to the police and they sent [assigned] civilian patrols to provide security, patrols at night. It [the security detail] lasted for one month.

My younger sister, like me, has also suffered psychological trauma. During the entire month of April [the most intense period of the three-month commemoration period] she refuses to talk. Every April. She does not say a word to anyone. She was born in 1988, so today [this year], she is twenty. When she experiences this trauma, she usually stays at home and does nothing. When she absolutely refuses to talk to anybody we take her to the hospital. She often stays there for a week or more. At the hospital they give her an injection with medication and she sleeps. When she comes home, a counselor comes and helps her.

I live in Butare Town now, but I still go back to Nyanza to see my cousin who still lives there. I also see friends. I go about three or four times a year. About one thousand people live in my former village. It is called Ntyazo today. It still has genocide ideology today. Survivors who have remained have told me that it is so. For example, if you are a farmer and plant beans, people [who are suspected of being former extremists] steal the beans. Only the survivors have patches attacked like this.

A genocide survivor was killed there in May 2007. He gave information during gacaca. Only this man was killed in our village, but in the Nyanza District other genocide survivors—three persons—have been killed for also giving information to gacaca.

Today I am sad because of what I lived through and lost. My mother, father, and my brothers and sisters are not here. I am very sad about not knowing where my mother, younger sister, and father are [where their bodies were dumped after they were murdered]. I have not been able to provide them with a proper burial.

Of my six brothers and sisters who were killed during the genocide, we put in cement [provided a proper burial place] only two. In 2004, we put them in cement. In April, we put in cement an older brother and in July we put in cement an older sister. During [the] commemoration [period] some people showed us where their bodies were [dumped after being murdered]. Other people helped us find the bodies [the remains] and return them to Nyanza. We found their skeletons covered with sod. We put them in cement in Nyanza during a ceremony during commemoration. About one hundred people attended. Other people [the remains of those who had been murdered] were also put in cement by their family members on the same day. Many others were put in cement [the same mass grave] with them [her siblings].

MURORUNKWERE

DATE OF INTERVIEW: January 29, 2009

LOCATION OF INTERVIEW: Huye

INTERVIEWER: Samuel Totten

INTERPRETER: Rafiki Ubaldo

LANGUAGE IN WHICH INTERVIEW WAS CONDUCTED: Kinyarwanda

BIRTH DATE OF INTERVIEWEE: Does not know (She is approximately thirty-five years old.)

AGE DURING THE GENOCIDE: Approximately twenty years old

PLACE OF BIRTH: Huye

PLACE OF RESIDENCE DURING THE GENOCIDE: Bujumbura, Burundi

ETHNICITY PRIOR TO THE GENOCIDE: Tutsi

NUMBER OF IMMEDIATE FAMILY MEMBERS KILLED IN THE GENOCIDE: Mother, father, sisters, brother

CURRENTLY RESIDES WITH: Husband and six children

Even before I left Rwanda in 1992, the war between the government soldiers and the RPF [Rwandan Patriotic Front] was going on and people were being labeled as accomplices of the rebels [the RPF].

I left Rwanda in 1992 to go to Burundi to visit relatives. Since my parents were healthy I didn't see any reason to come [return] to this porch [small house in the countryside], and it was the first time I went to a big city, Bujumbura. I was living with the family of my brother who had moved to Burundi.

In 1994 I thought I should come back home because I was missing my parents, but then I decided to stay [in Burundi] because the [Rwandan] president's plane got shot down. It wasn't just a Rwandan problem, but also Burundi's because the president of Burundi [Cyprien Ntaryamira] was on the airplane. So, after the plane was shot, the Rwandans were not allowed to go to the market.

If you went to the market, people would take your belongings, on purpose. So the Hutu-Tutsi problem [there] started up again. In Bujumbura there are people of many ethnic backgrounds—Senegalese, Sudanese, Ugandans, Congolese, Rwandans—and the facial profile is a signal of whether you are one or another. We all have the same color of skin, but we have different attitudes, different ways about us, and distinct styles of life. In Burundi, it's not like Rwanda; when there is a problem in Burundi, a conflict, it can end in a month, and then we could relax somewhat.

All that time, my brother and I followed the radio and sometimes the television and we could see what was happening back home. The only thing that could help me with the images [the piles of hacked up bodies and the rivers running red with blood and bloated bodies] was I was raised Pentecostal, and I believed then, and I believe now, that when my time did come there was nothing I could do. Of course, even if I mention God it does not mean I didn't think of my family, and so it was very depressing.

Radio Burundi reported what was happening in Rwanda. Let me ask you a question: Who didn't know what was happening in Rwanda? Every radio was reporting on that.

The radio reports said that the RPF and government troops were fighting, and I just kept thinking that the conflict was a war [not something like mass murder]. But then we began hearing the stories and seeing the images of what was happening in Rwanda. And . . . let me put it this way: when I left Rwanda in 1992, I was eighteen and I had reached puberty and I had breasts and when I went to Burundi I had a very good life and I became a really beautiful girl. [Interviewer's note: To this day her face is strikingly beautiful, with high cheekbones and luminous eyes. She is tall, graceful, and shapely.] So for you to understand how I was feeling in 1994, I was so depressed that my breasts shrank. To hardly anything. They were no longer full, no longer those of a young woman. Only those who pass through the night can tell you what it was like.

At that time, I was a teenager and I was going through the emotions of a teenager, and that was a very difficult period. And I was a teenager in a different country. Then the news came from back home. I was a good Christian, a strong believer, and I thought praying was going to ease my desperation.

After the plane crash, I realized I was going to become a refugee and that I wouldn't be able to go back home. I was also wondering about my family back in Rwanda, whether they were alive or dead. There was no way to tell. I was also seriously wondering what my future would be like.

On Radio Burundi we heard the Swahili edition of "Five in the Morning," and the news was saying the president of Rwanda [Juvénal Habyarimana] and the president of Burundi were killed in an airplane crash, that they were shot down by the RPF. I knew that this would worsen the situation and I began to worry even more about my family. [At this point in the interview, the interviewee informed us that she wished to end the interview for the day, as she was tired. She sat with her back to us, looking sad and depressed.]

[But then, continuing, she said] you know when you were here last time [six months previously, during which the interviewer had asked her if she was willing to be interviewed in regard to her perspective about the gacaca process] and the country was in the middle of gacaca, and I wouldn't talk to you about gacaca? Then, I had too much on my mind. Remember, I was not here during the genocide and only knew that my family members had been killed, so during gacaca I was finding out exactly what happened to them, and at the time I was traumatized and couldn't talk.

Also, my husband is a judge in gacaca and he would come home and we would talk because he was having difficulty with what he was hearing. So, I . . . couldn't talk. It was too much.

After a gacaca session, I also asked him [her husband] about the testimony, hoping I could find out more about who killed my family.

I came back [to Rwanda] in March of 1995 and the war [genocide] in Rwanda was over, but war was raging in Burundi and it was difficult for Rwandans to remain in Burundi. I knew other Rwandans who were going back home because we knew it was more peaceful back in Rwanda than it was in Burundi. On the bus, we went from Bujumbura to Butare. The bus stopped in front of the [Hotel] Faucon , which is located on the main street in Butare Town, and that was when I began to worry about what I was going to do. The bus got in quite late and it was not possible to go to the village [Huye, several miles outside of Butare Town] because while war had stopped, it was still not peaceful and thus dangerous to travel at night. By coincidence, I met a woman of a family I knew and she let me stay at her home for the night. That night we did not, could not, sleep, because we were so excited to be back home, and so we talked all night.

They [the female friend and her family] started giving me details of how people were killed. So and so was killed by a machete in the head, children were dumped in [outside] latrines. At that time it was very difficult because people began to dig up latrines to try to locate bodies.

That night they told me what had happened here in Butare. If someone dies when you are away and you're not at the burial and you are not there to bury the person, you cannot accept they are dead; you are always waiting for them to come back. [At this point, she stopped talking as she breastfed her baby.]

They told me about what happened to my family. My father had stayed at home while everyone else went to Huye [to the commune of Huye about two miles away from the hillside village of Gasharu/Sector Nyanza, where her family resided] because they thought it would be safer there. My father, though, stayed here in our house in order to care for the cows. That afternoon, the killers attacked and he defended himself, but they managed to cut [hack off] his two arms. He ran off trying to escape and they chased him and it was not easy to find him in the dark, but they kept searching for him and found him and killed him that morning

My mother and my younger brother and sister were killed in Huye. They were among the mass of people [who went there,] and [they] were killed by grenades that were thrown into the crowd by Interahamwe, soldiers, and the local population [of Hutu].

So the following day I came home to the village [Gasharu/Sector Nyanza, Huye Commune]. I walked up to my home, which had been made of bricks with a tile roof, with my aunt, and saw the ruins. I was fearful to come up here, but the Hutu were fearful, too, and during the day[light] they couldn't kill me. Our home had been destroyed completely.

Most of those people [her neighbors] thought we were dead, and when they saw me they thought I was a spirit coming back to haunt them for what they had done. And this was because they truly thought no one was alive. Many were so shocked that they came up and asked for forgiveness.

The whole house had been destroyed and all of the bricks and tiles had been stolen. All there was left was the foundation and rubble. But I didn't care because I already knew about my family members, and I didn't care about anything else.

No one came forward to say they had killed my family, but they said, "I'm sorry for taking your things from the house," and others apologized for helping to destroy the house and stealing the bricks. They were telling me empty words. I was expecting to hear them apologize for the killings, but they were just talking about material things and so I answered with empty words. I was physically unable to retaliate, but I wanted to do so.

The banana plantation was still there, but the local people had divided up the land and claimed it for themselves. Eventually, I got the land back.

I'm not considered a survivor. [Interviewer's note: She explained that the Rwandan government does not consider her a survivor since she resided in Burundi during the genocide. Thus, even though she is an orphan as a result of the genocide and lost most of her extended family, technically she is simply a returnee from Burundi.] And I think that's fair; I can't ask for help when there are people who have been injured, traumatized, and missing limbs.

I left and went to live with my aunt in Cyrwa. Over the next month, I went to the village on those days the authorities [designated] for families to dig in the latrines, weeds, and ditches to try to locate their loved ones.

Later, we found my father who had been dumped into a ditch. That was April 1995. Some neighbors finally came up and told me they knew where my father was buried. We dug and found his bones. I identified his clothes, and saw that both his arms were missing.

He had not gotten far, only about two kilometers, and that's where we found him. We buried him in Huye at a memorial site. We had a formal burial for him with a priest.

My son does not like to go up to our banana plantation where my family had its house because we told him that's where his grandparents lived. When he goes up there [to work] he listens to the birds and it makes him sad. I would like to build something there so it looks like a home, but that is just a wish because I can't [afford to] do that.

In the beginning, I kept the ruins as we were thinking we would build a house there, but over time people began to steal more and more of the bricks to build their own houses. You know, when people kill you once, they can kill you again. If I kill and destroy you and I come back and steal such things as the ruins of your home I am killing your memory; they want you to be forgotten. Now, it's not only the ruins; now, people steal my banana plants—not because they need food, but just to hurt me.

After burying my father, I looked for a job. There was a project in Gihindamuyaga financed from abroad that involved planting and harvesting flowers and I worked there for one year. In 1996 I got married. We met through church services. My husband was a preacher at ADEPR (Association des églises de pentêcote du rwanda). They sent him to another parish so we moved near the border with Burundi. In 2001 we built this house. The house is right next door to his parents' house. [Both are about five hundred square feet, made of concrete with rough dirt floors, heavy wood shudders, and faded and cracked tile roofs surrounded by banana plants and dirt trails.]

A problem living here is that our neighbors don't like us. For example, my children don't play far from this place [house] because it's not safe. And those people who killed my family are not happy I am here. And even today you can imagine, my husband, who is a judge in gacaca, they are mad at him. My neighbor says my husband has been eaten by a dog [meaning, he is married to a Tutsi]. [Interviewer's note: Her husband is considered a Hutu. Many years ago his family "changed" from being Tutsi to Hutu in order to be part of the majority and to access the privileges of the majority. Over and above that, since her husband married her, a Tutsi, he is no longer trusted and those who are Hutu refuse to talk to him. They claim that she has destroyed him. The neighbors also saw that he didn't take part in the killings, and thus consider him a traitor.] Neighbors pass by and insult me without any reason; they don't come to visit us, and we wouldn't feel welcome visiting them.

Before I got married, I was so desperate. I didn't think anyone would be interested in me. Imagine, after 1994 I was a grown-up girl, without a family, without hope for a dowry, without relatives who would come to my wedding. How could I expect to get in a relationship with a man? And when I would meet people with family members and relatives I would get very jealous because I was alone. So, when I got married I wanted many children.

The worst part of my life is that I am an orphan. And when thoughts of that [arise] I am saddened because even though I have my own family I am still an orphan. You see, in the Kinyarwanda culture when you become a mother, when you have a newborn, your family comes to congratulate you. They bring beer, they bring bananas, they bring milk, and there is a ceremony. And the new mother brings the newborn to her family. But where can I go?

As for gacaca, I never expected anything from it. We live close to the prison and prisoners come out to do community work and they go to their families as much as they want, and to me they are not prisoners. Also, I see them as representatives of the killers of my family, and they are free but my family does not come back. [So,] the fact that the prisoners are brought to gacaca and are forced to answer questions is good enough for me.

The man who killed my father was in prison and confessed. So when they brought him to gacaca it was an easy trial because he confessed in advance and asked for forgiveness. You ask, Did I forgive? Well, Paul Kagame [the Rwandan president] forgave him so who am I not to? The man [who murdered her father] was at gacaca and looked me in the eye and asked for forgiveness; at that time, I believed he was sincere. I think he feels very guilty [for what he did]. I forgave him, and the rest he has to answer to God.

But, it is a fact he has been in prison and has been sensitized to confess. Also, prison can be very, very difficult, and having blood on your hands is disturbing, it can be traumatizing. The sincerity is not for life, forever, because I believe if you ask them to pick up machetes and slaughter us again they will do that.

I don't feel safe living here. As I said, my children don't go far from this place [their house]. I don't like Rwanda. I would go somewhere else if I had the means. If I had the means, I would be gone already. Look at me, one single individual on this ground, alone, and they [the Hutu] unite.

[An older woman walks down the steep dirt trail adjacent to the interviewee's house, and waves to the interviewee.] That is my aunt. She is traumatized as a result of the genocide. She had seven children and now she only has two. They were all killed, as was their father, her husband. She constantly cries and shouts a lot. The worst case we've seen was during a memorial service when she began shouting and it sounded as if she thought there was a war going on around her. That day she got help from a trauma counselor from FARG [Victims of Genocide Fund]. But the rest of the time she receives no help.

You only get help when you are traumatized [meaning, "acting out" in public]. Only when there are active signs of trauma [making incoherent sounds, running about in an unruly manner] can she get help. Other times, she can't get help because there are no signs. Crying is not enough of a sign. Besides, she does not have enough money to go get help every time she cries.

When my husband was a preacher, a woman stood up in church and demanded that another layman confess for having killed her children. Then later, during gacaca, this woman asked my husband, "Did I ask [meaning, in the church] this person to confess his killing of my children?" My husband said, "Yes, many times." From that point on, none of the Hutus will talk to him.

Prior to the genocide I was very happy. Now I am all mixed up. Sometimes I'm very happy, sometimes I am very sad. Sometimes I don't know.

I would like to see hatred between Tutsi and Hutu go away. You see, for example, in gacaca, when someone has been given a heavy sentence, all of his family identify themselves with him, and they see those who charged him as their worst enemies. They also say that later they will seek revenge. But they forget that our family is dead and buried, and we will never see them again.

If there had not been genocide I would've lived much better. I live poorly now. I've been forced to invent [there are different words for "create" and "invent" in Kinyarwanda and she used the term "invent" on purpose] a family. If you have a family [meaning, parents and brothers and sisters and aunts and uncles] in Rwanda it helps out a lot when you are about to choose your partner in life. After 1994 we were viewed as human beings with less value, and when anyone steps up to be with you, you don't think twice, you go.

MUGABO ARNAUD

DATE OF INTERVIEW: April 27, 2008

LOCATION OF INTERVIEW: 10 to 10 Paradise Hotel, Cyangugu

INTERVIEWER: Samuel Totten

INTERPRETER: Not needed

LANGUAGE IN WHICH INTERVIEW WAS CONDUCTED: English

BIRTH DATE OF INTERVIEWEE: December 3, 1980

AGE DURING THE GENOCIDE: Fourteen years old

PLACE OF BIRTH: Rutobwe, Cyubi Sector, Muhanga District, Southern Province

PLACE OF RESIDENCE DURING THE GENOCIDE: Rutobwe, Cyubi Sector, Muhanga District, Southern Province

ETHNICITY PRIOR TO THE GENOCIDE: Tutsi

NUMBER OF IMMEDIATE FAMILY MEMBERS KILLED IN THE GENOCIDE: Immediate family: none; extended family: grandparents, uncles, aunts, and cousins

CURRENTLY RESIDES WITH: ROOMMATE

In our village, among our friends and our neighbors, Tutsi and Hutu, we had no problems because we were good neighbors, helped one another, attended weddings and celebrations and like that. But at school we had problems. There, teachers made us stand up and tell if we were Tutsi or Hutu. Before I went to school, I didn't know that I was that [whether he was Tutsi, Hutu, or Twa] because my parents did not talk about such, did not tell us. At school, when I was first asked, I did not know, but since my teacher knew my parents, he wrote down what I was. And so when I went back home I asked my parents what we were. They told me that I am Tutsi. I don't remember if they explained it very well, what the differences were or what it meant to be one or the other. Later, I learned about all that at school.

In school, we began to learn about Rwandan history—and who and what Tutsi and Hutus were—in the fourth year [fourth grade]. Before that, though, in school, on the playground, among other children, I'd heard different things about Hutu and Tutsi and gradually, over the first four years at school, I began to have questions about why some were Tutsi, some Hutu. So, when I returned to my village from school—primary school—I would go and see my grandfather and ask him questions about why Tutsi and Hutu were different and about other things I had heard at school. See, in Rwanda, during the first three years of primary school you only go to school in the morning and in the afternoon I would spend the time with my grandfather and we would herd cows. And our grandparents, when you asked them questions, they could tell you everything because they were very wise.

My grandfather explained to me that he was Tutsi and his parents, my great-grandparents, were Tutsi and it became very clear to me that my father was Tutsi and I was Tutsi. And he also told me about [the forced] exile [of Tutsi] in 1959 and 1973, and how Tutsi houses were destroyed and how they [the Hutu] stole their cows and other property.

My grandparents were not forced into exile in 1959 or 1973, but in 1959 their village and home were attacked so they fled to an area where no one knew them. When they returned, everything was gone—their cows, beds, tables, everything. My mother's brothers, though, fled to Congo. Her brothers were not married and they did not want to be killed and so they went into exile. My grandfather and grandmother didn't leave because they felt it would be very difficult to leave their village, home, herd, and possessions and then try to come back [to Rwanda, their village and home] at another time.

In school from the fourth year to the sixth, we studied history. We learned what happened in Rwanda, who was king, who was Tutsi, who was Hutu, how they lived together, everything. Many times I was ashamed to learn that during the different periods [of history] it was said that Tutsi, when they were ruling, they treated the Hutu like slaves—they made them do all the work, they made them carry the king around [in a sedan chair]. But, at the same time, many things that we were told [taught] in school were different from what my grandfather had told me.

So, I used to go home and ask my grandfather—my father was at work at the school [where he was headmaster of the local primary school] and my mother was busy caring for all of the children—and so I would ask my grandfather, "Why did you, Tutsi, treat the Hutu like you did? And he told me, "We cannot deny that we used them [the Hutu] for work, as servants in our homes, but we did not treat them like slaves. They needed money and would work for us. But, you must understand, there were also educated Hutu who had served as chiefs [in what would be referred to as sectors in today's Rwandan society]."

In school, though, we learned that the history had been a very, very bad situation for the Hutu. I remember fifth year [fifth grade] when we were studying history and our teacher told us that the Tutsi treated the Hutus very, very bad, and a student asked, "Why did Hutu accept to be treated like that? Why didn't Hutu pay back [fight back]?" I remember that student and even many years later when I saw him, I would remember [laughing at] his question. He wanted revenge. I don't know why I remember those words [the words of the young boy in his class] out of everything.

The teacher, a woman, replied, "It's not good . . . when something bad is done to you, it's not good to do something bad back." She, the teacher, was Hutu, the wife of the bourgmestre [mayor].

But things changed in 1990 when the RPF [Rwandan Patriotic Front] attacked Rwanda. At that time, we, Tutsis, began to be called inyenzi [cockroaches]. We were called that in school by our fellow students and even in the village by our friends who were Hutu. I don't recall any teachers calling us inyenzi.

At that time, when I thought of the word inyenzi, I didn't think of the small animal [cockroaches] but of the RPF soldiers [because that was what they were commonly referred to by the Hutu]. On the radio, all the time, the RPF were called inyenzi and were said to be animals. And so, I feared even seeing a RPF soldier because we were told they were not human, that they even had tails. We—many Tutsi—feared if they came into Rwanda they would kill us. Yes, even Tutsi feared that because the radio made them sound so . . .

When we began to be called inyenzi I knew nothing about the RPF and their attacking Rwanda, but others would say, "You are inyenzi and supporting the attacks on Rwanda."

When I heard what was happening up on the borders far away I was surprised, shocked, to think that something that was happening so far away would have such an impact in the center of the country because we had nothing to do with such programs [actions]. It was very strange for me, for us, to be treated poorly and called inyenzi for things we didn't know about or do. Maybe my parents knew about it [the RPF attacks], but I, and the other children, didn't, so why were we ill-treated, I wondered.

In the village, people would say that the RPF were attacking Rwanda and that we, Tutsi, were helping them and that Tutsi men were going and joining them. Even in the village we heard that two of my uncles who lived in Kigali had joined the RPF, but they hadn't. They were simply living in Kigali.

When we would go to the center [the area where there were small stores and stands that sold food staples and supplies] and buy salt and rice and when we passed by people, they would say, in a very mad voice, "Those are inyenzi!" and, "You are inyenzi and your friends are attacking us."

They were fierce when they said such things. This made us afraid because people threatened revenge and so we didn't know what was going to happen [next, or to them].

People, also, were motivated by the radio. On the radio, it was being said that the enemy were the Tutsi, all the Tutsi in the entire country. I remember one time the chief of our village came to my grandfather and wanted to take my uncle, saying he was an enemy of the country—a RPF supporter—and my uncle went into the house and shut the door and refused to go because they wanted to take him to jail. I think that was 1993. The situation was very bad at that time.

In 1990, 1991, 1992, 1993, and 1994, every day the situation got worse. We would hear about other places where people, Tutsi, had been attacked and killed, and how the country was losing [spinning out of] control.

Even Radio Rwanda—before RTLM was established—would say bad things about Tutsi in Rwanda and how they, we, supported the soldiers [RPF]. However, when RTLM began [to broadcast], the messages about Tutsi became much worse. Sometimes we would listen to RTLM to hear what was being said [about Tutsis]. They used to say, "The enemy of the country are Tutsi. The Tutsi are attacking the country." They also said, "Hutus have to be together. They have to fight for the country because Tutsi want to take power." The radio also said things like, "You should not take a Tutsi for a friend because they are enemies!" They also said if a Hutu, at that time, got married to a Tutsi, they would be punished because all Tutsi were enemies. [The interviewee is referring to the so-called Hutu Ten Commandments which, initially, were issued by *Kangura*, the Hutu extremist newspaper.] But before, of course, Tutsi and Hutus married, but things changed.

I first remember seeing Interahamwe in the center. This was between the middle of 1993 and the beginning of 1994, and they [the Interahamwe] had traditional weapons—pangas and massues—and were attacking people who were supporters of the RPF, people who were members of the PL [the Liberal Party] because they [the Hutu] said this was a Tutsi [political] party. They beat them, and some were killed. They also attacked witches. Why they attacked the witches I do not know.

The Interahamwe were very crazy; they acted as if they took drugs. They screamed as they ran in groups, waving their weapons. Even if you were a long ways away you could hear them. They were screaming songs, about how they were going to kill the enemies of the country, how they had to be [band] together to fight for the country, how the RPF was not going to be able to hurt the country. These Interahamwe were from the villages in the area.

In my village, three [young men] became Interahamwe. They were older than me. Before the genocide they were nice, just like other villagers. But after they joined [the Interahamwe], they changed. They would stand in groups and talk about how they would kill all the Tutsi, how they would locate all the Tutsi and kill them, and I heard them say this when I passed by.

At school, even in early '94, during February and March, things were fine, but when we left the school we heard about the war, the attacks by the RPF, how all Tutsi were enemies, and the threats against Tutsi. In school, we were just studying. [At one point, the interviewer asked if the headmaster of the school was Hutu or Tutsi, thinking that if he or she were Tutsi this may have had a calming effect on the school, and the interviewee stated that his headmaster was Tutsi. Outside [during breaks and recess], though, kids who were Hutu would make comments about the war and how Tutsi were the enemy, but [they did] not [do] so in the class.

On April 7th [1994], in the morning, we heard from our aunt, who was our neighbor, that the president's plane had crashed and he had died. We were very surprised and afraid of what might happen.

My aunt was very afraid, not crying, just very upset, telling us she feared that we'd all, all the Tutsis, would be killed. Personally, I was just surprised to hear that the president had died, but my aunt and mother and others were talking about how the situation would change.

On the radio, too, we heard about how people, Tutsi, were being killed in Kigali. They even started reading off a list of those Tutsi who had to be killed. I heard this, on the radio. They would tell their names and where they lived. We listened to RTLM because they [the radio announcers] would relate what was happening [around the nation].

For three days we remained at home. After three or four days we saw people leaving their homes—lots of people, Tutsis, streams of people—going to Gitarama [the closest large town to their village]. I remember my father joining them and asking them, "Why? Why are you leaving your homes?" and they said, "Because they [the Hutu] began killing Tutsis in villages." In our village, though, the killing had not begun yet.

When my father returned home, he spoke to my mother about what he had learned and how we needed to leave. On about the 11th or 12th [of April], a priest, a white priest, my father knew, told my father that the situation was going bad and that our family ought to leave the village. So, my father and mother discussed how our family should leave the home [so as not to be conspicuous].

That same evening, my father sent me and my brother Faustin to hide at our neighbors—about one kilometer away from our home. My father didn't want anyone to know that we were planning to hide, so he sent me, as he usually did, with a bottle to fetch him beer. We took the bottle and then, instead of purchasing the beer, we stayed out our neighbor's, who was a Hutu, for one week. This man, this Hutu, was my father's friend, and my father believed that since he was his friend we could go there and be safe. We, of course, could not have gone to another Tutsi's home because they, too, were in danger of being attacked and killed.

From that evening through the week we were there we did not hear any news from the family. So, we had no idea what had happened to them, if they had been killed or . . .

At the man's home, we stayed in the house for three days, but then the man feared that those attacking Tutsi homes in the area might come to his house so he had my brother and me hide in the house for the rabbits [the rabbit hutch]. My brother and I were each in different sections of the [rabbit] house so we were separated and we could not talk. I was in, hunched up, with one big rabbit. My brother [as he told me later] slept, but I did not. There was a tiny hole I could look out and I just stared out that hole trying to see what was happening. The people let us out at night so we could wash.

As time went on, things got worse. The chief of the house [the man who owned the house where they were hiding] had been going around to see what he could hear about what was going on, and one day he told us that my father and the family had left our home and were in Gitarama, at Kagbayi Seminary. He had also heard that there was a teacher, a Hutu, who had worked with my father, who was planning to come to his [the chief's] house to look for the children of Bagabo [the interviewee's father] who were staying there. He [the teacher] didn't know for sure, but had heard that we were there. He was not coming to see if we were safe, but to kill us. He [the chief] told us that the next day—which was about the sixth day or the seventh [since being in hiding]—that we would have to leave the next night because the hiding spot was no longer safe.

So, the next night, about midnight, we left the house with the man and his daughter, and we joined his son-in-law who was living about five kilometers away and we stayed at his son-in-law's, all the rest of the night and all the next day. We met no one [while walking] because it was midnight.

The next night, with the man and his son-in-law, we started toward the seminary, walking. We didn't go through [via] the roads, but through the villages [on dirt paths].

On the way to Gitarama, to the seminary, we were arrested [accosted] in a forest near a village, in a place called Kivumu. We were arrested by two Interahamwe. Near the forest was a classroom [a place priests had built as a school for old people in order to teach the elderly how to read and write] where many people had come to hide, but had been attacked in the night and had been killed. There were about fifty to sixty bodies scattered around, on the ground, in the road nearby, and in the forest. It was the first time I had seen dead persons. Some had been killed with machetes as they were trying to escape. I remember seeing a very old man who had been slashed in the head with a machete.

They [the Interahamwe] asked us who we were and where we were going and if we were the men's sons, and they [the men the two boys were with] said, yes, we were their sons. They [the Interahamwe] asked the two men for their identify cards to see if we were Hutu or Tutsi and to see if we [actually] were the men's sons. On the identity cards [at that time], the children's names of adults [parents] were listed. When the two men gave their cards, the son-in-law had a son about the age of my brother and so my brother was safe. But the older man had a daughter and her name was on the card. The older man said that when he went to register my name when I was born the person writing my name got it wrong and put a girl's name. The Interahamwe said, "No, it's not true! We're going to find out from others [other Interahamwe] who you are." The two men said, "No, we told you the truth. We don't lie." But the Interahamwe said, "It's not true! You have to give us money or we will kill all of you!" But the two men we were with didn't have any money. The Interahamwe said, "If you don't give us money, you don't leave this area." Finally, the older man pulled out four hundred Rwandan francs and the other man pulled out 200 Rwandan francs, I think, and gave them to the Interahamwe. But the Interahamwe said, "No, you have more money! Take off your clothes!" So, the two men were forced to take off their clothes. They were forced to take all of their clothes off, everything, and the Interahamwe then checked the clothes, trying to find money. They found another three hundred francs, I think, from the old man only. After finding the money, they gave the men their clothes back and told us to leave the place.

So, we went on, and we arrived at the main road, and from there to the seminary we had no problems along the way. At the seminary we immediately sought out my mother and the other children. As soon as we found my mother, the old man [who had hid him and his brother and guided them to the seminary] began crying. I was surprised by that [that he was so emotional].

My mother and brothers and sisters told us they thought we had been killed. It had been about one week without their having any news of us and at that time people all over the country were being killed. They also told us that our father was hiding inside the seminary.

After some time, the old man and his son-in-law went back home, and we, my brother and I, went inside the seminary. We remained there, with our family, for about two months. We were saved by the RPF [on] 2 June.

Our father was inside a small room inside the seminary. Upon the arrival of my father, my brother Muhima, who was a seminary student there, helped him to find a hiding place. The Hutus used to come into the seminary to take people out and kill them so he, my father, was hiding in the room, an office, so they couldn't find him. My mother, brothers, and sisters stayed in a large room with all the others. At the time [early on], they [the Hutu] were taking out the men and older boys to kill them. Later, they would come and rape the women and girls and then kill the rest.

At the seminary there were more than five hundred people gathered, seeking safety. We slept with our mother and all of the other mothers and their children, and the older boys and men slept in another section of the seminary. Within the room we slept, there were about one hundred people. We ate in the seminary's cafeteria and some students who were seminarians, Tutsi, prepared the food—beans, rice, and maize—and served us. Also, the servants of the priests helped to prepare and serve the food.

At times, the [government's] military came in with their vehicles and they took men, Tutsis, away. We didn't know where they took them, but sometimes we heard [the firing of] bullets. But after the RPF saved us and we were able to leave the seminary—because during the genocide, we never left the seminary because if you did you didn't come back, they [the Hutu] would grab you and kill you—we saw many bodies outside the seminary and we figured that the gunshots we had heard were [caused by] the bullets that killed these many people we saw. Many times people, Hutu, from [surrounding] villages would come to the seminary and urge the military to kill people, Tutsis, from their village. That is the way they, sometimes, decided whom to take each day when they came in to kill people.

The bishop, his name is Nsengiyumva, who owned houses on the seminary grounds told the military and Interahamwe not to destroy his house but take anybody they wanted away. He was Hutu. He could have probably prevented anyone—the military or Interahamwe—from entering the grounds of the seminary, but he didn't.

Just after the RPF arrived, the bishop was killed. I don't know if the RPF killed him or some of the refugees [Tutsi] killed him in revenge.

Sometimes the Interahamwe and military came into the halls where the women and children were and would select girls and even women and take them away—we didn't know where or why—and later the women and girls would come back. Now, I believe they were taken out to be raped. Then, they [the military and Interahamwe] would return and take away men and older boys and kill them.

One evening my father was taken out to be killed. It was about six in the evening and they [the military] were pulling men out of different rooms in the seminary and made them stand outside as they collected men from other rooms. Somehow, I don't know how, my father was able to hide behind a roof of the building, and it was dark so they couldn't see him and they took all of the others and they put them on a bus and took them away and killed them. I even knew some families whose relatives were taken [away that evening and killed].

This [the roundup of men and older boys to kill] happened every single day. Sometimes they would bring a bus and take many people. Every day they [the Interahamwe and/or military] came into check, they said, to make sure there weren't any RPF among us and they would look for any communication devices because they believed we were in communication with the RPF.

One day a man came in and told us—my mother and brothers and sisters—that our father had been taken by the military and put on the bus. My mother began crying and screaming that she was going to go with him because she wanted to die with him. Other women held her back and said, "If your husband is killed, you must stay here and take care of your children." This happened in the morning, but my mother didn't know my father was already back in hiding.

About midday I heard from my mother that my father was alive. I don't know who told her. She went to see him and from that point on he kept hiding, hiding, hiding, always in different places so he would be harder to find. About two days later, we, the children went to see him and he came out of hiding and bought us tea and other things and then went back into hiding. Some refugees from Nyacyonga-Byumba were selling tea and cakes and potatoes and rice and he bought it from them. The food was better than the food we took from the cafeteria. At that time none of us asked about what [had] happened to him. You were just quiet [silent] about such things. He didn't say anything either.

My brother Muhima, the seminarian, we saw sometimes but not often. He would bring us milk and small amounts of good food—rice and meat—to help us get better because we, some of us—two of my brothers and two of my sisters—at that time were suffering from diarrhea. Also, the students at the seminary were often hiding from the military because they were young guys [the seminarians] who could've been taken away and killed at any time.

Outside the seminary many refugees were also gathered. My uncle and aunt—my mother's brother and his wife—were living outside the seminary [grounds] and they were taken away and murdered. We found out about their murders [the day] after the RPF came and saved us. They had been killed about one week before the RPF arrived.

The RPF arrived [at the seminary] in the morning, about seven, of 2 June. The night before, we heard guns shooting and we didn't know what it was. Then that morning the RPF arrived and opened the gates and told the people to leave the seminary. We were very worried though because we didn't know if they were RPF, Interahamwe or. . . . We didn't know if we should trust them or what they would do. So people refused. The RPF said, "Come out. We're here to save you." And gradually, people began to leave the seminary.

People were very, very happy, of course, that the RPF was there and that they [the refugees] could leave the seminary. But for me, I was very sick. I couldn't eat, I couldn't drink, as I was suffering from malaria.

The RPF took us all to Ruhango, in the direction of Butare, and we stayed there for two days and then we left. The RPF had us walk from Ruhango to Kinazi, where we stayed one day, and then we went, again walking, to Busoro, which is in the direction of Nyanza, where we stayed a long time, for two months, as the RPF had absolute control of it and they knew it was safe.

The program [situation] was good as we had enough food and we could go into the village, which was empty of people, and get what we wanted. We stayed in abandoned homes [those of Hutu who had fled out of fear of the RPF and/or to escape punishment for committing the genocide]. My entire family. All except Muhima, who was someplace else. Where, I am not sure. My two grandmothers were also with us.

The difficulty was that many people were ill with diarrhea and other sicknesses, and there was no help as we could not locate medicine. My grandfather, my father's father, died at this place. He had a very serious stomach illness. Before we left the village he had had an operation on the stomach but he was still ill and had been [recuperating] inside [at the time his family decided to flee from their village]. It [the trip from their village to the seminary and from the seminary to Ruhango, Kinazi, and Busoro] was the first time he had walked a long way, and he became ill and died at Busoro. My father's mother was killed in his village during the genocide.

During this time many young men who came to Busoro joined the RPF to help win the war. I didn't as I was only fourteen.

When we returned to the village we discovered that our home had been destroyed. All Tutsi homes all over the country had been destroyed. The entire village had been destroyed and everything had been stolen. Where our house was you couldn't even know [tell] there had been a house [there]. Everything was gone! Everything! No doors, no windows, no roof, nothing! All there was . . . it's like this [points to the grass on the ground at the hotel where we were conducting the interview], just the ground. You couldn't even say a house had been there. You couldn't! All of the houses in the village were destroyed. The Hutus took everything from the destroyed houses: the roofs, windows, fences, even the chairs.

When I was at Busoro I thought when I returned home to our village I would not talk to any of our neighbors, but when we got there our neighbors came up and told us what had happened and then [laughing incredulously] life seemed to go on as before. Some [Tutsi], of course, wanted revenge but the new government said, "There will be no revenge and people will be punished if they try to get revenge."

So, at that time, we found a house Hutus had left behind [as they had fled from Rwanda] and we lived there. We stayed there for about two years. It was big and we stayed there, our entire family. It was close to our house [where it had been before it was destroyed during the genocide].

In '95, the Interahamwe began throwing rocks at homes of Tutsi and even pulling people out at night and slitting their throats. Even our house was stoned in the middle of the night. They would stone it for about an hour and then leave. But then they would return in a week and do the same thing again. I don't know how many times they did this, but it was many times.

My mother, who is an Adventist [Seventh-Day Adventist] would pray really loudly, pray for safety for us and pray for them to stop their actions. [Interviewee laughs.]

No one could go out to stop them because they would kill you. They were throwing big rocks and also had machetes.

Then, the family who had left the house and fled to the Congo came back. They moved into another of their houses right next door to us. So we lived beside one another as neighbors for about six months.

But then it became more insecure in the village because the Interahamwe carried out a big attack. [During the attack] we all yelled trying to prevent them from breaking into our house and killing us. That is what we feared. All of this was happening after they had done all the killing, stolen or destroyed everything we owned [during the course of the genocide], and we didn't send them to prison or seek revenge and here they were doing this to us. So, we moved to Gitarama and lived there for two years. We moved there because there was no security in the village and we were afraid we would be killed if we stayed there. In town [Gitarama], we believed we would be safe because there were police and the military there who provided security.

[During the big attack] the Interahamwe wanted to burn the commune office because near the office, prisoners were held [Hutu suspected of having killed during the genocide]. So, they wanted to attack the commune office, burn it down, and free the prisoners. Before they could attack the commune building the RPF fought them off. It was a big battle. Many soldiers were hurt and killed and many Interahamwe were hurt and killed, too. The villagers, though, had all fled in fear and so they were not hurt or killed.

About three or four days after the battle, we, our family, moved from the Hutu's house to Gitarama. My younger brother and sister went to primary school in Gisarme, I went to secondary school [boarding school] in Butare, and my father continued to work at the school in the village. He continued as headmaster and traveled back and forth on moto [as a passenger on one of the scores of motorcycles that serve as a taxi-like service], hiking down and back up the long hill to the school each day and then returning to Gitarama in the evening.

As I said, my grandfather—my mother's father—was killed during the genocide. He was killed by his neighbors after the rest of the family had fled to Kagbayi. My grandfather was an old man and he was ill and could not walk so he had remained in the village. One of his sons stayed with him and the neighbors killed both of them.

When my grandmother returned to the village she already knew that my grandfather and uncle had been killed and. . . . She asked the neighbors who killed them, where they had put the bodies and they told her. The killers had dug a small hole and put my grandfather in it, and my uncle, too. The neighbors who had killed my grandfather and uncle showed her where the bodies were and helped dig them up. They had to because the authorities told them they had to do so. Then my grandmother had a ceremony to bury my grandfather and uncle and invited all of the family. They buried them at her home [about twenty-five to twenty meters away] and they planted flowers and a cross.

But there were other uncles whose bodies could not be found—three uncles from my father's side and one from my mother's—as we did not know exactly where they were killed. Also, my father's one sister who lived near Kigali was killed with her son. She and her son were killed in a church in Iruhuha, and their bodies were not found because the church was destroyed by the military and Interahamwe. They [the killers] came with grenades and guns and also rammed the church with a big tree trunk and their weapons.

If the genocide had not happened I would have a very different life. As I told you, our family lost many uncles, aunts, and cousins and we have many orphans in the family. And so, if I have a job [he works as an information technology specialist] I must be responsible for helping many in my family. I cannot just remain here [Cyangugu] and work at my job and enjoy my life and make plans for my life, but I must help many.

After the killing ended, we believed that the trouble would end, but it hasn't. After the genocide, the threats continued and, in some cases, the killing. And so I wonder, "Why?" and as a result, I keep thinking about the genocide, all the deaths, and why it is continuing [the genocide ideology and the threats] today.

The sister of my grandmother on my father's side was hacked in the top of the head with a machete and she lived, but she suffered terribly up to the day she died in about 2004. She suffered every single day from the pain for the entire ten years she lived after the genocide. She couldn't do anything because she did not have the force [energy]. She could not work; much of the time she was at home. She could talk to you, but that was about all. Doctors could do nothing for her because it was a head injury and . . .

Now, I cannot see my grandparents and uncles and aunts. When we were young we were happy to see them and be with them. Here in Africa, and particularly Rwanda, our life is based around the family. For holidays, we used to get together and all be together and it was so nice [tearing up]. And so, as I told you, one of my grandfathers was murdered during the genocide, and the other, who I helped to herd cows when I was young and who helped me understand life, died in the refugee camp.

In 1998, my aunt, the sister of my mother, was also forced from her village, Tambwe, and her house because of threats from neighbors. They would, for example, pound on her door in the middle of the night and threaten her and scare her. The night they made her leave her village for a year [was when] her neighbors pounded on her door, and push[ed] it open. She walked outside holding up her hands, and asked them to forgive her. When you are being threatened with being killed, you . . . you . . . you do anything you can to prevent it so she thought if she asked them to forgive her [for the anger she caused them] they might go and leave her alone. They rushed into her house and gathered up all of her clothes—and those of her children—and burned them and left. She had three children—one son and two daughters—but her husband had been murdered during the genocide.

Also, from 2000 to 2008, at least once a month someone has come to my family's house at night and disturbed it [by knocking on the door, making noises, throwing rocks, and then running way], and the problem is, one time they [those who are harassing the family] could enter and . . . [the interviewee did not complete his statement]. So, my parents and brothers and sisters feel unsafe, and ask, "Why are they [those who harass them] coming to the house like that?"

My parents even got a document [letter] warning my father to take care [be careful] about what he told our sector authorities about those who had attacked our family during the genocide. The letter threatened him, saying if he gave any more information that he would be punished, severely. My parents found the letter out on the path in front of our house. My father took the paper to the police. Nothing happened [as a result of the report to the police] because they did not know who did such a thing [wrote the letter]. But the police said that if our family was threatened or attacked again to come and report it, and they [the police] would come to the village and try to help make it more secure.

The disturbances at the house in the village continued for years and my whole family was feeling very unsafe so two months ago [February 2008] all of my younger brothers and sisters moved to the Northern Province to live with our sister to try to see if they could live and feel safe. My parents have remained in the village because of the house, our cow, land, and possessions, but we are trying to arrange for them to move to the Northern Province, too. But we need to find someone who will take care of the house, cow, and land for us. [Interviewer's note: Ultimately, the interviewee's mother moved to the Northern Province in early 2009 in order to escape the harassment, and in late 2009, the interviewee's father finally gave up and moved there as well.]

I have always been a very deep sleeper, but after the genocide my mother told me, "You must sleep with one ear listening for trouble." One morning my mother asked me if I had heard the stones being thrown at the house and I said, "No." She said, "That is not good! You must sleep less deeply and listen if anyone is approaching so you can be ready, prepared."

After the genocide, you can have no hope. I cannot know if my future is for a long time ... or not. The killing continued after genocide, the threats, the fear, and so I do not know [what life holds]. Yes, of course, I want to get married and have a wife and children, but I also worry about whether the killers can come, will come, and kill my relatives, my parents, brothers, sisters, uncles, aunts, or even my wife and children. It is not possible to know that that won't happen. So yes, I completed my university studies and have a job now, but it's ... I don't know if the killing will start again and ... No. I do not sit curled up saying, "I can't study or work" but there's ... worries of what might happen.

From 1994 to '99 Tutsis were killed every single day and it was very, very bad. From 2000 to now [April 27, 2008] it is much better, but some killing still goes on.

I get nervous and feel unsafe when I hear on the radio that they—sometimes they are Hutu neighbors, or former prisoners—have killed Tutsis, because then I think it can happen to my village, or even [to] me, at any time.

So, yes, I have a job today but I could wake up in the morning and hear about survivors who have been killed [during the commemoration period of 2008, in April, some survivors were killed by their Hutu neighbors], and so I think why can't this happen to me as well, because I, too, am a survivor.

In general, I like how Rwanda feels today—how you can go out and travel around Rwanda [freely and, largely, safely] but people, Tutsi, still are being killed [by the extremists] and that makes me not feel safe, sometimes.

After the genocide it was like starting life from zero. You've lost just about everything. Grandparents, uncles, aunts, your cows, everything at home. Everything! It's like starting life all over again, at zero.

Both my younger sister and my cousin, who lost his two brothers, suffer [ongoing] trauma, feeling sad, not wanting to talk to anyone, and having difficulty in life. Even at home she [his sister] is very quiet, and sometimes angry. My mother says, "Every day you are angry!" My sister won't say anything, she just stays like that. Even when we ask her, "What is wrong? What is the matter?" she replies, "No, I'm not [angry]. Nothing is wrong!" But it's obvious that something is, but she will not say, not talk about it, even refuses to talk.

Survivors continue to live in difficulty—as I said, they've lost everything—members of their families, everything from their houses, even their houses. Up to now some survivors still do not have homes, but the government is working as fast as it can to build homes for those who are without.

I think it would be good to help survivors start small businesses, [but I do not think] that it is good to give them money. If you give some money, they just go out and spend it here and there and it's gone, but if you train somebody and they start a business, then they can generate money.

I have been many times to gacaca—once in my village, and many times in Gitarama and Butare. For the country, overall, it is good, but the gacaca itself, when they [the alleged killers] are in front of it, they don't want to tell what they did, but they tell [testify] because it is an order. As someone who has attended gacaca it is my belief that they [the alleged génocidaires] do not tell the truth—not the whole truth. They change parts and they leave parts out.

In gacaca, the génocidaires are supposed to ask for forgiveness but, again, when they do it, many do it because it is an order [not an order, but required if they hope to have their sentences cut in half]. There are even those who ask for forgiveness and then when they get out of prison they go back to their villages and commit the same crimes; they kill, so how can they say that their asking for forgiveness was genuine?

There are some cases where gacaca has helped to reconcilate [sic] people, but for instance, out of five hundred who committed crimes, maybe one hundred out of the five hundred who ask forgiveness return to the village and there is reconciliation with the survivors. But the other four hundred who ask for forgiveness return to the village and there is nothing [no reconciliation]. They keep in their mind their willingness to kill. Many go back to the village and they mistreat the survivors, threaten them, and even kill survivors.

And justice! Some people who killed continue to live in the village [where they did the killing], but have not been brought to justice. Others in the village make excuses for them, saying these persons did not kill, but they did! So, what is needed is a way for the government to find out the truth and then . . . [hold the perpetrators accountable].

I think the government has helped to support survivors. The young survivors are in school, and this is of most importance to me.

One of the most rewarding aspects of my life was when my name was published in the newspaper that I would go to the university [meaning, he had scored well on the national examinations and thus would earn a scholarship]. In our country very few students go on to university, and I was one of the few to be accepted.

After the genocide, the government funded health care for survivors, but now [in 2008] it is not going well. The fund for survivors [FARG] says that it is paying a lot of money for students to study, and [thus it] doesn't have enough funds to pay for health care as well. I don't know [if that is true], but that is what I hear. The funds for health care are still available but not as good [plentiful or forthcoming] as before. Before, FARG would give you a card and you could go to the hospital and everything was cared for [all the costs were covered], but now, this began in around 2006, some hospitals won't even take the card.

I am happy I finished university studies and that I found a job because before I was worried about the family and how it can live. I used to think, "What can I do to help my family?" My family is large—nine members [in the immediate family], [plus] my cousins who are orphans and my aunts who have no husbands. And so, with my university education, I gave my family hope—only three persons out of our entire village went to university—that the future will be better because I can get a job. And while I cannot help everybody, even if I can help only a small extent it is good.

Today, I'm in between happy and sad, because life before [the genocide] is different from [life] today. During genocide it was the first time to see someone who had been murdered, and that scared me. Before, I didn't think my parents could die; I didn't think about that. Or [the murder of] my relatives. Before, I didn't think our friends or our neighbors could betray us, do bad things to us. I thought we had neighbors who were our friends, yeah? I've seen many things. I saw killings, we lost many things, our house was destroyed. Even though my parents and brothers and sisters were not killed, my relatives were murdered and this can [when he thinks about it or memories of the genocide are relived] make me sad.

At other times life continues; for instance, I'm here in Cyangugu and I am with people here in Cyangugu and we can share life, share a drink, meet friends from the university, meet friends from here. This is the life now. And at such times, I can be happy.

I can say that if my neighbors came and apologized and said, "I am sorry for having done this and this to you and your family," I think I could accept that and forgive. But many do not admit what they did. You can tell them what they did and they will say, "No, I didn't do that. I was at home."

Before 1994, I was, we were, Catholic, and I went to church. Today, I still believe in God, but I do not go to church, especially the Catholic Church.

I saw and I heard so many bad things about the Catholic Church. When we were at Kagbayi Seminary there were so many priests and nuns and they didn't do anything to save us. So many people were dying there, and they didn't even negotiate with the Interahamwe—[attempt] to give them money. They could do [have done] that! But they didn't even try. And I heard about priests who participated in [the] killing. And [I even heard] that they [the priests] raped, too, raped girls and women.

What happened in our country, it happened. People use to say, "Never again," and now I think the nations of the world have to truly make sure it [genocide] never happens again.

I also think the nations of the world should help survivors. There are different ways to help—to help them improve their health, to help them overcome the problems caused [by the genocide], and to help judge those who are living free but killed during the genocide—like the priest, Wenceslas Munyeshyaka, who is living free in France. I know they cannot get people to forget what they lived through, but [they can help to] reduce their problems.

AFTERWORD

It is vital for survivors of genocide to tell their stories. This is as true for survivors of the 1994 Rwandan genocide as it is for survivors of the Khmer Rouge-perpetrated genocide of their fellow Cambodians (1975–1979), the Holocaust (1933–1945) or the Ottoman Turk genocide of the Armenians (1915–1919).

Talking about what happened to themselves and their loved ones during genocide help many survivors feel less alone in the world. For many, it is comforting when others take the time to truly listen to what they experienced and continue to deal with in the aftermath of the mass killing. When they are listened, and responded, to with genuine care it encourages them to try to trust humanity again (and this is not easy to do when one recognizes the fact that most of the world stood by silently as they [the survivors] and the members of their group were targeted for annihilation). Ultimately, to share their stories and have them read by others all across the globe constitutes, in an odd way, an affirmation of life, in that it provides survivors with a sense that others care about their fate. In that regard, at least some survivors may begin to feel that they no longer reside in a world filled with apathy and indifference.

To paraphrase one interviewee in this book, in the aftermath of genocide, life must be reinvented. The accounts in this book certainly attest to that. It is not, of course, easy. And, in fact, for many survivors life itself, bereft of loved ones and marred by memories of the horror they lived through, is harrowing. But people are, if anything, resilient, and the survivors of the Rwandan genocide are certainly that. That doesn't mean they are happy all the time, or even most of the time. It doesn't mean they don't carry their sadness with them like a heavy weight. What it does mean is that they have gotten on with their lives: returned to school, married, had babies, returned to work, and, try as they rebuild their lives, to contribute to rebuilding their country in the hope that genocide will be avoided in the future.

However deeply sad and depressing it is to read the stories included in *We Cannot Forget*, these accounts are bound to be useful to students, teachers, and researchers across the globe. These stories help one to appreciate the diverse set of circumstances individuals and families faced prior to and during the genocide as well as what they now face in the post-genocide period. Among some of the many unique aspects about the genocide in Rwanda highlighted in the accounts herein are as follows: how Tutsis were demonized prior to the genocide; the use of radio to issue propaganda against the Tutsi and to encourage Hutu involvement in the genocide; how victims were killed by their neighbors and, in some cases, by their very own relatives; how, after the genocide, survivors have had to cohabitate with perpetrators and their families; and how the new government continues to wrestle with bringing the survivors and former perpetrators back together in a way that minimizes conflict and in the hope that reconciliation will win out—and what survivors think of such efforts.

We sincerely hope that the accounts in this book will stimulate deep thought and thoughtful discussions on university campuses and other platforms of learning across the globe, with an eye toward opening new ways of examining the past and the present so as to confront and effectively deal with potential seeds of genocide. We also hope that it prods readers to contemplate what is needed to assist survivors in the aftermath of genocide so that they regain a modicum of stability in their own lives—not only so they can lead fruitful and satisfying lives but also contribute in their own ways to constructing a healthy and just post-genocide society.

Neither relating nor reading these stories will reverse the course of events that led to the perpetration of the Rwandan genocide. It will not bring back those who were brutally murdered. It should, however, force us all to think about what it means to be a bystander when crimes against humanity are being perpetrated and/or a situation is slouching toward genocide. It should help us all to consider the sagacity of the words and thoughts inherent in the dictum "Do unto others as you would have them do unto you" and what it means to be, or to fail to be, our brothers' and sisters' keepers, particularly for those who face dire straits and need, in the most desperate of ways, a helping hand.

GLOSSARY

Akazu: The Akazu (which means "little house" in Kinyarwanda) was a close-knit and radical extremist circle within a larger network that supported Rwandan president Juvénal Habyarimana. It held immense power within Rwanda. The president's wife, Madame Habyarimana, and her relatives maintained iron-fisted control of Akazu.

Arusha Accords: A set of five agreements signed by the Hutu-dominated government of Rwanda and the Rwandan Patriotic Front (RPF) in Arusha, Tanzania, on August 4, 1993. The talks leading to Arusha were cosponsored by the United States, France, and the Organization of African Unity, and addressed a wide range of issues: refugee resettlement, power sharing between the Hutu and Tutsi, the introduction of an all-embracing democratic regime, the dismantling of the military dictatorship of President Juvénal Habyarimana (1937–1994), and the encouragement of a transparent rule of law throughout Rwanda. In the months that followed the signing of the accords, numerous negotiations were set in motion. The negotiation meetings required the various actors to travel extensively, sometimes by road and at other times by plane. It was after one of these meetings, on April 6, 1994, that the jet carrying Habyarimana and the president of Burundi, Cyprien Ntaryamira, was shot down by a missile fired on the outskirts of the Kigali airport. All on board were killed, triggering the genocide of Rwanda's Tutsi population and the murder of moderate Hutu over the next one hundred days. To this day it is not known who shot the plane down. Among those suspected of doing so are: the extremist Hutu, the RPF, and the French government. Each entity categorically denies responsibility and has accused one or the other groups.

AVEGA: Association des veuves du genocide, or Association of Genocide Widows, was founded in 1995 by a group of fifty Kigali women widowed as a result of the 1994 Rwandan genocide. It is estimated that there are approximately twenty-five thousand members. AVEGA focuses on health and social problems faced by widows of the genocide. It also offers limited financial assistance to its members.

bourgmestre: The administrative leader of a commune. Basically, the equivalent of a mayor of a town.

CDR: Coalition pour la défense de la république, or the Coalition for the Defense of the Republic, was the hard-line Hutu nationalist political party; virulently anti-Tutsi, it periodically collaborated with MRND.

cellule: Prior to 1994, a cellule (or cell) constituted the smallest administrative unit in Rwanda. A committee of members oversaw and administered each cellule. The individual who led the committee was referred to as a *responsable*.

commune: An administrative unit, equivalent to a town.

councilor: The administrator, or leader, of a sector.

double genocides: *See* two genocides.

FAR: Forces armées rwandaises, or Rwandan Armed Forces, the Rwandan government army under the Habyarimana regime.

FARG: Created in 1999, FARG (Fonds national pour l'assistance aux rescapés du génocide, or Victims of Genocide Fund) is primarily financed by the Rwandan government and is responsible for providing homes, health care, and schooling for the impoverished survivors of the 1994 Rwandan genocide.

FRW: Francs rwandais, or Rwandan francs, the Rwandan currency.

gacaca: An indigenous form of local justice used in precolonial Rwanda that was adapted in the late 1990s and implemented in the early 2000s to try alleged perpetrators of the 1994 Rwandan genocide. The term *gacaca* (pronounced ga-cha-cha) is derived from the Kinyarwanda word meaning "grass"; over time, gacaca came to mean "justice on the grass" due to the fact that during the precolonial period gacacas took place out in the open, on hillsides, under trees on grass.

Contemporary gacaca sessions tried the vast majority of the génocidaires, with the exception of the planners and leaders who were tried either by the International Criminal Tribunal for Rwanda (ICTR) or in national Rwandan courts. Among the more notable goals of the new gacaca system were as follows: to provide a means for the victims to tell their stories, to allow the victims to discover how and where their family members and friends had been killed and/or were buried, to allow perpetrators to confess and ask for forgiveness, to convict and imprison those génocidaires who were found guilty and did not confess or ask for forgiveness, and to help bring about reconciliation of the nation's peoples (perpetrators and victims/survivors alike).

génocidaire (French): Participant in the 1994 Rwandan genocide.

Habyarimana, Juvénal (1937–1994): President of Rwanda from 1973 until his assassination on April 6, 1994. On April 6, 1994, while returning to Kigali, the capital of Rwanda, from one of the negotiation rounds of the Arusha Accords, President Habyarimana's plane, carrying Habyarimana as well as Burundian president Cyprien Ntaryamira (1955–1994), was shot down by two missiles fired from just outside the perimeter of the Kigali airport. All on board the Falcon 50 jet were killed. The shooting down of the plane triggered the killing that ultimately resulted in the hundred-day genocide of Tutsi and moderate Hutu by extremist Hutu and others.

Controversy continues to swirl around who might have been behind the shooting down of the plane. Some assert that extremist Hutu blew the jet out of the sky. The Hutu, it is argued, were angry with Habyarimana for capitulating to the Rwandan Patriotic Front as they (Habyarimana and the RPF) carried out plans, under the auspices of the Arusha Accords, to implement a peace agreement that revolved around the shared governance of Rwanda. There are others, such as scholar René Lemarchand, who argue that the RPF downed the jet. Still others, such as British journalist and author Linda Melvern, claim that French government personnel shot down the plane.

Hutu: Majority ethnic group (about 85 percent) in Rwanda prior to the 1994 genocide.

Hutu Power: A movement that promoted Hutu exclusivity. Alison Des Forges (1999) asserts that "The movement known as Hutu Power (pronounced Pawa in Kinyarwanda), the coalition that would make the genocide possible, was built upon the corpse of [Burundi president Melchior] Ndadaye. The doubts about RPF [the Rwandan Patriotic Front, the political movement of the Tutsi in exile] intentions, sown by the February 1993 attack and fed by the extent of RPF gains at Arusha, ripened following the assassination [of Ndadaye] in Burundi. As one political leader commented during the genocide, 'Who didn't have his eyes opened by what happened in Burundi . . . [where they] elected President Ndadaye [a moderate Hutu], who really wanted Hutu and Tutsi to live together, but you know what they did [to him] . . . ?'

"First announced at a meeting in Gitarama, Hutu Power drew widespread support at a rally in Kigali on October 23, 1993, where adherents met to deplore Ndadaye's assassination and to draw lessons from it. . . . The second vice-president of the MDR [Democratic Republican Movement, an integral part of the Parmehutu, the party that headed up the revolution of 1959 and dispelled the Tutsi aristocracy], Froduald Karamira, took to the podium to declare that the RPF, including specifically its leader General Kagame, were among the plotters who had killed Ndadaye. Asserting that Kagame was depriving the people of Burundi of democracy, Karamira went on to say he would do the same thing in Rwanda because 'he lied to us in Arusha when they were signing for peace and democracy. . . . ' Karamira called for all Hutu in Rwanda to stand up and take 'appropriate action' which he said does not mean 'uttering words just to "heat heads" but rather unifying into one effective Hutu mass'" (137–138).

Hutu Revolution: 1959 saw the creation of the Hutu movement (MDR Parmehutu), which was duly influenced by the publication of the Bahutu Manifesto in 1957 that called for the abolition of the rule of the Tutsi king by the Hutu majority. The winds of change led to the so-called Hutu Revolution in 1959.

A series of incidents instigated violence. First, King Mutara III Rudahigwa died under mysterious circumstances in Bujumbura, which lead the Tutsi elite to believe that he was assassinated by the Belgians, who had begun to establish close ties with Hutu elites. In November 1959, a MDR-Parmehutu Hutu leader, Dominique Mbonyumutwa, was believed to have been attacked by a young Tutsi in the village of Byimana in Gitarama, and this sparked killings of Tutsi on every hill in the country. Thousands of Tutsi were killed and many others fled into exile. Those who remained in Rwanda lived in a constant state of fear as both the Hutu regimes of Kayibanda and Habyarimana regarded the Tutsi as foreigners and/or second-class citizens.

Hutu Ten Commandments: A list of admonitions that were to be adhered to by every Hutu in order to destroy Tutsi influence over Rwandan society and guarantee Hutu hegemony. Published by Hassan Ngeze (b. 1961) in issue number 6 of the extremist Hutu screed *Kangura*, in December 1990, the "Ten Commandments of the Hutu" were written by Hutu extremists. The Hutu Ten Commandments were as follows:

1. Every Hutu male should know that Tutsi women, wherever they may be, work for the interest of their Tutsi ethnic group. As a result, a Hutu who marries a Tutsi woman, befriends a Tutsi woman, or employs a Tutsi woman as a secretary or concubine shall be considered a traitor;
2. Every Hutu should know that our daughters are more suitable and conscientious in their role as woman, wife, and mother. Are they not beautiful, good secretaries, and more honest?;
3. Hutu women, be vigilant and try to bring your husbands, brothers, and sons back to reason;
4. Every Hutu should know that all Tutsi are dishonest in their business dealings. They are only seeking the supremacy of their own ethnic group. Any Hutu who engages in business dealings or partnerships with the Tutsi is a traitor;
5. All strategic positions—political, administrative, economic, military, and security—should be entrusted to the Hutu;
6. The education sector should be majority Hutu;
7. The Rwandan armed forces must be exclusively Hutu.
8. The Hutu should stop having mercy on the Tutsi;
9. Hutu, wherever they may be, must have unity and solidarity and be concerned about the fate of their Hutu brothers;
10. The 1959 revolution, the 1961 revolution, and the Hutu ideology must be taught to Hutu at all levels. Every Hutu must spread this ideology widely. Any Hutu who persecutes his brother Hutu for having read, spread, and taught this ideology is a traitor.

Ibuka: An umbrella organization for all of the survivor organizations in Rwanda. The various organizations represent survivors at the national and international levels. Ibuka, a Kinyarwanda term, means "remember." Ibuka was established in 1995 in order to address a host of issues (ranging from justice and memory to social and economic problems) faced by survivors of the 1994 Rwandan genocide.

identification cards: Prior to 1994, every Rwandan citizen was required, by law, to carry identification cards, which stated their ethnic affiliation (Hutu, Tutsi, Twa). During the 1994 genocide, those Hutu breaking into homes, accosting strangers on paths and at roadblocks frequently demanded to see an individual's identification card. In many cases, if the card identified the accosted individual as a Tutsi, or the accosted individual claimed to have lost his/her card, the result was death.

The current Rwandan government, under President Paul Kagame, banned all Rwandans from considering and referring to themselves as Tutsi, Hutu, or Twa; rather, in order to encourage a focus on citizenship over ethnicity, all citizens are instructed to consider themselves Rwandans and only Rwandans. In private, many continue to differentiate between Hutu and Tutsi (particularly in regard to both the pre-genocide and genocide periods), but in public most are careful not to use the banned terms.

impiri: A club; traditionally made of wood and used to defend oneself, especially during nighttime. In 1994, there emerged a type of impiri with nails in its round, bumpy head. These nails expedited the killings, as the nails created deep wounds.

inkotanyi: Members of the Rwandan Patriotic Front (RPF), a term that harkens back to the powerful and significant armies of nineteenth-century Rwanda. A common translation is "fierce warrior."

Interahamwe: MRND youth militia ("Those who stand together" or "Those Who Attack Together"). Beginning in early 1992, Rwandan president Habyarimana's government provided military training for the young members (largely teenagers) of his party. Such youth served as a vicious militia for the Hutu-dominated government, carrying out much of its dirty work. More often than not, the roadblocks established in Rwanda prior to and during the genocide, where many Tutsi were caught and slain, were manned by Interahamwe.

ICTR: International Criminal Tribunal for Rwanda. The ICTR tried those persons suspected of planning and/or directing the 1994 Rwandan genocide and/or conducting other major violations of international humanitarian law committed in the territory of Rwanda between January 1, 1994, and December 31, 1994.

inyenzi: A Kinyarwanda term that, literally, means "cockroaches." It was a derogatory term used by extremist Hutu to refer to the Rwandan Patriotic Front (RPF) and, ultimately, all Tutsi.

Kangura: An anti-Tutsi periodical published in Rwanda prior to the 1994 genocide. Its first issue appeared in May 1990, and its last in February 1994, just two months prior to the outbreak of genocide. *Kangura*, which means "Wake them up" in Kinyarwanda, served as a means of propaganda to disparage the Tutsi and inflame the Hutu population against them. *Kangura* was published by Hassan Ngeze, a Muslim of Hutu ethnicity, who was later prosecuted by the International Criminal Tribunal for Rwanda (ICTR) and convicted for facilitating genocide.

The most infamous piece published in *Kangura* was the Hutu "Ten Commandments," a set of inflammatory anti-Tutsi principles that every Hutu was admonished to follow. Their repeated appearance in the pages of *Kangura* served as a major means of stirring up Hutu hatred against the Tutsi.

Kangura constantly published material that referred to Tutsi as inyenzi (cockroaches) and drove home the message that inyenzi (including those from the outside, the inkotanyi, or rebels, from the Rwandan Patriotic Front) were about to enslave all the Hutu or exterminate them. To avoid the latter, it goaded its Hutu readers to preempt the Tutsi onslaught, protect themselves, and wipe out the Tutsi attackers. *Kangura* also published the names of those Hutu who were purportedly willing to live on equal and friendly terms with the Tutsi, suggesting that they were dangerous and merited the same treatment as the Tutsi.

massue. *See* impiri.

MDR: Mouvement démocratique républicain, or Democratic Republican Movement. The MDR led the revolution of 1959 and unseated the Tutsi aristocracy. It constituted the largest domestic opposition political party in Rwanda, with its largest contingency of backers residing in central, southern, and southwestern Rwanda.

MRND: Mouvement républicain national pour la démocratie et le développement, or National Republican Movement for Democracy and

Development. Founded and led by Juvénal Habyarimana, MRND constituted Rwanda's ruling party. Its strongest following resided in the north
and northwest.

Murambi: The site of a large-scale massacre of Tutsi during the genocide.
Estimates of the number killed there range between twenty and seventy
thousand. In 1999, Des Forges asserted that "Estimates of persons killed at
any one site are widely off, often by a factor of ten or more, perhaps because
most have been made by untrained observers" (16).

panga: a traditional large cleaverlike cutting tool used in Rwanda. It looks
like the modern machete.

People of Integrity: The common term for the panel of individuals who
served as gacaca judges. Judges were chosen based on their honesty by their
fellow community members. By law, the judges were not to take part in cases
involving their relatives, friends, or enemies. The judges collected information on the cases, heard the cases, and issued final judgments. The People of
Integrity were not university-educated lawyers, and the training they received
was extremely minimal.

PL: Parti libéral, or Liberal Party. PL was an opposition political party
that was largely supported by Tutsi residing in Rwanda prior to the 1994
genocide.

préfet: The leader of a prefecture, the equivalent of a governor of a province
in today's Rwanda.

Presidential Guard: The fifteen hundred Presidential Guard served as an
elite force recruited almost exclusively from northwestern Rwanda, President
Juvénal Habyarimana's birthplace. They were instrumental in carrying out
the 1994 Rwandan genocide.

PSD: Parti social démocrate, or Social Democratic Party. An opposition
political party whose base of support was largely in southern Rwanda.

Radio Muhabura: "Soon after the start of the war, the RPF [Rwandan
Patriotic Front] established its own station, Radio Muhabura, but its signal
did not reach throughout the country. At first, many Rwandans were afraid

to listen to it, but its audience grew steadily during 1992 and 1993. Although it glorified the RPF, it did so in a nationalist rather than an ethnic context, consistent with the general RPF emphasis on minimizing differences between Hutu and Tutsi" (Des Forges 1999, 68).

Radio Rwanda: The national radio station during the Habyarimana years. It generally toed the party line, but in the pre-genocide period, particularly in 1993, its reporters began reporting more accurately what was taking place in society, due to a change in the directorship. More specifically, "Following the establishment of the coalition government in April 1992, the MDR, PL, and PSD insisted on a new direction for Radio Rwanda. Ferdinand Nahimana, a stalwart supporter of the MRND, was removed from his post at the Rwandan Office of Information (ORINFOR), where he had supervised Radio Rwanda. Several months later, Jean-Marie Vianney Higiro, a member of one of the parties opposed to Habyarimana, was named director to steer the radio towards a more nonpartisan stance. By December 1993, Radio Rwanda had agreed to include the RPF [Rwandan Patriotic Front] among the political parties participating in its broadcasts, although the decision had not been implemented by the time the genocide began" (Des Forges 1999, 68). By December 1993, Hutu extremists considered Radio Rwanda far too liberal. In this regard, Prunier (1997) reports that "the CDR extremists had felt ill-at-ease with the gradual slide of Radio Rwanda into liberalism. They felt that the national radio journalists were opportunists who were betraying 'the Cause' and toadying to the opposition" (189).

RPA: Rwandan Patriotic Army, the military wing of the Rwandan Patriotic Front (RPF).

RPF: Rwandan (also Rwandese) Patriotic Front, an armed force/movement initially composed of Rwandans living in exile. It served as the political arm of the anti-Habyarimana guerrilla force. It attacked Rwanda in 1990, thus igniting a civil war. The RPF is credited with bringing the genocide to an end in Rwanda in July 1994.

RTLM: Radio-télévision libre des mille collines. Co-owned by members of the Akazu and colleagues/friends of President Habyarimana, it broadcast scurrilous messages about the Tutsi, urging Hutu all across the country to take part in the "work" or the killing of the Tutsi. It often informed génocidaires when and where to attack Tutsi during the genocide, in certain cases providing actual addresses.

sector: An administrative unit smaller than a commune but larger than a cellule.

Ten Commandments of the Hutu. *See* Hutu Ten Commandments.

TIG (pronounced *teege*): Travaux d'intérêt général, or Work of General Interest. TIG is an alternative punishment program for people who confessed to and sought forgiveness for their role in the 1994 genocide. TIG ranges from the construction of houses for survivors and other people without shelter to fighting against soil erosion and cutting stones for paving roads. It is a program whereby former génocidaires work for the public good by undertaking supervised work designated by the government. The three key goals of TIG are fighting impunity, promoting unity and reconciliation, and contributing to the nation's sustainable development.

Tutsi: Minority ethnic group (about 14 percent) in Rwanda prior to the 1994 Rwandan genocide.

Twa: The original inhabitants of Rwanda, the Twa are a Pygmy people who currently comprise approximately 1 percent of the Rwandan population.

two or double genocides: Some individuals and groups assert that in addition to the Hutu-perpetrated genocide, the RPF committed genocide prior to and during the early 1990s. While it has been established that some RPF soldiers did carry out massacres (a select few have been tried in Rwanda for such massacres and been found guilty, but many more alleged perpetrators have not been held accountable according to various sources, including reputable international human rights organizations), there is no evidence that the RPF committed genocide. In regard to RPF-perpetrated massacres, Lt. Gen. Romeo Dallaire (2005), who served as commander of the UN force in Rwanda prior to and during the 1994 genocide, reports the following in his book, *Shake Hands with the Devil: The Failure of Humanity in Rwanda*: "Reports of massacres of Hutus who were former government agents and employees, along with their families, continued to come in. The massacres were mainly conducted in the areas of Byuma and Ngarama. . . . To make matters [worse,] the RPF had put heavy restrictions on where our UNMOs

[United Nations Military Observers] could go. The last line of [a field] report read, 'It has been established that the restrictions imposed on us are done to conceal their [RPF] activities, especially massacres'" (378).

ubuhiri: *See* impiri.

umuganda: Community work as a collective activity accomplished by members of a village in Rwanda for the public interest. Such activities range from cleaning up the neighborhood and streets, upgrading (through fixing, painting, or cleaning) a local neighborhood, and building common buildings.

UN: United Nations.

UNAMIR: United Nations Assistance Mission for Rwanda, the peacekeeping force established under the Arusha Accords. Undermanned and under-resourced, UN headquarters and the UN Security Council prevented it from doing all it could to avert, and then halt, the 1994 Rwandan genocide.

UNHCR: Office of the UN High Commissioner for Refugees.

"work": During the genocide, Radio-télévision libre des mille collines (RTLM) regularly issued broadcasts cajoling Hutus to engage in "work" hunting down and killing Tutsi across the country. The word "work" came to be widely understood as the synonym and euphemism for "killing" during the genocide.

BIBLIOGRAPHY

Dallaire, R., with B. Beardsley. 2005. *Shake Hands with the Devil: The Failure of Humanity in Rwanda.* New York: Da Capo.

Des Forges, A. 1999. *Leave None to Tell the Story: Genocide in Rwanda.* New York: Human Rights Watch.

Hatzfeld, J. 2005. *Into the Quick of Life: The Rwandan Genocide: The Survivors Speak.* London: Serpent's Tail.

Hatzfeld, J. 2005. *A Time for Machetes: The Rwandan Genocide: The Killers Speak.* London: Serpent's Tail.

Kroslak, D. 2008. *The French Betrayal of Rwanda.* Bloomington: Indiana University Press.

Melvern, L. 2004. *Conspiracy to Murder: The Rwandan Genocide.* London: Verso.

Newbury, C. 1988. *The Cohesion of Oppression: Clientship and Ethnicity in Rwanda, 1860–1960.* New York: Columbia University Press.

Prunier, G. 1997. *The Rwandan Crisis: History of a Genocide.* New York: Columbia University Press.

Reyntjens, F. 1996. "Rwanda: Genocide and Beyond." *Journal of Refugee Studies* 9 (3): 246.

Straus, S., and R. Lyons. 2006. *Intimate Enemy: Images and Voices of the Rwandan Genocide.* Brooklyn, NY: Zone Books.

ABOUT THE EDITORS

SAMUEL TOTTEN is a genocide scholar based at the University of Arkansas, Fayetteville. He served as a Fulbright Scholar at the Centre for Conflict Management, National University of Rwanda, from January through July, 2008.

RAFIKI UBALDO is a journalist. Currently, he is studying political science at Stockholm University, Sweden. He is a survivor of the 1994 genocide against the Tutsi.

CPSIA information can be obtained
at www.ICGtesting.com
Printed in the USA
LVHW110012120719
623878LV00001B/23/P